FROM WATER TO WINE

FROM WATER TO WINE

Becoming Middle Class in Angola

JESS AUERBACH

Teaching Culture: UTP Ethnographies for the Classroom

UNIVERSITY OF TORONTO PRESS

Toronto Buffalo London

© University of Toronto Press 2020
Toronto Buffalo London
utorontopress.com
Printed in Canada

ISBN 978-1-4875-0641-4 (cloth) ISBN 978-1-4875-3411-0 (EPUB)
ISBN 978-1-4875-2433-3 (paper) ISBN 978-1-4875-3410-3 (PDF)

All rights reserved. The use of any part of this publication reproduced, transmitted in any form or by any means, electronic, mechanical, photocopying, recording, or otherwise, or stored in a retrieval system, without prior written consent of the publisher—or in the case of photocopying, a licence from Access Copyright, the Canadian Copyright Licensing Agency—is an infringement of the copyright law.

Library and Archives Canada Cataloguing in Publication

Title: From water to wine : becoming middle class in Angola / Jess Auerbach.
Names: Auerbach, Jess, author.
Series: Teaching culture.
Description: Series statement: Teaching culture : UTP ethnographies for the classroom | Includes bibliographical references and index.
Identifiers: Canadiana (print) 20190206039 | Canadiana (ebook) 2019020608X | ISBN 9781487506414 (cloth) | ISBN 9781487524333 (paper) | ISBN 9781487534110 (EPUB) | ISBN 9781487534103 (PDF)
Subjects: LCSH: Middle class—Angola. | LCSH: Angola—Social life and customs 21st century.
Classification: LCC HT690.A54 A94 2020 | DDC 305.5/509673—dc23

We welcome comments and suggestions regarding any aspect of our publications—please feel free to contact us at news@utorontopress.com or visit us at utorontopress.com.

Every effort has been made to contact copyright holders; in the event of an error or omission, please notify the publisher.

University of Toronto Press acknowledges the financial assistance to its publishing program of the Canada Council for the Arts and the Ontario Arts Council, an agency of the Government of Ontario.

*To the memory of my grandfather, Franz, who set the direction;
to my parents, Christina and Raymond, who raised me,
hugged me, and let me go;
and to Aarvin Jahajeeah, for bringing me home.*

Contents

List of Images xi

Acknowledgments xiii

Interview Report xvii

Preface xxi

~ Proprioception ~
Introduction: Where Petrol Is Cheaper than Water: Life in *Capitalismo selvagem* 1
    The Back Story 1
    Representing "Africa"? 4
    On Making Sense in the Writing 6
    What the Book Is Actually About 7
    How the Research Was Done 10
    How to Read This Book 14
    Core Concepts 15

Interlude ~ A Brief History of Angola 23
ILLUSTRATED BY ELINOR DRIVER

~ Smell ~

1 The Smell of Success: Perfume, Beauty, Sweat, Oil 31
Read with Your Nose 31
Conditioning the Air: Space and Control 34
Class, Perfume, Dream: Aspiration and Authenticity 42

Interlude ~ Recording Fieldwork: Notes, Objects, Structured Observations of Space 50
Notes 50
Objects 51
Structured Observations of Space 54

~ Touch ~

2 Touch and the Tactile: The Textures of Scouting in *Capitalismo selvagem* 57
Seeing through the Skin 57
Making the Mafia 59
Stitching *Pano* Pants 61
Catching Slipping Children 63
Lighting the Fire as Service 66
Building the New Man 68
Choosing Appropriate T-Shirts 71
Practicing Peace 75

Interlude ~ Poems 1 77
Fatherhood 77
Radio Building 78
Seven Women 79
Buying Cloth 80
Fátima's Mother, on Christmas Day 2013 81
The Cuban Help 82
The Driver 83

~ Taste ~

3 Changing Tastes: Palates and the Possible 85
Recipes 86
The Man Who Made Cake, Dona Maria, and the Sushi Chef 87
Oral Histories: The Stories of Two Lives 93

Interlude ~ Photo Essay 1: The Flavors of Peace 106

Interlude ~ Photo Essay 2: Choices and Consumption 108

~ Sound ~
4 Music, *Fofoca*, and the News: Sound, Space, and Orientation 111
    Sound Readings: Spectrographs, Annotation, Language   111
    Cold War Echoes: Higher Education, Ideology, and Contested Duties   118

Interlude ~ Poems 2   137
    Estrelinha (Little Star)   137
    Birds on Campus   138
    João, Collapsing   139
    Dona Maria Serving Soup   140
    Dona Inês   141
    Two Photographers   142
    Cinema Church   143
    Yoga Teacher   144

Interlude ~ Photo Essay 3: Childhoods   146

Interlude ~ Photo Essay 4: Leisure   148

~ Sight ~
5 National Rebranding 151
    The Selfie and the Other   151
    National Rebranding: Guarantee Your Children a Better Past   154
    Biopolitical Screens: Frames of Vision   158
    Laughing on the Internet   162
    Insta Lies or Insta Truths?   164
    Fieldwork Ethics: Seven Afterimages   166

Interlude ~ Photo Essay 5: Art   176

Interlude ~ Photo Essay 6: Architecture   178

~ *Curiosity* ~
Conclusion: Attending the Beautiful in the Light of What We Know 181
    Capitalismo selvagem in Uncertain Times   186
    The Government Has Gone on Holiday,
       but Maybe João Lourenço Will Bring It Back   188
    Practicing Peace ... Again   191

Notes   195

Indicative Bibliography   201

References   209

Index   221

Images

P.1 Computer monitor, beer can, dodgem   xxii
I.1 Map of Angola and surrounding region   2
I.2 Map of the Atlantic Ocean   12
1.1 Notebook pages and voice memos   51
1.2 Fieldwork objects   53
3.1 Dono Oniko   95
3.2 Lino Espelanga   99
4.1 Spectrographs   112
C.1 Vedran Smailović and cello   192

Photo essays appear on pages 106–09, 146–49, and 176–79.

Acknowledgments

It takes a community to raise an anthropologist, though in my case it has taken several, in six countries. The names I could acknowledge go far beyond those listed in these pages. I hope that everyone who has contributed knows the impact that they have had, and the value that I place on our relationships.

First, my parents, Christina and Raymond, have gently supported my curiosity and provided a refuge to which I could always return. My sister Elinor Driver has been a friend, interlocutor, and commentator who holds me to high standards and shares great insights of her own. She has added so much to this book through her illustrations and her attentive questions as she drew. Her husband Casey has become a much-loved brother. My aunts, Margaret Auerbach and Liebe Kellen, have hosted me again and again in Johannesburg, and watched me grow, and around them all is a broader extended family who have given me roots in the world—however much I move across it.

I left Durban for Cape Town for my undergraduate studies, and relationships built there have withstood time and absence. After a decade away, I am so happy to be moving home as this book enters into production. My mentors Sally Frankental and Fiona Ross at the University of Cape Town have continued our discussions, and continued to demand the best from me. Their comments on this manuscript made me appreciate afresh how lucky I was to have received my early training there, and in the South African academy as a whole.

Lesley Green, Divine Fuh, Carolyn Hamilton, Jonathan Jansen, Dilip Menon, Shannon Morreira, Francis Nyamnjoh, and many others have fundamentally shaped my outlook on the world, and I hope to one day reach the high bar that they have set.

At Oxford academic life was complemented by a richness of friendships that was profound and unique. I thank all of those at St. Antony's College and in the Rhodes community for dialogues that also susurrate throughout this text. In particular I acknowledge Edwin Cameron, Nina Hall, Charne Lavery, Noelle Lopez, Bonolo Mathibela, Nanjala Nyabola, Emma Preston, Christopher Trisos, Carina Venter, and Anya Yermakova.

At Stanford, I was enormously privileged to work under James Ferguson, whose patience, guidance, insights, and humor made the process one that was mostly a lot of fun. A course on graphic novels with Lochlann Jain completely changed my thinking in my first year there, and allowed me to slowly find my own academic voice. Teresa Caldeira, Kathy Coll, Shelly Coughlan, Paulla Ebron, Laura Hubbard, Liisa Malkki, James Lorand Matory, Grant Parker, Richard Roberts, Krish Seetah, Anna Tsing, and Sylvia Yanagisako all contributed significantly to my intellectual development. It would have been so much harder without a community of friends: Julia Cassaniti, Hillary Chart, Nisrin Elamin, Cordelia Eriksen-Davies, Mark Gardiner, Maron Greenleaf, Vivian Lu, Sarah Quesada, Joanna Richlin, Nethra Samarickwema, Victoria Saramago, David Stentiford, Kathryn Takabvirwa, Anna West, Tunç Yilmaz, and so many others, including all those in the DARE community that enabled the completion of my degree. Hannah Appel and Ramah McKay were wonderful "older sisters."

In Angola, I thank first the Mouzinho family for everything they did to support me. The research was funded by grants from the Social Science Research Council, the Susan Ford Dorsey Fellowship, the Bucerius ZEIT-Stiftung Foundation, the Brazilian National Science Exchange Program, and Stanford University. I was hosted by the Economics Department at the University of Katyavala Bwila, and none of this work could have been done had Dr. José Nicolau Silvestre not ensured the documentation was ready, and then offered every possible support in the process. I also thank Dr. Bonifácio Tchimboto at the University of Jean Piaget, for conversations that I have continued to reflect on and that have helped me to chart my own life path, and Loide Chivinda for the same. Ana Duarte made the connection with

UKB and other relationships possible. Isabel Bueio was the core link in so many chains, and also remains a much-loved friend. Aires Walter Dos Santos, Pedro Kaputa, André Macala, and José "Zeto" Patrocínio all opened up worlds. Zeto died just as this book was completed; his passing leaves a chasm in Angolan civil society. I will think often of the many cups of tea I enjoyed in his house in Bairro da Luz, the conversations we had there, and the courage, conviction, and strength of character that he modeled for the country he loved.

From my scout *irmãos* I learned the meaning of service. I thank all of you, *Sempre Alert*. To Luis, who struck a bargain that served us both well, and to Gu, for rolling with it. To Rafael Chitanda, for his integrity and his friendship, and to the many other friends not listed here, as well as the parents, teachers, and students at the College of Stars. Without Justin Pearce, I never would have made it to Angola in the first place, and his curiosity, integrity, and knowledge continue to inspire: RAO to the max, *querido*. A wonderful community of scholars of and in Angola have also supported and deepened this work. I thank again Ana Duarte, and acknowledge the critical input of Claudia Gastrow. In addition, I thank Dorothée Boulanger, Chloe Buirré, Mariana Candido, Ricardo Cardoso, Mathias de Alencastro, Maria de Encarnação Pimenta, Aaron de Grassi, Iracema Dulley, Imke Gooskins, Selina Makana, Rafael Marques, Estelle Maussion, Cheryl Meiting Schmitz, Marissa Moorman, Susana Santos, Jon Schubert, Ricardo Soares de Oliveira, António Tomás, and all the others for generosity in community that raises us all. In Brazil I thank Roberto Kant de Lima, Julie and Ricardo Lill, Marta Patallo, Frederico Policarpo Mendonça Filho, Lígia and José Saramago Pádua, and the members of the Angolan Consulate who helped me so much.

After finishing my doctorate, I took a job at the African Leadership College in Mauritius. It was a fascinating challenge, and I acknowledge the support and friendship of Gaidi Faraj, Mlungisi Dlamini, Janice Ndegwa, and Efemena Odu amongst others. The students made it all worthwhile, and this book is written with all of them in mind. Let us tell stories of "Africa" in a way that is nuanced, and makes us proud. For their comments on early versions of this text, I acknowledge the students in African Studies 2, 2018, and in particular Rosemary de Moor, Ahmed Konneh, One Pusumane, and Amina Soulimani. In 2019 I transitioned to the Open University of Mauritius, where Dr. Kaviraj

Sukon, supported by the Mauritian Tertiary Education Commission, provided the space for the completion of this manuscript, and a collegial environment that was nourishing and refreshing. Myriam Blin's thoughtful conversation in our shared office sustained and enriched the text at so many levels.

Anne Brackenbury at the University of Toronto Press understood my vision and encouraged me to write the book I wanted, rather than the book I thought I should in order to prove myself an anthropologist, and Carli Hansen and Janice Evans saw me to the finish line with enthusiasm and professionalism. Ken Wissoker at Duke University Press helped me along the way. Many people already named gave insightful comments on the manuscript. I also wish to acknowledge the input of Simon Abbott, Abena Asare, Hannah Baumesiter, Melinda Griffiths, Jenny Hough, Zandile Kayabonda, Siphiwe Gloria Ndlovu, Mary Pipes, and Michelle Reddy. Their reflections have helped to make what follows more widely accessible. Thanissara, Kittisaro, and the Dharmapala community in South Africa and elsewhere have given me the confidence to write my own truths quietly, and Nobantu Mpotula has helped me to feel seen. Finally, Aarvin Jahajeeah entered my life at a moment when I was completely distracted by all the other things, and somehow became its center. His pragmatism, insight, and terrible jokes have completely transformed this process, and brought so much laughter and happiness.

Interview Report

How do we assess the validity of social science findings pertaining to countries and contexts we might know nothing about? In an era of fake news, and increasingly deep fakes as well that build on a long history of stereotype we might not even be aware we subscribe to, it seems helpful to show readers what this book is based on. Later on I explain the methodology more comprehensively, but here I show the formal interviews. These were discussions that happened, that were recorded, on these places, on these days, and they form the skeleton around which the book has emerged.

No.	Place	Date
1	Lobito	131106
2	Lobito	131112
3	Lobito	131112
4	Lobito	131119
5	Lobito	131120
6	Lobito	131121
7	Lobito	131122
8	Lobito	131124
9	Lobito	131202
10	Lobito	131210

(continued)

Interview Report

No.	Place	Date
11	Lobito	131211
12	Benguela	131212
13	Lobito	131212
14	Benguela	131213
15	Lobito	131216
16	Lobito	131217
17	Lobito	131217
18	Lobito	131217
19	Lobito	131218
20	Lobito	131220
21	Lobito	131230
22	Benguela	140108
23	Lobito	140109
24	Lobito	140110
25	Lobito	140112
26	Lobito	140116
27	Lobito	140117
28	Lobito	140118
29	Lobito	140207
30	Benguela	140216
31	Catumbela	140221
32	Lobito	140224
33	Benguela	140302
34	Lobito	140308
35	Lobito	140309
36	Benguela	140314
37	Lobito	140318
38	Lobito	140321
39	Lobito	140326
40	Lobito	140327
41	Lobito	140328
42	Lobito	140402
43	Lobito	140403
44	Catumbela	140424
45	Lobito	140425
46	Benguela	140503

No.	Place	Date
47	Lobito	140507
48	Lobito	140513
49	Lobito	140515
50	Lobito	140519
51	Lobito	140521
52	Lobito	140522
53	Lobito	140526
54	Luanda	140527
55	Luanda	140527
56	Benguela	140528
57	Lobito	140603
58	Lobito	140603
59	Lobito	140605
60	Lobito	140606
61	Lobito	140606
62	Rio de Janeiro	140729
63	Rio de Janeiro	140821
64	Rio de Janeiro	140823
65	Rio de Janeiro	140824
66	Rio de Janeiro	140828
67	Rio de Janeiro	140829
68	Rio de Janeiro	140905
69	Rio de Janeiro	140907
70	Rio de Janeiro	140908
71	Rio de Janeiro	140910
72	Rio de Janeiro	140911
73	Rio de Janeiro	140912
74	Rio de Janeiro	140918
75	Rio de Janeiro	140921
76	Rio de Janeiro	140922
77	Rio de Janeiro	140922
78	Rio de Janeiro	140923
79	Rio de Janeiro	140926
80	Juiz da Fora	140927
81	Rio das Ostras	140929
82	Rio de Janeiro	140930

(continued)

Interview Report

No.	Place	Date
83	Rio de Janeiro	141001
84	Rio de Janeiro	141002
85	Rio de Janeiro	141002
86	Niteroí	141003
87	Rio de Janeiro	141004
88	Rio de Janeiro	141008
89	Rio de Janeiro	141010
90	Rio de Janeiro	141016
91	Curitiba	141018
92	Curitiba	141019
93	Curitiba	141020
94	Curitiba	141021
95	Curitiba	141021
96	Curitiba	141022
97	Curitiba	141023
98	Rio de Janeiro	141030
99	Rio de Janeiro	141030
100	Rio de Janeiro	141030
101	Rio de Janeiro	141031
102	Rio de Janeiro	141106
103	Rio de Janeiro	141110
104	Rio de Janeiro	141110
105	Lobito	141209
106	Lobito	141211
107	Lobito	180514

Preface

Português

MÁRIO ROMBO: Não contes a ninguém, Nadine.... (Triste.) Mas tu não imaginas a vontade que eu tive hoje de me dar encontro com um bom peixe frito....
NADINE: Com muito limão e cebolada?
MÁRIO ROMBO: E jindungo! Para dar um certo ritmo....
Os Vivos, O Morto e o Peixe Frito (Ondjaki 2014)

English

MÁRIO ROMBO: Don't tell anyone, Nadine.... (Sad.) But you cannot imagine the desire I had today for a meeting with a good fried fish....
NADINE: With a lot of lemon and dressing?
MÁRIO ROMBO: And chilli! To give a certain rhythm....
The Living, Death and Fried Fish (Ondjaki 2014)

Image P.1. In December 2013, I went for a walk on the beach near my house at dawn. I came across these objects, set together on the sand: a computer monitor, an empty beer can, and an old dodgem car dragged several kilometers up the beach from what was once a fair ground, then a refugee camp, now a neighborhood of Lobito, Angola. Who assembled them and what took place that night are not known to me, but they capture something of the essence of this book, and so I set them here to think with.

This is a book that is written to trip you out of your eyes, away from your screen. As Angolan playwright Ondjaki suggests on the previous page, a little chilli gives a certain rhythm. That acknowledged, it is also a book that is written to mimic the Internet: things change quickly, styles and form of content move around. There is a central argument about the importance of attention to beauty, and the significance of everyday acts of triumph and happiness. The goal of the book is to "unflatten" (Sousanis 2015) the way outsiders think of Angola, and also Africa, and the definition of middle class is cumulative and flexible—mimicking reality. There's no fake news, but history moves: by all means, fact-check it.

In this book I tell stories about how I experienced everyday life in a small town on the coast of Angola. It is divided into sections based on senses—more as a literary device than as a contribution to what scholars might call sensory theory, although sensory theory is woven through it too, a subtle thread. I am not claiming that this is how *Angolans* experience their world, but I am sharing how I did, when the country let me in, and how I learned to feel "with" my friends and colleagues by participating in their lives and asking questions.

Anthropology is a discipline that has been said to "make the world safe for human difference" (Wheeler 2017), and in the interests of safety, and difference, I think it is important to acknowledge upfront what this book is and what it is not. It is not a definitive text. It is not a text that claims to speak for anyone other than myself. It is not a text that shies away from the felt and perceived experiences of difference—both mine and amongst the many people who contributed to this work.

Those differences manifest on many axes: national, racial, religious, gustatory, educational, aesthetic, and a host besides. Some are structural, some personal, some cultural. These differences enrich our world, and open many pathways to knowledge, understanding, and compassion. Sometimes knowing how to ask questions in a way that makes others feel respected can be difficult, and having models of how to do that can be helpful. The question I asked as a PhD student beginning the research that lead to this book was "How can I research what's *working* in Angola, what makes people happy?" The question I asked when I was putting what I learned into this book was "How can I write this in a way that an eighteen-year-old university student or my mum's best friend or my colleague in engineering would not find boring, and that might help them *care*?" I think that caring is important.

In addition to being about difference, this book is also about the things that most people in most places can relate to: humor, stress, friendship, love, betrayal, assistance, money, responsibility, sickness, Facebook and Instagram, dealing with change, and the big question that hangs constantly over most of us: Are the people I love okay? Are they going to stay okay? What will I do if something shifts? It's not common practice to start a book born out of academic research with a discussion about love, but at this moment in history it seems important. To be able to love someone, we have to do our best to understand them—and in a world where global systems affect us all in record-breaking time, it's important to open up the possibility of care toward those we do not know.

I recently read Yuval Noah Harari's (2018) *21 Lessons for the 21st Century*, and one section in particular left me with chills. In a chapter on equality he observes that perhaps people in different regions of the world have totally different futures—much like George Orwell (1949) wrote in *1984*. Preparing for what is to come, Harari says, "Maybe in some parts of the world you should teach your kids to write computer code, while in others, you had better teach them to draw fast and shoot straight" (77). Harari is one amongst many who feels that in places like Angola it's hard to become a computer programmer—and he's right at a very broad level (even if some individuals will always overcome structural barriers). The thing is, that's not inevitable.

Global separations exist because we have allowed the world to be this way. Our political and social systems make the world we live in—in Angola as everywhere else—and they are closely connected, from human rights to climate change to the manufacture and regulation of oil and the cleaning of air. We need to do more to understand each other, to recognize shared humanity as well as the structures and belief systems that make us different. That way we can work together, in global teams, from a place of respect. This work must be toward the world we actually want—not just the one that we have now.

~ Proprioception ~

INTRODUCTION

Where Petrol Is Cheaper than Water: Life in *Capitalismo selvagem*

The Back Story

I was born on the 21st of March, 1985, in a rural South African town, inland to the southeast of the border with Lesotho. This, too, is not how academic books usually begin, but stay with me, because it is relevant. Twenty-five years earlier, on the 21st of March, 1960, South African police had opened fire on protesting civilians, killing sixty-nine people. The event, which became known as the Sharpeville Massacre, was just one of thousands of acts of violence committed by the South African state, which at the time upheld the political system of apartheid. *Apartheid* literally means apart-ness, and in South Africa the people to be kept apart were those of different "races."[1]

Apartheid had a profound effect on all South Africans, but what is sometimes forgotten in popular memory is that the South African government had far grander ambitions. Not content with dominating South Africa, it wanted to extend its control throughout the region, and engaged in what were colloquially known as the "border wars" to try to increase its reach and influence. To this end, from August 1987 to March 1988, just as I turned three years old, the battle of Cuito Cuanavale raged in Angola between South African, Cuban, and Angolan armed forces, paid for with money from the United States and the former Union of Soviet Socialist Republics (USSR). This was one of the decisive events in a three-decade war that I will shortly explain in more detail.

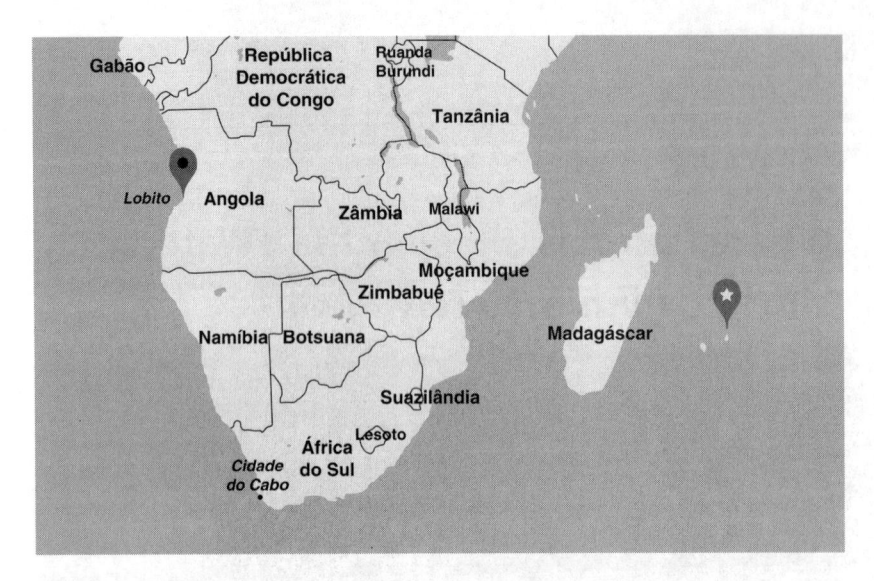

Image I.1. The pin on the left represents the town of Lobito, Angola, where most of this book is based. The star on the right indicates the island of Mauritius, where most of this book was written. Cidade do Cabo (Portuguese for Cape Town), at the bottom, is the city where the author studied for her undergraduate degree and now lives. The map has been left in Portuguese, because that is how the world of this book has been perceived.

By the end of the 1980s, the cracks in apartheid were beginning to show, and when I began primary (elementary) school in 1992, it was almost over. In 1994 South Africa had its first democratic election, and Nelson Mandela was made our president. My childhood was marked by the hope and deep joy of that time, and also by its fears. I was of the last generation to begin school in a segregated system, and no amount of rainbow nation posters could compensate for the absence of black classmates nor change the fact that our generation had parents who, in different ways, had been shaped by a system that had taught them to fear one another profoundly.

Even in the liberal, alternative school that my parents selected, in first grade my classmates and I practiced identifying different kinds of bombs and grenades, and drilled repeatedly what we were to do if shot. Nobody knew if, after so much violence, the elections could possibly be peaceful, and so in addition to color wheels and number boards, I vividly remember the tactile feeling and shades of olive-green-brown-red-edged weapon identification boards used at that time to teach children, and the feeling of the grass on my bare knees on the sports field as we practiced things like "being shot at in a bus" (as a six-year-old I found this puzzling: our parents all had cars, none of us took the bus, it seemed a very strange thing to learn).

Almost all of our fathers had been forcibly conscripted into the military structures of the South African Defence Force (SADF)—the same army that fought in Cuito Cuanavale, in Angola—and in diverse ways that people far more eloquent than I have described (Jansen 2009; Krog 2000; Malan 2000) we, as children, absorbed something of their trauma, which we have all now woven into the threads of our adult lives. Just before the elections there was a craze for T-shirts with the emblem of peace, blue-and-white doves—it felt like everybody was wearing white flags that said, "please don't shoot me." History unfolding had textures, smells, and sounds, and they marked my childhood profoundly.

A significant national dialogue began at that time, to try to make sense of our past and prepare for our future, but the border wars were hard to speak about. My own father was not part of the thousands of white South African men who went to fight in Angola, but many of my friend's fathers were, and as children we already knew better than to ask too many questions about it. Angola was a place of violence and trauma worse than our own, and it was better to ignore it. What we had done to ourselves was bad enough; what we had done to other countries was too much to confront (de Vries 2016; Morris 2014; Scholtz 2016).

Then, just before I finished high school, the war in Angola ended; peace "broke out" unexpectedly in 2002 (Pearce 2005) with the death of a man named Jonas Savimbi.[2] During my undergraduate training at the University of Cape Town, I had become fascinated by Portuguese colonialism and the different ways in which decolonization had taken place. By then, Angola was beginning to "open" to the outside world. Due to its civil war, for almost three decades it had been extremely difficult to get visas to go there. "All Angolans are enthusiastic [because] peace is here to stay" (Cerqueira and Schul 2008, 8) claims the introduction to a 2008 photo book entitled *Angola: A Country Reborn.* I decided that I wanted to go there too, and to observe a country other than my own, learning how to translate pictures of doves into everyday actions of peace.

It took me some time to get to Angola. After undergrad, I did a master's degree to help me understand returning refugees: What had changed in them and in the country while they had been away? I read everything I could that had been produced in English about Angola. At the time I did not speak Portuguese, never mind Umbundu, Kimbundu, Chokwe, or any other language that might have been useful. As expected, what I read about was suffering: hunger, deprivation, violence, and so much ugliness that a Scandinavian NGO took it upon themselves to stage a beauty pageant entitled "Miss Landmine Angola" to try to invert the way both Angolans and outsiders perceived themselves (MacKinnon 2008). If this scholarly literature and media were to be believed, Angola was a country damaged beyond all hope.

Representing "Africa"?

Part of what I had learned in my own childhood was that even, or perhaps especially, in contexts of transition and sometimes violence, everyday life continues. People go on dates, argue, celebrate the birth of children, or help them with their homework. Whilst dramatic events of historical significance may shape the contours of a life, its textures will be composed of everyday acts between present people: kindness, cruelty, care, neglect, and all the rest of it, and I chose to do a PhD in anthropology because it is one of the disciplines that sees those everyday acts as interesting and fundamentally important.

Typically, powerful media-houses based in the "global north"[3] present a vision of Africa that continues tropes of backwardness, neglect, and violence that were once deemed necessary for the justification of slavery (Smith 2006) but have since continued largely uninterrupted and arguably now serve the interests of extractive capitalism. Nigerian author Chimamanda Ngozie Adichie made this point very powerfully in the public domain in her 2016 TED Talk "The Dangers of a Single Story," but Adichie's work is grounded in a long tradition of work by other African scholars that has been saying much the same for years (e.g., Du Bois 2005 [1903]; Mbembe 2001; Mudimbe 2008; Ogunnaike 2017).

Going into this research, I was very aware that one often sees what one is looking for, and that the "danger of a single story" in practice could mean that in the context of postwar Angola I might see only suffering, just as in the context of a holiday to the United States, I might only see wealth (when anyone who has walked down a street in any major US city with their eyes open knows it is far more complicated than that). The suffering of human beings is extremely important, and throughout this book I grapple with the fact that many people I knew—and even more whom I chose not to get to know—suffered profoundly. The final section of the book reflects on a disciplined, focused curiosity that takes one beyond expected tropes and into observations of lived realities, with how one can be curious with strangers in a way that is respectful, that leads to dialogue, that is based on a premise of fundamental shared humanity. Before I get there, it is important to note the deliberate choice to focus on what is working, and to share that, in part as a political contribution toward changing the single story of "Africa."

"Focusing on what is working" is an extremely vague suggestion, and in practical terms this book is about the emergent Angolan middle class. Historically, Angola was run by a small group of elites (Corrado 2008), and though that still arguably continues to a certain extent (cf. Schubert 2017; Soares de Oliveira 2015), changes in the country after the end of the civil war meant that during the time of my fieldwork it was increasingly possible for people who were *not* of established families or politically well connected to nonetheless begin to enjoy a much higher standard of living than had previously been possible. That meant changes in education, consumption, and way of living, and it is these changes that the book explores at a granular level.

A note on terminology: I, like many scholars of the continent of Africa and its diaspora, become quite distressed when the entire continent is referred to as if it were a country. That acknowledged, many of us ourselves refer to one particular country as if it were not one but two entire continents: "America." Throughout this book, when I refer to the United States of America, I say so, and use the adjective "US American"; I only use "America" or "American" in the continental sense, from Chile through to Canada. That might seem strange to readers not used to interrogating the linguistic and psychological impact of the dominance of one particular country within two continents, but it is standard practice in many parts of Latin and Southern America and should, I believe, become standard practice throughout the world. Why? Because it is accurate, and because there is power in naming, and because it is a disservice to the citizens of the United States as well as to those of all other countries in the Americas writ large to homogenize and to flatten. An Argentinian likely has as little in common with a person from Canada as a Liberian has with a Zimbabwean—in both cases, we need to know how to tell the difference.

On Making Sense in the Writing

Relatively few people interrogate bodily senses in everyday life, but they are some of the most important tools that human beings have to know the world around them. The phrase "making sense" of something is so commonplace in everyday English that most readers will not have paused to consider it. "Making sense" of something makes it comprehensible through the body, and allows people to act based on knowledge that might have been obscure before giving sensory attention to it. It is precisely because the senses are so foundational that we learn about them when we are tiny, and from that point build up our understanding of both the material and the social context in which we live. It is at least in part on this basis that we come to "common sense," the taken-for-granted ordering of the world that is far from universal (let alone "global").

For many people, reading this book (understanding its logics, its convention, its flow and style and order) in the first place is a result of a sensory training that emerged during Enlightenment Europe. That training was based on a rationalist interpretation of the world and the foundations of modern science and ways of learning. Above all, it prioritized the sense of sight. Seeing was said to be believing, and sight could be "trusted" as empirical, which sounds remarkably like "empire" (though the two have different Latin roots), but the system also recognized and valued hearing, touch, taste, and smell (Classen 1993). These five senses have dominated what might be considered capitalist[4] ways of knowing ever since (extractive, domineering, often deeply patriarchal), but they are by no means the only options available. Many scholars—including in the so-called hard sciences—have done wonderful work that shows how different societies value other entry points to understanding our experiences of life (Desjarlais 2003; Geurts 2002).[5] Even within existing "Western" knowledge frameworks, there are many disciplines that recognize, for example, balance, nociception (the ability to identify and experience pain), and many others.

Here, I use the senses as entry points into understanding a country that many readers will know nothing about. The objective is twofold: first, to help readers imagine more fully the spaces and interactions that are being described, and second, to provide methodological insight into the processes by which social science research is undertaken. In the chapter on touch, for example, the material does not analyze touch as a sensory phenomenon per se, nor does it suggest that some or all or any Angolans experience the tactile in a way that is particularly unusual. Instead, it gives attention to the textures that surround bodies, and what these textures reveal about class, belonging, membership of social groups, health, and education. My intention is that readers therefore "immerse" themselves more fully in the space that they can imagine through the page, but that *is* real, in all the three-dimensionality that that entails. By making constant reference to embodied knowledges, readers will imagine their own bodies in the spaces being shared, and consider how they might respond were they there. Let's call it low-tech virtual reality (;-)).

In the current chapter, I foreground proprioception to bring attention to how one makes sense—literally and figuratively—of movement, balance, orientation, and space, and how individual biographies and experiences of place, travel, and the journeys between them inform our receptivity toward new narratives and experiences. This book came about after a journey that took me from Kokstad to Cape Town (a relatively short distance at 1,351 kilometers[6]) via California and Cuba and Curitiba, not to mention Oxford, San Francisco, East/ Palo Alto, Luanda, Benguela, Lobito, Rio de Janeiro, and Réduit, Mauritius. That is a very, very long distance indeed, and in the section entitled "Fieldwork Ethics: Seven Afterimages" I reflect on the implications for the planet of that amount of movement.

What the Book Is Actually About

The book's title, *From Water to Wine: Becoming Middle Class in Angola*, is a play on the subject of transformation, hope, and consumption. The majority of Angolans identify as some denomination of the Christian religion (Péclard 1998), and the first public miracle that Jesus is said to have performed is the transformation of water into wine at a wedding. That transformation was the proof that many of his disciples needed in order to believe in him. The play on this subject I make in the book is that as everyday people's consumption power increased, they were able to afford not only water to drink, but also wine. This marked a change in their material circumstances that helped everyday people to "believe" in peace far more than, for example, symbols such as T-shirts with doves on them.

Readers may have noticed the title of this chapter, "Where Petrol Is Cheaper than Water: Life in *Capitalismo selvagem*." More will be said on this subject later, but for now note that in Angola in 2013 and 2014, a liter of potable water cost *more* than a liter of processed gasoline.[7] This was indicative of what my interlocutors (the people who shared their lives with me in Angola) called *"capitalismo selvagem,"* a phrase that I have wrestled with in terms of translation. The obvious translation from Portuguese is "wild capitalism," but that does not quite capture the element of savagery that the term implies. "Jungle" capitalism gets closer, but comes with the terrible weight of the word "jungle" as a stereotype of Africa and African identities that has been inscribed in popular culture in much of Europe and North America for the better part of three centuries (e.g., Conrad 2010).

When I asked interlocutors who were bilingual in English and Portuguese to translate the term, they invariably chose "jungle" because they wanted to emphasize that the version of capitalism they were experiencing followed *"a lei da mata"*—the rules of the "jungle" (i.e., only the strongest and smartest survive). To soften their analysis of their own country for the sake of my liberal sensibilities would not be appropriate, but if the word is read in a way that reinforces stereotypes, I would also be deeply upset. I therefore use the original term, *capitalismo selvagem*, as much as possible, hoping that the italics will remind readers to cut through whatever biases they might hold—however unconsciously—and approach the data presented in the text for what it is.[8]

This introduction gives the reader the background information that will be needed to make sense of the country, how the book was written, and how to read it. The book is then structured in five chapters, which can be read in any order, though sequentially is probably the easiest. Each chapter ends with a brief reflection on why it matters that we read this material, and what it can do. Following each chapter is an Interlude, where the text transforms into different tools of communication and knowing.

Each of the following chapters deep-dives into aspects of everyday life in Angola, highlighting both similarities and differences with other experiences of the world, and emphasizing a particular sense. Chapter 1 considers scent, and in particular perfume and air-conditioning as tools of managing the environment and bringing about positive change. Chapter 2 explores touch, and the textures of Scouting in the context of *capitalismo selvagem*, specifically how the texture of uniforms, the heat of fires, and the "feeling" of togetherness create strong bonds of belonging and community in a country at peace. Chapter 3 is about taste, flavor, sweetness, and acidity and the class positioning of eating certain foods, as well as the cultural significance food often carries. In Chapter 4, sounds are brought to the fore, and in Chapter 5, readers are invited onto Instagram and Facebook to explore national rebranding and knowledge through sight, as well as the "afterimages" of the ethical challenges of fieldwork.

The concluding chapter is about curiosity, and the many ways in which we might strengthen a feeling of connectedness and shared human experience by asking good questions and truly listening (and not just with our ears) to the answers. We need to do this whilst simultaneously acknowledging the structural and cultural differences that set us apart and ensure the world is interesting. This is of relevance not just to students in the social sciences, but to anyone who works in international teams or in fields that influence people far away. Whether you are an architect or a zookeeper, an engineer, a lawyer, or a sportsperson, curiosity about how people different from you think can only lead to better work that is able to meet the very different needs of different people.

Angola has been a very important stage for world history, and I believe strongly that it has much to teach us all. Before it was a state in the modern sense of the word, the ancestors of those alive today were part of some of Africa's most important polities (Thornton 2012; Vansina 1966). These ancestors were caught up in the Age of Empire, spreading across the South Atlantic and beyond and playing a critical role in the emergence of modern-day Brazil and the development of sports such as capoeira and zumba and religions such as Candomblé (Alencastro 2000; Freyre 1933; Matory 2005).

More recently, the country underwent a profound period of upheaval through decolonization from the Portuguese. This quickly morphed into the Cold War Proxy Conflict that I described above, which saw Cuban and South African forces combining with rival Angolan counterparts and fighting one another as part of the global contestation of socialism and capitalism (Hatzky 2012; Marcum 1969, 1978; Soares de Oliveira 2015). In 2017, José Eduardo dos Santos, who had been president of Angola since 1979, stepped down, and a new era has been initiated under the leadership of President João Lourenço.

Recent changes in political leadership throw yet more light on how a country attempts to be at once modern and peaceful, technologically up to date and democratic, globalized and nationalist, all in the context of relative real-life poverty in actual terms, and real-life wealth in speculative oil futures.[9] Comparing Angola with other countries can be useful, as in many ways the rawness, and newness, of Angola's "peace" allows dynamics to be visible that in other places have been made opaque by the layering of history, bureaucracy, and even national myth (think of the "rainbow nation" metaphor in South Africa, or the rebranding of post-colonial, post-genocide Rwanda as Africa's star success story, or even the "rise" of China).

How the Research Was Done

This work was begun in 2009 as I pursued my UK master's degree, researched in Angola and Brazil through the duration of a PhD in anthropology undertaken in the US, written in 2018 whilst teaching at two Mauritian universities, and completed in 2019 as I moved back to South Africa after a decade away. From 2009 onward I began to actively read about Angola, and from 2010 I began to study Portuguese. I visited the country for a few weeks for the first time in 2011, on an exploratory journey where I had hundreds of conversations that helped me to understand what questions to ask if I hoped to study "the emergent middle class." "The emergent middle class" in Africa was, at the time, a concept very much in vogue. A McKinsey & Co. consultancy report had made much of the "lions of Africa" (Roxburgh et al. 2010), and I was far from alone in wanting to tell a cheerful story about life on parts of the continent. It seemed a sensible way to approach the reality that is obvious to most Africans (but less so outside Africa due to selective media reportage), that many people across the vast swathes of territory comprising the continent are doing just fine.

When I first went to Angola, I immersed myself in the smells, tastes, textures, and moods of Luanda, Lobito, Benguela, and Namibe—all coastal cities that fit my broad interests—settling on Lobito as a site of long-term fieldwork for reasons that I describe below. In 2011, I also went to Brazil for intensive language training, and there I realized that to study Angola would not be quite enough—I needed to include time in Brazil, where many Angolans went temporarily to acquire education, skills, and merchandise for sale and resale. Understanding Angola in the context of the Atlantic Ocean therefore became an important orientation, and for a long time I kept the map shown in Image I.2 on my wall as a reminder to think in fresh ways about how geography both connects and separates.

In the same period that I immersed myself in Brazil, I was also privileged to be able to visit Cuba, which helped me to understand some of the broader historical context of the conflict that is described in the graphic history provided at the end of this chapter. I then developed a proposal, sought and was awarded research funding, and had my work evaluated for ethical approval by the relevant authorities in both the United States, where I was studying at the time, and Angola.

From 2013 to 2014 I lived in Angola full time, interspersed with three months of fieldwork in Brazil. In Angola I became a primary school music teacher at a private school, a Scout leader, and a university faculty member, which allowed me to develop a rich social and intellectual network. I got to know people at a local NGO and regularly attended their meetings. I worked out at the local gym, attended concerts, spent time at coffee shops and bars quietly watching the goings and comings of those with some disposable income. This technique is called "participant observation"—one participates fully in life, but observes it carefully as well, keeping detailed notes along the way.

Participant observation was structured and deepened by 107 full-length semistructured interviews, focus group interviews, a survey undertaken with strangers aimed at obtaining statistically significant data on middle-class definitions, and social media analysis.

Image I.2. A map of the Atlantic Ocean designed by Kyle Williams.

Angola's recent history included many people informing on one another during the war, and in part as a result of this few individuals wished to be recorded. In some cases it took a long time to build relationships of trust. I therefore rarely used a voice recorder, though occasionally I captured sound bites on my phone, and the interviews that I used for the oral histories in Chapter 3 were recorded—again on my phone. All files were kept embedded in a password-protected Excel sheet, and where possible off the main hard drive of my personal computer because I was regularly warned by friends that the authorities might confiscate it at any moment (they never did).

I wrote hundreds and hundreds of pages of notes, sketches, and questions, transcribing them every night on my computer. I often switched between Portuguese and English in the same set of sentences. Each interview was allocated a number, and all fieldnotes were recorded by date using the convention of Year, Month, Day, Place. They were recorded in this way because of the filing system I used on my computer. For example, were I to complete the 108th interview today, I would record it as Interview #108, 191018, Hermitage, Mauritius—that is, 2019, October 18, in Hermitage, Mauritius, where I am currently typing. These interviews are listed at the beginning of the book, and referred to throughout by interview number (e.g., Interview #21).

Sometimes I wrote by hand, sometimes I wrote notes on my phone, often I sent WhatsApps or texts to myself if there was something I was worried about forgetting, because typing on a cell phone proved to be far less obtrusive than writing by hand in a paper notebook. I took photographs with both a camera and my phone, and kept tickets, papers, and random artifacts; where possible these were scanned. Every person I worked with was asked to choose a pseudonym, and in my fieldnotes I referred to them only by that pseudonym, with the original name recorded on a password-protected Excel sheet to protect their identity. Informed consent was obtained in all situations beyond broad public events (I could not get everyone's permission to be part of my study at a rock concert!), and interlocutors always had the right to withdraw, though nobody did. When details were needed—such as the type of car an individual drove—I have, as much as possible, kept to the spirit of the truth but not its letter. For example, Aimé, whom I describe in Chapter 1, did not in fact drive a white Honda, but a car equivalent in value and status of a different color. To say what car she *actually* drove might identify her to those in the community, but the broad point of the argument I make using her car as an example remains valid either way. The detail about keeping the plastic on the seats is absolutely accurate.

I could not afford a car myself, but was able to purchase a motorbike in Angola (in Rio I took the bus or walked). It was rare for women to ride motorbikes in that part of the country, and the experience of my daily commute in this way opened up many conversations. This was compounded because—largely in deference to my parents and some concerned departmental administrators—I brought with me an extremely good motorbike helmet that earned me the nickname of the "astronaut from South Africa." As I explore later in this introduction, a motorbike was *not* a normal symbol of middle- or upper-class status, but whiteness was associated with wealth, and in that way I was often quite confusing for people. I also speak Portuguese with a strong Brazilian accent, further disrupting expectation, stereotype, and reality, which often did not quite converge. I found this productive, rather than disruptive, as it opened up many conversations.

Whilst doing my fieldwork, I felt increasingly that my efforts to capture "data" were incomplete when I focused only upon what I had been taught comprised ethnography: that is, the monographical, the singular anthropological gaze. In searching for ways to record experiences of insight and learning generated not only by ethics-committee-approved informants, but by my subjective responses to friends, children, and strangers within the fieldwork environment (Auerbach 2017), I began to write poetry alongside my fieldnotes. I have included some of that work in this book as well. The poems allowed me to explore ideas that later enriched my formal interviews and observation, and at the end of the process, it was the poems I liked the most.

I completed my fieldwork in December 2014 and returned to the United States. I finished my doctorate two years later, and in January 2017 began a job at the African Leadership College, where I taught for two years. In 2018 I returned to Angola to do follow-up research toward the completion of this book.

The 2018 fieldwork trip allowed me to observe the impact of the oil price crash that took place in December 2014, just as I was finishing my major fieldwork, and I did follow-up interviews with most of the people who appear in this text, also visiting the school and university where I had taught. In 2017, Angola also experienced its first change in presidential leadership since 1979, leading to both negative and positive shifts that affected everyday lives in significant ways. The book is mostly about what I learned from 2011 to 2014, but does take into account the changes that took place after that period.

How to Read This Book

This book does not follow the conventions of academic writing. It includes long sections of text, such as this one, and also a graphic-novel-style history of Angola, recipes, poetry, photo essays, and prose that opens itself to different types of analyses. It is informed by texts such as Nick Sousanis's (2015) *Unflattening*, which asks readers to interrogate how understanding is often shaped by the form of the material presented, and the limitations that such material inevitably has. Sousanis draws attention to understanding the "whole," which I do not think is actually possible. Nonetheless, his suggestion of a broader, more inclusive perspective, does seem useful.

In anthropology, we often use academic theory to structure our work and use the work in turn to build upon the theory. This can be very powerful. Theory, however, as Liisa Malkki and Allaine Cerwonka (2007) have written, is something that needs to be constantly "improvised" to be responsive to the needs of society, and the needs that this work is responding to are very much grounded in everyday discourses and everyday realities.[10] I have written in a particular way in these pages because of what I want this book to *do*. I want it to shift the way that readers imagine people in parts of the world that they don't know, and the nation-state categories that supposedly define, divide, and unite us. To shift thinking, there must be some engagement with emotion—one needs to "care" in a way that requires and compels more than clicking a link to something on the Internet. The feeling, far more than the thought of the particular contents of what we explore, is what is likely to stay with us, but acting purely on the basis of feeling and abandoning thought may have terrible consequences—as certain high-ranking tweeters regularly demonstrate. So, feeling and thinking need to converge. This at times can be difficult or uncomfortable, but difficulty and discomfort are arguably at least part of the point of learning—the sand that makes the pearl.

Core Concepts

The Angolan Middle Class

This is a book about the Angolan middle class, but what does that actually mean? I will argue that it can be understood as *those with a house, a car, and an education*. This understanding will be *cumulative*: each chapter reveals further dimensions of class membership and class mobility. First, it's important to understand the broad parameters of what class, or social stratification, means.

"Middle class" is a term that is frequently used in everyday language to include people who are neither starving nor flying around the world in private jets. For those interested, there is extensive scholarship in economics, sociology, and political philosophy (see the Indicative Bibliography) that takes into account the relativity of middle-class membership. In 2014, when this research was undertaken, Angola was 149th out of 185 countries on the Human Development Index, a United Nations tool that assesses countries based on three criteria: "a decent standard of living," "knowledge," and a "long and healthy life" (UNDP 2014). By 2018, only 11 per cent of the labor force were deemed by the same organization to have "skills," infant mortality was at 54.6 deaths per 1,000 births, and malaria was 120 cases for every thousand (UNDP 2018).

In this context, income is important. How much money does one make, how many people does that money support, and how far does that money go? Importantly, does a person get paid in US dollars—which are technically illegal for day-to-day purposes but widely used anyway—or in Angolan kwanzas (the abbreviation for which is AOK)? For example, in Angola during my fieldwork, US$1.00 bought a can of beer. You can't buy a beer for a dollar in most of the US, but there are other things in the US that are much, much cheaper than in Angola—like drinking water, or cars. At the end of the day, income itself is almost meaningless unless it is put in the context of the people concerned, and its source is also considered.

Is the money one earns coming from one job, or from many jobs? Are those jobs in the "formal economy" (by which I mean subject to labor regulation, protection, taxation, and law) or are they side gigs, that might be untaxed, unregulated, and unprotected? How many people contribute to money coming into a household, and how is the labor divided, both in terms of unpaid work, like chores, and in terms of paid work outside the home (Chant and Sweetman 2012)? Toward whom does an individual have financial responsibility? In Angola, like most of the world (excluding much of Europe and North America), "family" tends to mean more than parents and children, and it is unwise to assume universal models—of family or of finance—that are actually Euro-American exceptions to global chains of response and responsibility (Chakrabarty 2000). In Angola almost everybody had, and still has, side gigs, but increasingly that is becoming the global norm. Think of people who drive for Uber on the weekends, or babysit the neighbor's children, or sign up to www.taskrabbit.com if they live in the US or Canada.

Assets are very important. Later chapters in this book consider the experiences of some of the many people who entered the Angolan middle class by occupying buildings abandoned by Portuguese colonizers and then using those buildings to leverage capital. In the Angolan context, assets also include cars, computers, jewelry, and so on: things can be sold if necessary, or maintained in different ways to secure a future. Shailja Patal's (2010) exquisite *Migritude* is a meditation on the experiences and conditioning of migration, and the role that saris, jewelry, and money played in the financial lives of a family of Kenyans of South Asian descent. Very differently, Jane Guyer's (2004) *Marginal Gains* explores exchange of different *categories* of goods in parts of West Africa, and what can and cannot be converted into categories of wealth. In this book, the chapter on smell explores how, in the context of Angola-Brazil, perfume became an important asset to some individuals—in terms of both financial and symbolic gain.

For decades, social scientists have shown that just as human beings invest value in financial capital, we also place tremendous importance on "cultural capital"—which is understood as habits, mannerisms, and knowledge that enable us to show belonging in a given space, often leading to class mobility (both upward and downward). The latter is not monetized, but the irony is that it is often precisely what leads to money being consolidated, because of the symbolic meaning that cultural capital has. The sociologist Pierre Bourdieu has most famously written about this in his book *Distinction* (1984), but there has been a long history of analysis in the literature that started when a Swede named Thorstein Veblen (2009 [1899]) explored European holidays in the 1800s. Cultural capital has to do with taste, with circles of knowledge, and with one's ability to "traffic in influence" (described below). In Angola it is about language, style, music, literature, social media, and more.

For most Angolans along the urban coast, houses were critical. If one had one, one had a claim to land, and to stability. Many inherited or occupied their houses when the Portuguese fled the country in 1975, unsure if they would ever be back. At that time, whole buildings were left unoccupied, and though the processes of distribution have been to some extent controlled by the state (Croese 2012; Gastrow 2015; Tomás 2014), many people simply moved in and effectively secured the financial future of coming generations—a kind of modern-day equivalent of what Karl Marx (1999) has famously referred to as "primitive accumulation."

Public transportation in Angola is rudimentary at best, dangerous at worst, often entirely missing. Walking takes time, and energy, and dirties the body. Motorbikes are a decent intermediary but the risk of death is high, and few would argue that they are an optimal way to transport children (though many have no option but to use them for that). A car represents capital in the form of an object, to be sure, but it also represents freedom of time and control over the environment. Cars can be air-conditioned and they can be used at one's own convenience. Social life can, and does, take place in them. Holidays, as Henry Ford so powerfully intuited, can be experienced with cars, and the world quite literally opens up. To have a car was to have control, to become a master of one's destiny in terms of daily life.

Finally, on education: in Angola, as the coming chapters will demonstrate, much attention goes to what is "authentic" and what is "fake." Many houses had been procured through occupation or networks, and the only necessity for car ownership was sufficient cash. But to be *truly* "middle class," I was told repeatedly, one needed a "quality education"—the kind of education that enabled one to think independently of political party logic, or even orders from military structures (for many years, these had been much the same thing). Education also meant networks, and networks were critical for getting by. Without education, one could be duped or controlled. Furthermore, education streamed individuals toward particular futures. A striking example was that at the school where I taught music, children were expected to carefully separate their rubbish into categories appropriate for recycling, despite the fact that no recycling facilities existed in the country at the time. This is indicative of an expectation of skills and *habitus* that had no grounding in local reality, but were nonetheless deemed by the teachers to be essential for these particular children (from fee-paying households).

Being in possession of a house (or a house-under-construction), a car (or perhaps, at a stretch, a motorbike), and an education (or an education-in-progress) were the criteria that emerged again and again and again for middle-class membership. These were what was needed to ensure thriving—not just surviving—in contemporary Angola. Having one of those was good, but not enough. Two meant possibilities were opening, but three meant stability. Often, of course, this was generational, as parents who owned their homes and had access to transportation worked jobs that paid just enough for their children to attend private schools. They almost universally spoke of their desire for their children to attend university thereafter. A degree remained an extremely important guarantor of both status and stability, and those who had completed undergraduate degrees were often given the title "Dr." as a mark of respect.

Capitalismo selvagem

Capitalismo selvagem has already been referenced in this introduction and refers to the economic experience of Angola circa 2014. It was a term used by everyday people to describe a context in which there had been an explicit shift in national policy from socialism to capitalism with the end of the Cold War. Chapter 2, on touch, goes into this in much more depth, but for now some broad features of *capitalismo selvagem* as it was experienced by my interlocutors can be laid out.

Capitalismo selvagem is a system that takes place in a weak state, where *a lei da mata*, or the "rules of the 'jungle,'" play out in economic life. The state, broadly established in the context of socialism, purported to offer free schooling, health care, police protection, and so on—but in reality was able to do very little. Two visits to a family who lived at the economic periphery of Lobito drove this point home forcefully for me. On the first visit, I photographed the children at their grandmother's request (Fieldnotes 131204). I returned some time later with the images. The grandmother began to weep, and explained that the middle child—about three years old—was now deceased. When I asked how, the answer given was that "children just die sometimes" (Fieldnotes 140611)—the human face of a 54.6 per 1,000 infant mortality statistic (UNDP 2018). In the conditions of *capitalismo selvagem*, this is at least acknowledged as a likely possibility.

The Angolan currency, the kwanza, has fluctuated significantly throughout its history (see also Schubert 2017), and the informal currency of the state has largely been US dollars. These dollars, however, could be changed for very different rates on the streets as in the banks, indicating a powerful alternative financial space in which much of the country's economic activity took place. For example, at one point during the civil war, a crate of imported beer could be exchanged for a round-the-world ticket on the national airline (Interview #27), and though in 2014 the situation was much less dramatic, financial instability and unpredictability were basic conditions of *capitalismo selvagem*, making it very difficult to budget, bank, or buy. By 2018, when I returned to Angola, the kwanza had depreciated significantly, and those who did not have access to an external source of income were suffering profoundly.

Finally, many cultural and intellectual traditions say something to the effect of "it is not what you know, but who you know." In Angola under conditions of *capitalismo selvagem*, this was taken to an extreme. People spoke regularly of "trafficking influence," and this book explores how life could get very complex if one didn't know the right people, and by the same token, with the right contacts everyday needs could be easily met. For example, one of my neighbors worked in an important government department that issued personal documents. The queues to get in were usually impossibly long and necessitated an entire day off work. Other neighbors would occasionally take a commission after introducing an individual to the bureaucrat concerned, who "helped" those individuals as part of his after-hours labor. Was this corruption, or was it the logic of the market, whereby supply reacts to demand at the highest price? "Corruption" is, I will argue, far too lazy a term for making sense of the ways in which resources were mobilized at all levels of Angolan society; the "traffic of influence" is a more helpful phrase.

I have now laid out the ground on which this path progresses. The book does not offer a detailed historiography of Angola, although relevant works are suggested in the Indicative Bibliography. Instead, with Elinor Driver, I present an illustrated history of Angola. This history is brief but captures the essential details that are necessary to understand if one is to make sense of what follows. The first chapter prioritizes the sense of smell, and immerses readers in the space the book will ask them to inhabit. It is about perfume and sweat, air-conditioning, and subtle indicators that help people place one another in terms of influence and prestige. The second chapter feels into touch, the tactile, and the textures of everyday life, as experienced by members of the Angolan Scouting association. The third offers an analysis of taste—both gustatory and aesthetic—through two life histories of very different men: a chef and a tailor. In the fourth chapter readers are invited to "hear" the echoes of cold war ideology, the noises of contemporary capitalism, and how these manifest in the classrooms and halls of local universities. The last ethnographic chapter, sight, looks at selfies and the use of social media, as well as what are framed as "ethical afterimages;" moments of ethical complexity that have stayed with me as a researcher ever since. Finally, the conclusion speaks to curiosity, and the importance of asking good questions, even after research has formally "ended." It updates the text with what has happened in Angola since the work was undertaken, and draws together the themes of the book as a whole. My hope is that through an appreciation of an ethnography of that which is working in contemporary Angola, readers might find in themselves a desire to know more, and to ask people there (and elsewhere) to explain how it is that their lives are lived, heard, witnessed, and experienced, with regard to the good, the bad, the ugly, and the beautiful.

> **Why does it matter? (proprioception)** *Orientation*
>
> The purpose of this explanation is to orient the reader. At the end of each chapter, there is a short section, like this one, on why—in my opinion—a particular concept matters, and what I hope readers might think about after going through the material. The section is not meant to be conclusive but rather to form the basis for a discussion. Some readers need a reason to engage with ideas, others do not. Some might find it helpful to read this section before reading the chapter, or all of these sections at once before reading the book. This text *can* be linear, but it doesn't have to be.

A BRIEF HISTORY OF ANGOLA
Illustrated by Elinor Driver · Text by Jess Auerbach
Selma, Isabel and Joaquim are attending their first camp-out with the Angolan Scouts for Africa Day. Hundreds of children and young people have come together in the big church at the centre of town to celebrate.
Joaquim is scared to spend the night outside the church, but he doesn't tell the girls that!
They are greeted by Chefe Alex, one of the most important teachers in the whole of Benguela province.
Welcome!
Chefe Alex gathers all the cubs around him in the courtyard outside the church and lights a fire.
Now cubs, let me tell you about the history of Angola!
Selma yawned, she wasn't sure if she liked history.
Selma querida, Why are you yawning? Tell me, when your father was young, what did he do?
My dad fought in the war.
And your mother?
She was also in the war but then she ran away. She walked from Andulo to Lobito.
Sumbe
Andulo
451 km
Kuito
Lobito
Benguela
Huambo
But why?
UNITA?
Oil?
MPLA?
O Povo?
Diamonds?
The children mumbled a few words but they were not sure, and so, around the fire Chefe Alex began to tell them a bit about their story...
Long ago, before countries as we know them existed, there were people living on these lands...

24   From Water to Wine

A Brief History of Angola   25

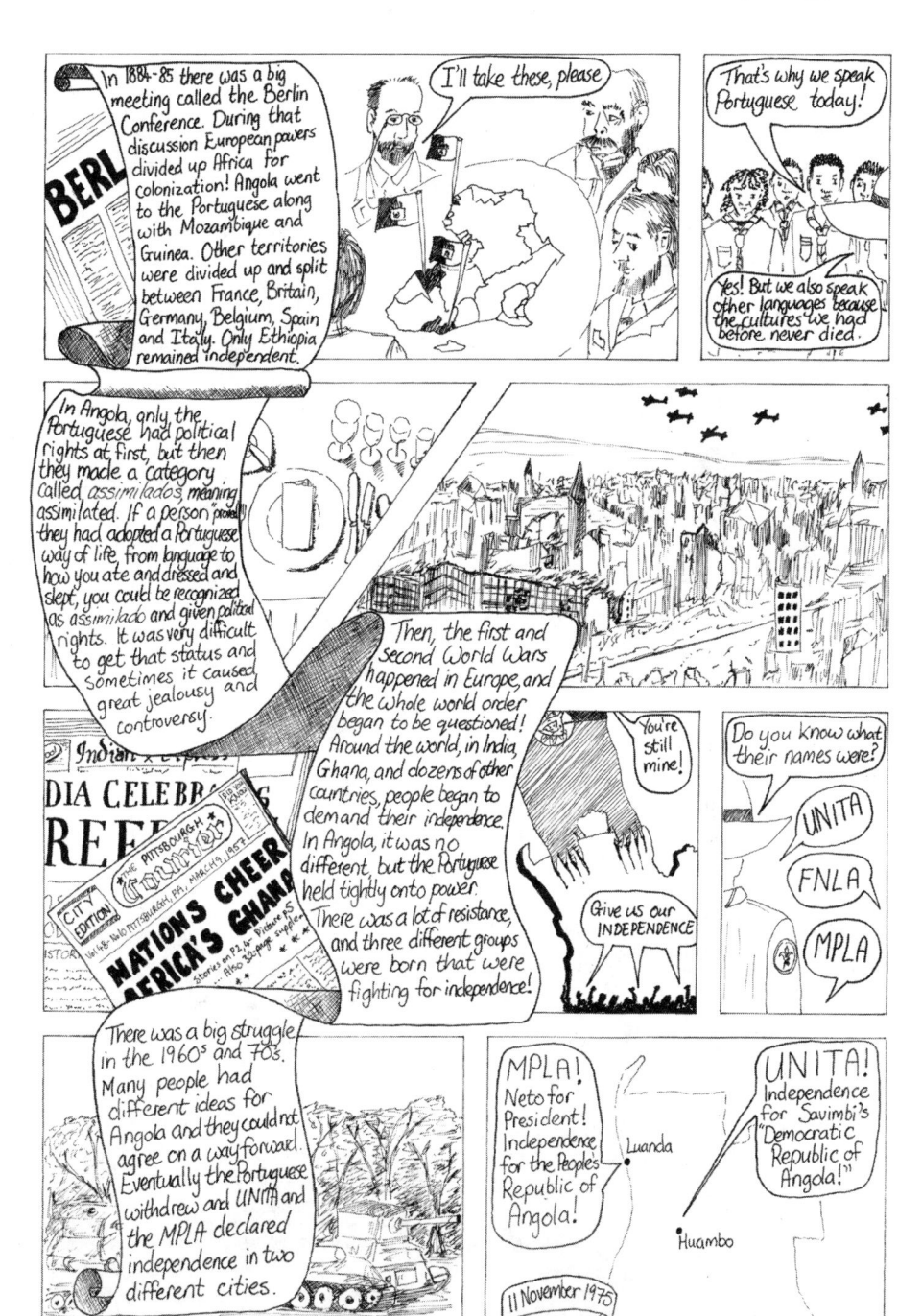

In 1884-85 there was a big meeting called the Berlin Conference. During that discussion European powers divided up Africa for colonization! Angola went to the Portuguese along with Mozambique and Guinea. Other territories were divided up and split between France, Britain, Germany, Belgium, Spain and Italy. Only Ethiopia remained independent.

"I'll take these, please."

"That's why we speak Portuguese today!"

"Yes! But we also speak other languages because the cultures we had before never died."

In Angola, only the Portuguese had political rights at first, but then they made a category called *assimilados*, meaning assimilated. If a person proved they had adopted a Portuguese way of life, from language to how you ate and dressed and slept, you could be recognized as *assimilado* and given political rights. It was very difficult to get that status and sometimes it caused great jealousy and controversy.

Then, the first and second World Wars happened in Europe, and the whole world order began to be questioned! Around the world, in India, Ghana, and dozens of other countries, people began to demand their independence. In Angola, it was no different, but the Portuguese held tightly onto power. There was a lot of resistance, and three different groups were born that were fighting for independence!

"You're still mine!"

"Give us our INDEPENDENCE"

"Do you know what their names were?"

UNITA
FNLA
MPLA

There was a big struggle in the 1960s and 70s. Many people had different ideas for Angola and they couldn't agree on a way forward. Eventually the Portuguese withdrew and UNITA and the MPLA declared independence in two different cities.

"MPLA! Neto for President! Independence for the People's Republic of Angola!"

"UNITA! Independence for Savimbi's 'Democratic Republic of Angola!'"

Luanda
Huambo

11 November 1975

Then the former USSR, Cuba, the USA and South Africa got involved, and suddenly the war went from being an internal struggle over power to being a proxy conflict for the cold war. Most of the Portuguese left in the space of a single week! Tens of thousands of soldiers from South Africa and from Cuba came to Angola to fight. South Africa (with money from the USA) supported UNITA. Cuba (with money from the former USSR) supported the MPLA. Almost all Angolans were drawn into the war.
As well as soldiers, Cuba also sent nurses and teachers. The education system in Angola was not strong at the end of colonialism, now most of the teaching happened in Spanish! On the 10th of September, 1979, one week before his 57th birthday, Antonio Agostinho Neto lost his battle against cancer. His birthday, 17th September, is still celebrated today as National Heroes' Day. After Neto's death, Eduardo dos Santos took over the MPLA and became the next president of Angola.
Jose Eduardo Dos Santos
Is that the same Eduardo who was president until 2017?
Yes! The same one! Zedú, as he was known, stayed in power for 38 years!

A Brief History of Angola 27

The change in leadership did nothing to ease the conflict between the MPLA and UNITA. The war was hard. Many people died, many had to flee their homes, people were often very hungry because infrastructure was destroyed and fields were filled with landmines.
Millions of people left the country as refugees.

28   From Water to Wine

In 1991, it looked like the war was going to end, and for a brief period there was peace. That is when we set up the Angolan Scouts! But the peace did not hold and the country went back to war. This time, it was even worse.

Then, on the 22nd of February 2002, UNITA's leader, Jonas Savimbi, was killed. By then, the population was so, so tired. Suddenly, there was peace in the country and slowly people began to rebuild their lives. Angola is a country that is veeery rich in natural resources, so lots of people wanted to "help". Zedú became known as the "architect of peace" because he made a plan to turn Luanda into Africa's Dubai!

There were so many in Luanda after the war that space came at a premium. For years, it has been one of the world's most expensive cities to live in!

In December 2014 the price of oil fell. Angola had been rebuilding quickly because it has so much oil, but suddenly there was a crisis!

A Brief History of Angola   29

Angola had been so long in a state of war that everybody had to learn how to live in a period of peace. It wasn't always possible to speak freely, like in the case of 15++ but that is a story for another day.
Today Angola is still a major diamond and oil producer but is also known for lots of other things. Dance is a huge part of Angolan life — Zumba, a world-wide exercise, comes from a dance. Kizomba, and the Latin American Samba originated from our Semba. Kuduro has also travelled widely.

João Lourenço (MPLA) became president in 2017 and many things are now changing in the country. For the first time ever we are even developing tourism!

We don't know what will happen in the future, but for now, it's good that children like you are able to play freely...

To be continued...

~ Smell ~

CHAPTER 1

The Smell of Success:
Perfume, Beauty, Sweat, Oil

This chapter begins with an olfactory experience, before moving into an analytic essay about scent and stench in contemporary Angola.

Read with Your Nose

Welcome to Lobito. As the newly built hot-tar road reaches the entrance of the city, there is a wall with a mural painted on it. The wall smells of mud, trash, urine, and salt. Everything in Lobito smells slightly of salt, as it is located by the sea on a bed of sodium chloride.

There is a faint smell, too, of hot plastic in the sun from the signage that was put up to mark the countdown to the one-hundred-year anniversary of the city in 2013. It no longer works, except for a random flashing strip of light half-way down that is simply an early indication as you enter the town of whether the electricity is working.

Continuing our drive, we pass the port, where machinery is manufactured for the oil rigs that pump the economy, and which always smells of petrol and exhaust fumes from the trucks that carry equipment in and out. Our noses clog with dust from cement, and we cannot help coughing.

Along the main road is the *Africano* roundabout, marked by a pink concrete statue of the city's token: a flamingo. Blue-and-white minibuses called *candonguieros* ferry people between the formal city, near the sea, and the hills up above it, where buildings are haphazard and mansions lean up against homes of corrugated iron sheeting and thinly plastered concrete brick.

Inside the *candongueiros*, the geographies of human passage mix together in an odiferous stew created by bodies packed tightly next to one another. Subtle battle tactics are employed by many in efforts to avoid being placed next to the almost inevitable plastic bucket of fresh (or less than fresh) fish.

In the upper zone of the city, a huge concrete elephant with a trunk that doubles as a slide offers shade to pedestrians and motorbike taxi drivers, and laughing children who scamper like ants across its back.

Here, the city's outbreaths rise upward in the mornings and the evenings when cooking takes place at home, and a hundred thousand mosquito coils repel the ever-present threat of malaria. Neighbors rest with one another over beer and starchy *funje*[1] and peanut-spiced chicken.

Dust clogs nostrils with a smell of dehydrated earth. It is everywhere; new schools being built, level by level, also new houses, each bag of cement thrown down on the floor leaves a cloud in the air to inhale. In the center of the city workers refuel their bodies at the magical Aurea's restaurant, where the scent of sugar lingers in the air for blocks around. During the war, the old white man never stopped baking cakes. This is regarded as an act of civic heroism. We are told that he is "more Angolan than Angolans" in the eyes of the city's populace, Portugal a footnote in his history.

Now to the market, which smells of old clothes and mud and the sweat of vendors sitting in the sun, of fermenting meat and vegetables, of layered global commerce coming together: palm oil and tinned tuna from Jakarta, electronics from Guangzhou, motor parts from Delhi—these all smell of hot metal. More pungent the odors of local pineapples and goats. "Kony 2012"[2] T-shirts hang like defeated flags on a string: good will from the United States, for sale on the open market at a very low price; and damp kwanza bills unfolded from pockets close to the skin give off the subtle odor of hundreds of finger tips, tens of palms.

Following a wisp of acrid sweetness, we find ourselves at the personal hygiene section. Boxes of scent vie for our attention, stamped "Made in China" or, for double the price, "Product of Emirates." Everybody around us is anointed, and here the afterscent is one that stings a little and potentially burns the skin, but that is sweet, intense, and pungent.

We leave, and on our way out we pass by Lino. Hunched over a foot-powered sewing machine, he is making dresses in a makeshift shelter at the side of the road; at twenty-eight his reputation for design precedes him even to Brazil. His booth smells of freshly cut wax-print cloth.

Though it feels a world away, just up the road is Aimé's shop. She travels to New York each year, and to Lisbon and São Paulo, to buy clothing for special clients, and transports the goods in reinforced suitcases carefully locked. In my mind her shop smells of frankincense and myrrh (I don't know what these things really smell like); it is otherworldly. It includes a cabinet of perfumes: French and North American, and special shampoo for babies and Disney-branded plasters for children's cuts. Prices are all in US dollars. I am told that dollars, kept in locked drawers, smell fresh—to me they smell only of paper.

Aimé drives a white Honda that was imported to the country last year. Plastic still covers the seats to preserve the new-car smell for longer. She lives with her husband and her children in a house with an open veranda and an avocado tree in the garden; the fruits make everything smell green, verdant, lush.

Now we are on the city's concrete artery again; here dirty flamingos dream of the mangrove that used to cover this place. Their population was nearly decimated, but at the last gasp the newly opened chapter of the Rotary Club launched a campaign to save them. Because of where they live, they smell like feathery trash and skinny fish (I think).

Here is the old whisky factory that still makes bootleg liquor, here is the gym where the odor is of purposeful sweat. Gym sweat distinct from the sweat from labor—is it from mingling with spandex as opposed to rubbing against thick cloth that offers protection from the sun? Is sweat fuelled by Poweraid different from sweat fuelled by sugared water, or is it the space that shapes the way my nose perceives them?

Here is the river Catumbela, gushing toward the coast. It was the conduit for hundreds upon thousands of enslaved people once, who were taken from here to Brazil. It flows right past the former slave market. Few people remember what the structures used to witness, though the sensitive might say they smell at times the cloying stench of bloody history. It is largely overpowered now anyway, by the hot-old-oil smell of frying chips at the newly opened drive-thru.

The hot-old-oil smell of frying chips comes from heated sunflower oil. Absent in all these smells is that of the new black gold that replaced humans, coffee, sugar, cotton as a source of extractive revenue. The oil flows off the coast in rigs that never come to land, its only presence felt in the low cost of petrol that spills, red, into the vehicles of those who clog the roads.

In Daniella's rented apartment the atmosphere is one of work and flame-retardant-covered furniture, and her memories of life are marked by her collection of perfumes. She is building her own house in a suburb under construction that is called "Grace," that smells of bricks, cement, and paint, marked by infrastructure newly arriving.

Infrastructure also smells: supermarkets, with their curious odor of packaging mixed with vegetables mixed with chemical cleaners and filtered through air-conditioning and refrigeration technology that smells the same but different across the world.

Tar roads are unfurled, steel bridges welded and coated with polyvinyl acetate. New fantasies are built alongside decaying relics of the past. So often, these fantasies smell much like glass. Banners glued to trees and to the walls say we are growing, growing in peace. They invite us with all our senses into the dream of the future, to focus on that, not the past that lies littered all around us.

And the future smells good: it is mangoes next to iPhones at Carnival, it is freshly cut grass on manicured university lawnscapes, it is the wind on the sea carrying the scent of hot espresso and grilled, fresh fish. It is the knowledge of the smell of duty-free, which lies at the border of the known, the owned, and the desired.

Conditioning the Air: Space and Control

Usually we do not think about the air, we just breathe it. We tend to notice it only if it gets too hot or too cold or something is *wrong*, and then we *really* worry. Most of the people reading this book might never have thought at all about the air before: Why would you? It is the invisible emptiness that gives us life, and surely if there's one thing we could hope to take for granted in the world, air would be it.

Anthropological methodology is grounded in what we call "participant observation." This is just as simple, and just as complex, as it sounds. We participate in everyday life around us, and we observe it. We combine presence, empathy, and curiosity with discipline and a commitment to truth. We use our bodies as our research instruments with which we come to know the world, using all our senses and all our skill to earn trust and to make connections, to weigh and to reassemble the world around us and to weave from our experiences the kind of text you are now reading. We take up space. We breathe.

Anthropologists, and other social scientists as well, are far from neutral. We acknowledge that our presence itself is usually enough to change reality. Yet rarely, in methodology books at least, is the subject of our own smell raised.[3] Perhaps this is because the systems of knowledge that we work in largely emerged during the Victorian era, when discussions of bodily functions were deemed impolite. Perhaps it is because, in the broad epistemology of whiteness (from which many of these disciplines first emerged), an embedded assumption was that white people did not smell, but other people did. Those interested in this point would benefit from Mark M. Smith's (2006) book *How Race Is Made: Slavery, Segregation, and the Senses*. Whatever the reasons, few would deny that scent is often the key to our deepest memories, and with them emotions, and through the smells of others we make snap judgments that inform trust, attraction, or fear (Classen 1992; Classen, Howes, and Synnott 1994).

During my fieldwork, I had no choice but to engage with scent when I began teaching music at a private primary school, which I call in this book the College of Stars. The College of Stars was founded by a pair of entrepreneurs in Lobito who did not want their little girl Catarina to go away to school. Until the end of the civil war, families with means sent their children to be educated abroad from as early as six years old, and the rest did what they could in the strained national system, which was free but of wildly varying standards.

Mr. and Dr. Diego had the money to send Catarina to Portugal, but chose not to, as her birth coincided with the arrival of peace in the country, and they felt it was time for change. Instead, they set up a school in their living room that, by 2014, catered to several hundred children from ages two to seventeen. Of course, by then it had moved to its own big building in the center of town, and when I returned in 2018 it was one of the few private businesses that was still thriving—it had just added a swimming pool.

The College of Stars offered an alternative to the two previously existing options: Angolan government education or education in a religious institution, and in 2013–14 it dominated the local private-school learning market. The teachers at the time were mostly Portuguese, promising "quality" education with an "Angolan curriculum," so that children could, in the words of the school's director, have the "best of both worlds" (Interview #61).[4] Mr. Diego and I had met by chance through a mutual friend, and when he learned that I had been classically trained in music, he immediately offered me a job.

The deal was simple: I worked at the school as a music teacher for a minimum wage, teaching students from age five to thirteen how to play the recorder and read music notation. In exchange, I would meet their parents and, after seeking appropriate consent, could interview these parents about their backgrounds, lifestyles, aspirations, and experiences in Lobito. I did not interview the students nor make them part of my study as individuals, but of course getting to know them informed my broader understanding of the emerging middle class. The affiliation also made the world of difference as it made me socially legible. Instead of riding around the city on my motorbike with my astronaut helmet as a stranger, I gained legibility, gravitas, and a social role in my teacher's coat (bright white, like a lab coat).

When I announced the job enthusiastically to my friend Victoria, whom readers will come to know well in the pages that follow, she was supportive but also mildly concerned. As an upwardly mobile young professional and born and bred Lubitanga (a person from Lobito), Victoria was infinitely more sensitive to social expectations than I could ever hope to be. Her response was to warn me that should I accept the job at the College of Stars, one of the first things that I would need to do would be to purchase perfume (Fieldnotes 131121).

Shortly after that discussion, Victoria and a colleague from the school marched me over to Aimé's shop (described above), which was located near the school. There I somewhat reluctantly exchanged US$150 for an apple-shaped bottle of Nina Ricci's *Nina*, which collective wisdom had concluded was an appropriate scent for me to wear. I was told gently, firmly, and repeatedly that if I wanted to teach in a private school in Angola, I had to smell right. And "right" in this case meant I had to smell of imported perfume—French or US

American—which would enable students to trust that the knowledge I was imparting to them was indeed of "quality."

Writing of Hong Kong's notoriously polluted air, US American anthropologist Timothy Choy asks, "How are Hong Kong's *air spaces* distributed?" (2010, 38, my emphasis). He continues, "Who gets to occupy those [spaces] with the cleanest air? Who breathes the street? Who breathes mountains? Who breathes the sea? Who breathes flies?" Choy is concerned with questions of what he calls "atmospheric ontology," or how the atmosphere—both literal and in its poetic form—is understood and is experienced. Importantly, he acknowledges that even within the space of one city, the atmosphere is not the same, but rather is differentiated according to social, political, and economic power.

In Lobito in 2014, some little children went to school and breathed the scent of Nina Ricci perfume during their recorder lessons in air-conditioned classrooms with smartboards and wireless Internet. Most, however, carried tin cans or plastic chairs into overcrowded spaces where government-provided furniture did not even begin to meet the needs of the number of pupils, and quite often children were turned away from school entirely due to lack of space (Interview #68). Norms of hygiene and self-presentation were fastidiously maintained and socially reinforced, but average temperatures on Angola's coast are about twenty-seven degrees Celsius and people packed together smelled distinctly of humanity.

Singapore has a climate similar to Angola's, and its founding prime minister, Lee Kuan Yew (2015), is said to have claimed that air-conditioning was the most important invention of the twentieth century. Smell transmits differently in hot versus cool environments, and air-conditioning lessens the body's need to self-regulate through perspiration, limiting "competing odors" that might otherwise intrude. To be in an air-conditioned environment, be it a school, a car, an office, a shop, or a recreational space, was to be able to control both one's own and other's odors to a large extent. Air-conditioning further enabled higher levels of certain kinds of productivity, and kept mosquitos (and with them malaria) at a relative distance.

One could argue that air-conditioning enabled the creation of what can be imaged as an "olfactory blank canvas"—a kind of neutral space in which to create a very literal sense of oneself. Those who were poor[5] had little ability to exert that kind of control outside their homes. The odors of others and of the environment mixed with their own, and one had no way of knowing, for example, who else would board a given *candongueiro*. To show what that control *could* look like, it is worth considering the experiences of a woman I call Flávia.

Flávia was a successful Angolan postgraduate student specializing in gynecology at a prestigious Brazilian university. She and I met at a gym in Lapa, a busy district in the center of Rio de Janeiro. Sometime after a friendship had been established, we spoke about how I'd identified her as Angolan—something she had been curious about. I had approached her in the locker room when we were both changing, and said something like "Forgive my rudeness, but I heard your accent and I wondered if you are from Angola? I'm South African, and I miss spending time with other Africans a lot." All that was true, but accent was actually the least of it, I had just listened carefully to triangulate my intuition—a point I readily admitted to her when we finally spoke about it.

"I knew you were Angolan," I explained to Flávia, "partly because of the pink handbag that is just the style of people from Luanda, but partly just because of how you *are*, you know what I mean? Your hair, your clothes, but there's something more to it than that as well, something about *ser* and *estar* that is difficult to pinpoint" (Interview #75). *Ser* and *estar* are Portuguese verbs for "to be" that do not translate in English. *Ser* is to be existentially, unchangeably: I am South African (and *feel* South African, in the sense of "imagined communities" [Anderson 1990]). I am a woman—in my case this is not in fluctuation, though it could be. I have certain core beliefs that *could* change, but probably won't, and so on. Nothing is entirely fixed but these are the things we assume will not change. *Estar* is much more transient: I am hot, I am hungry, I am amused or grumpy or tired—but it will pass.

Flávia did know what I meant, though, and she explained it far better than I. She said it was important that as a black[6] woman working as a doctor in Brazil, she was not only immaculately dressed, but that the *sense* she gave was one of "radiance." She managed this, she said, through her choice of perfume. In her words:

> I adore perfume. The one I like most, maybe the five that I have now that I really like, they are Nina Ricci, Carolina Herrera,

Fantasy by Britney Spears, it's part of her cheaper range, Paco Rabanne, and I also like Del Pozo, Jesus's, *In Black,* which is for men but I really like it, and that cheaper one called Midnight, and also a Calvin Klein. And I have something from that other line of Britney. Oh, that's more than five but it's okay. And I like cologne and moisturizing cream, too. And I use Victoria's Secret sometimes, when I need something cheaper. I buy them at duty-free, or I get other people to buy them for me when they travel. Most of the good products come from Europe, though the USA does have some good things too.

Every moment of the day, I have scent [on me]. I use the cheaper ones, colognes, for sleeping, for the bath, the gym. I have perfumes for work. The more expensive ones of course I keep for a night out. (Interview #75)

Flávia's collection of perfumes, she estimated, was worth well over US$3,000, a remarkable sum given her life as a graduate student on a Brazilian government scholarship. (Like many others, her undergraduate degree had been paid for with a scholarship from the then Angolan president's private philanthropic foundation, Fundação José Eduardo dos Santos [FESA]). At first I thought she was exceptional in this regard, but when I asked other interlocutors, both male and female, most had extensive—if not always quite so expensive—collections of fragrances, and many spoke of how they layered perfumes upon one another to create unique olfactory signatures. Celestino—a close friend of Flávia's—worked in the Brazilian music industry. He explained that, in general,

> Angolan guys are very vain [*vaidoso*], but vain in the good sense, not the arrogant sense, but the sense of appreciating good clothes. And perfume *é primordial em Angola* [is primordial in Angola]. We consume so much of it there! We *auto afirmar atravez o cheiro* [self-affirm through scent]. I have a friend who takes maybe twenty days to a month to use a bottle of perfume! He gets through it so fast, because he wants to be at every moment *o homem mais cheiroso de pedaço* [the most fragrant person on the stage]—and in Brazil [with regard to perfume] that's just not the case. Maybe some or other guy will have that habit, but it's very rare, very rare

to find a Brazilian man who takes such care of himself. They—Brazilian men—are much more simple. (Interview #106)

Celestino's wife, and several other female friends in fact, often complained of the vanity of their husbands and how their pursuit of fine perfumes and clothes consumed too much of the family budget. Nevertheless, the "practice" of using began young. Celestino, like Flávia, grew up in Angola but had family who lived abroad, who would send frequent gifts to the little boy, including perfumes. He moved to Brazil as an adolescent, and told me that he always wore perfume to school, as his own four-year-old son did regularly now. Celestino's little boy had already acquired a sensibility to perfume that for him would later likely become an unquestioned part of his identity, whereas those who began using perfume later in life would need to learn the appropriate way to balance different kinds of scents. Celestino's perfume in the classroom as a migrant child in Rio de Janeiro in the early 1990s had at first caused some consternation, and he said that even the teachers would stop in the classroom and say, "Hey, what's that nice smell? Oh, it's the Angolan." "They would call me the Angolan to not give me respect with my name, it really drove me crazy," he explained.

Perfume had marked Celestino from childhood as different, and globalized, but what really troubled him was that Brazilians often failed to respect him by not calling him by his name. Many Angolans had come to Brazil during the war as refugees, and tended to live in the poorer parts of cities such as Rio de Janeiro and São Paulo. Having almost all served in the Angolan military, they were known to be good with weapons and were quickly co-opted into the city's gangs (Interview #89). As such, "Angolan" was a term that had negative connotations, and to use it of Celestino folded him into prejudicial associations with racial perception and denied his class sensibilities. This practice echoed the long history of discrimination based on slavery and colonial occupation that shaped Brazil as much as it shaped Angola (Alencastro 2000), but illustrates its specificities in the moments of a dark-skinned Angolan child interacting with Brazilian society. Indeed, many Angolan residents in Brazil placed tremendous emphasis on ensuring that they "looked different" (and smelled different, as Celestino's example illustrates) from dark-skinned Brazilians, explicitly to avoid police harassment. On a lighter note, when I asked Flávia if she would date a Brazilian, she shrieked with horror: "Are you crazy?!!" she replied, "Brazilian men smell *terrible*!" (her emphasis, Interview #75).

In many ways, Flávia's and Celestino's experiences with perfume represent the ideal of the upwardly mobile in Angolan society. Both their childhoods were marked by frequent visits from relatives outside Angola, who brought with them not only basic consumer goods deemed necessary to middle-class existence (household appliances such as kettles, clothing, certain kinds of food such as Swiss chocolate or dried fruits) but also perfume. The latter anointed both Flávia and Celestino as different from their peers and prepared them for lives of upward social mobility.

Important to keep in mind is that during the civil war (1975–2002) Angolan cities struggled desperately to cope with the influx of Internally Displaced People (IDPs), as well as urban maintenance such as rubbish disposal (Cardoso 2015; Gastrow 2015; Tomás 2014). Soon after the war began, cities began to smell, such that what urban planners understand to be a "neutral scent" (Henshaw 2014; Quercia, Schifanella, Aiello, and McLean 2015) was rarely achieved. Traces of scent from buses, markets, and other people lingered on the body, marking ones' movement through geographic and social space, so *what* one smelled of emerged as vitally important. Flávia's and Celestino's relatives ensured that anyone who caught a whiff of them knew that these were children whose odor connected them to a particular world—much as the Nina Ricci was supposed to do for my young students in Lobito.

Controlling the air, and the scent and sense of oneself that other people absorbed, was a way of managing "atmospheric ontology" and proactively engaging with the expectations of others. This section has shown how on both sides of the Atlantic, smell was shaped by cultural norms that themselves were deeply embedded in historical processes, as well as infrastructures that enabled or impinged upon individual projections. The section that follows builds upon those processes, exploring how aspiration and authenticity were communicated and tested primarily through smell.

Class, Perfume, Dream: Aspiration and Authenticity

Celestino and Flávia were both well established in Brazil, and as their life stories show, they had been raised with the social and financial capital to succeed as migrants and consolidate already existing class status. For others, though, it was much more complicated. It's one thing to just do what one has been taught, but what if one has not been taught these skills from birth? For example, how did somebody like Victoria (her mother a teacher, eight younger siblings, her father deceased) come to have such intimacy with expensive perfumes? The answer, I was told, was simple: it was through duty-free. In duty-free, one could purchase perfumes much more cheaply than in local boutiques, and wearing them afterward would communicate to others that one was globalized (*globalizado*), had the means to travel, and therefore was knowledgeable about the world. Let me illustrate ethnographically:

Returning from Brazil to Angola for the final segment of my fieldwork, I arrived early for my flight from Rio de Janeiro to Luanda. In the queue, I met a woman in her forties, Joyce, traveling with her *cassoula*, her youngest child (Fieldnotes 141130). Joyce worked in the check-out section of a Luandan supermarket, and that day marked the second flight of her life—the first being her arrival in Brazil some weeks before. She explained that she had come to visit her daughter, who was coincidentally a classmate of Flávia's in medical school. For the return flight, she had come early to ensure that she had time to purchase perfumes for her young twin boys in duty-free. "What perfumes?" I inquired. She said it did not matter, it was only important that they came from duty-free. With perfume from duty-free on them, she elaborated, her boys would be constantly reminded of the life that awaited them if they stayed out of trouble and worked hard—just like their elder sister.

Brazil is expensive and by the end of her journey, Joyce's budget was constrained. Eventually she found two bottles of cologne that were on special for US$25 each, and settled on them for gifts. "Now people will ask them why they smell so good and they will be able to explain that they have a sister studying medicine in Brazil, and that their mother went to visit her," she said with satisfaction, pulling her four-year-old gently away from the plush teddy bears on display at her child's eye level (Fieldnotes 141130).

For Joyce, the value in perfume did not lie only in the substance itself, but *also* in the kinds of social interactions it would enable. When her adolescent sons encountered the response to the perfume from others, they would be prompted to describe their upwardly mobile familial relationships, to articulate substantive links to the world of global higher education and jet-fueled travel. The smell was something both to be enjoyed for itself and to remind them to stay out of trouble, to inspire them to work hard, and to keep them focused on academic goals. It was to be an unguent of good influence that communicated with the boy's interlocutors without their ever needing to open their mouths.

In the case of Joyce's twins, smell was to communicate something positive that would open up opportunities for them, but it could also do exactly the opposite. Here it is worth considering the case of a man I call Aníbal, who lived in Luanda but whose brother was part of the same social milieu in Brazil as Joyce's older daughter (that is, Angolan university students on scholarship in Rio de Janeiro). Aníbal himself had recently graduated from a prestigious university law program in Luanda. However, in our conversation on the phone before meeting, he told me that a year after graduating, he was struggling to find a job.

Visually, Aníbal was the picture of New Angolan success: tall and physically strong, with neatly pressed clothes, highly polished shoes, a wide smile. As he drew nearer, though, I found myself all but recoiling from his scent—an experience so taboo in social science that my instinct was to freeze entirely. I ignored my internal reaction and did not let it show on my face or in my body language, and we spent a pleasant afternoon together. I promised to pass his details on to the few people in my network who I thought might be able to help him. I knew very well, however, that unless he changed his smell, it was highly unlikely that he would find himself employed. I considered asking him about it, but quickly changed my mind—surely, I thought, that would be far too rude? So I said nothing.

As I wrote up my dissertation in California more than a year later, the experience continued to bother me. Why had nobody just *told* Aníbal about his smell? Surely people knew? I knew from Facebook that he was still unemployed, and the cost of that lay heavy on him and on his family. I wrote an email to Victoria to ask her what she thought, and her response is worth repeating:

[10 February 2015, 10:35 am]

[Subject: *Cheiro*]

[From: victoria@imaginaryemailaddress.ao]

[To: jauerbach@postgraduatestudent.com]

There are two reasons why nobody would say to him what is going on. Firstly, it's necessary to be a very good friend of somebody to tell them they smell bad, because people get really offended. Even family members sometimes won't say, we learn here to be very careful with words, you know. Oftentimes we prefer to make comments behind people's backs instead of saying the truth to their face. And the other reason is that perhaps he doesn't care for himself properly, doesn't look after himself, or because of his house he *can't* look after himself, like with no running water. Maybe somebody told him [he smells] but he doesn't know how to address it, or he tried things that do not work. And then it could be that he just doesn't have the habits or the resources to buy the things you need to be clean, as you said he wasn't working [and so has no salary]. Everything becomes about self-care and hygiene, which is something very important in Angola.

Alfred Gell is one of the most important anthropologists to have written about perfume. In his famous essay entitled *Magic, Perfume, Dream* he writes, "We do not discover the meaning of a certain smell by distinguishing it from other smells (we have no independent means of codifying these distinctions) but by distinguishing contexts within which particular smells have a typical value" (1977, 27). Victoria's email reminds us of exactly that: that smell is important, and has consequences, but context is crucial for determining how people communicate about it, and in Angola, like in most places, telling someone they are stinky is unlikely to strengthen a friendship unless done in a very particular, nuanced way.

The second point to draw attention to is the simple fact that cleanliness can be costly. Aníbal lived in a house in one of Luanda's largest *musseques,* or informal settlements. It had neither running water nor electricity, and seven people lived in three rooms, only one of whom was formally employed. If one has grown up in a household with running water, electricity, and an abundant supply of toothpaste, it can be hard to remember that for many people, deodorant might be considered a luxury item. If it was that or a meal for two people—which one would you honestly choose?

Many of our deepest memories are stored in smell, both positive and negative (Marks 2008), and coming across those smells can often trigger powerful emotional reactions. Dr. Daniella was a university professor who, like Aníbal's brother and Joyce's daughter, did her undergraduate degree in Brazil on government scholarship. She returned to Lobito and quickly climbed the ranks in the local university and business sector, receiving promotion after promotion and opening several "side businesses" that generated significant revenue. Petite in stature, she wore precipitously high heels, and combined an easy charm with a steely will.

One evening, after dinner at her house, she showed me the box in which she kept her perfume collection. About thirty centimeters square, and shallow, it held a wide variety of small bottles of colored glass. Tenderly lifting each one, and smelling some of them, she explained:

> I remember them all. I went through a phase where I would put a label on the bottom of each with its story, but now most have fallen off. I leave a little, always, so I can keep smelling it and the smell takes me straight back. For example, this one was what I wore when I first started working at [...]. And this one [a long slender green bottle] was a present from that first boyfriend, and this one here was the one I wore when I went to Brazil; it's Boticário [a Brazilian brand]. This one is the one I wore when I was doing an *estágio* [internship] in Brazil, trying to earn money. I had none, so it is very cheap. And here is the most expensive, Coco Chanel! Oh, in that time I was very rich and I thought, let me buy this! This one I wore when I had my first customers with my business, some Chinese. And this one I have been wearing now, but now it is so nearly finished, I will find another. Yes, I wear perfume every day, but only in the morning. I only put it on one time per day. (Fieldnotes 141206)

Dr. Daniella insistence that she only used perfumes once a day was a reaction to the conspicuous consumption of scent she saw around her. She, like others, warned me not to take too seriously somebody who smelled *too* strongly (or dressed *too* well, or drove *too* good a car) because often that person might be spending "all of his salary on that, and meanwhile he lives in a shack and his cupboard does not even have any food in it" (Fieldnotes 141206). Dr. Daniella was a busy, organized professional, and ==she wanted to smell good, but not so good that she might be deemed frivolous or fall prey to male objectification.== It was a fine balance, she explained, laughing, but people who encountered her would *know* that she was neither poor nor uneducated, that her living conditions were good, but that she was also neither vain nor shallow, and certainly not the type of woman to chase a man for his money, especially—she elaborated, rolling her eyes—if he was *estúpido*. Scent for her therefore communicated aspects of one's character that were linked with morality and taste; with discernment and with internal value. These qualities, however, would only be picked up if one attended to that which was subtle: too much odor, or too little, might run the risk of attracting fools.

What the experiences of Joyce, Anibál, and Dr. Daniella collectively make knowable is ==the importance of smell as a component of upward social mobility—both one that enables, and one that potentially limits.== Where odors hold memory, they also capture in a subtle way the power of dream and aspiration, both material and intangible. Pausing for a moment to imagine one's ideal future home, asking "What will it smell like?" is likely to reveal far more than if we ask "What colour will be painted on the walls?" precisely because ==scent lies at the border of the internal and the external, the body and the world around it.== To invoke new futures using scented products was also to invite them: onto one's body, and into one's home, and to learn to use them well, and to communicate one's message effectively such that the dream translated from that which was singular to that which was shared.

Fieldwork teaches us a great deal, and there were many things I learned while I was in Angola that I did not anticipate. The importance of smell was probably the most significant. Before I arrived in Angola I had read about class, social mobility, and lusophone (Portuguese-speaking) history, but not much at all about smell. That meant that when I started learning about it from my interlocutors,

I did not have a pre-existing theoretical framework in which to place what I was observing. That has pros and cons: pros because it meant my mind was open and unbiased by the literature, but cons because I had not read any other studies of smell, and so I wasn't sure how to turn my observations and intuitions into questions that lead to "data"—particularly because thinking, speaking, and writing about bodily odor can be so delicate.

I was able to engage in what Clifford Geertz (1973) has famously called "thick description," meaning my notes were detailed and precise and allowed me to unravel entire social histories from a few particularly rich events (as I've done above). That said, I did not think to ask for the localized vocabularies of smell—including words such as *catinga*, meaning a terrible bodily stench—until toward the end of my fieldwork period, and as a result my data only scratches the surface of what could be (and I hope one day is) written on this topic. I kept my attention almost entirely on perfumes, soaps, and creams whilst I was doing research, but perfume is just one aspect of smell (in Angola as elsewhere), and there is a whole set of language, practices, substances that go into teaching children how to smell "right," into managing adolescence and the changes that happen in that time, into controlling the body's reaction to climate and context, that my work only partially addressed, and that is not recorded here.

Perfume was fun to focus on, in the same way that middle-class identity was fun to focus on. For the most part people enjoy speaking about that which is good, that which makes them feel good, that in which they find a sense of self-affirmation (returning to Celestino, quoted above). That acknowledged, it was much more difficult to ask about, write about, and even *think* about bad smells in this context, in part because it was one of the times when my white identity became very important. There is a long, long history of white people suggesting that non-white people smell not only different, but bad, that that difference comes from uncleanliness, and that because "cleanliness is next to godliness" non-white people are therefore somewhat lesser (see Burke 1996; McClintock 1995), and I found I needed to be extremely careful.

Care and sensitivity during fieldwork were manifest in strong core or key relationships in which relevant questions of race, class, and religion had been addressed directly through dialogue and where

I felt that the person knew me as well as I knew her or him—that we had formed bonds far beyond fieldwork and research. Victoria and Dr. Daniella were both key interlocutors (outside of academic contexts, I call them simply my friends). We had built trust between us, and we could comfortably explore subjects that were often taboo—such as, for example, stinky feet or how to wash one's armpits, or why nobody had told Aníbal about his bodily odor.

Victoria's email on Aníbal, reproduced in part above, included other interesting details and suggestions that I cannot share here because of context: the relationship of trust between reader and writer is relatively fragile and the opportunity for further explanation almost nil (though feel free to email, or find me on Twitter @jess_auerbach). I am aware that this is an area where many readers may be easily triggered—with historical justification—and where this book adds one more instance to the thousands of white people writing about people of color. If care is not taken in the writing, negative stereotypes can easily, and subtly, be reinforced, and that is certainly not my goal.

Yet smells are as complicated—and as subjective, and culturally encoded—as colors and textures and tastes and sounds, and so to do them justice, I ask simply that readers reflect on *all* smells: the good, the bad, the ugly, and the beautiful, and in that exploration take into consideration the nuances of history, commodities (e.g., deodorants: Where are they manufactured? Who profits from them? Who decides what counts as a "good" smell? Where do the empty cans end up?). I will end this chapter with a quote from a novel entitled *Créole*, in which Angolan author José Eduardo Agualusa explores the life of a man named Fradique who traveled throughout the lusophone world at the height of the Portuguese empire in the nineteenth century. My hope is that the quote, and everything that has preceded it, will inspire an interrogation of what Lalaie Ameeriar (2012, 2017) has referred to as the "sanitized sensorium," in which only a limited number of smells are deemed culturally acceptable, or even speakable, in the context of late capitalist Euro-American society. Introducing the main character of his novel, Agualusa writes:

> Everything about [Fradique] gave off a strange scent, warm and sweet, so intensely that one of [the Angolan] girls ran off covering her nose. "Savage!," young Arcénio cried after her. "This perfume

comes from France!" In those days the Luanda night-time used to smell of *jinguba*, the peanut plant, since from that plant came the oil they used to light the streets. Fradique used to say that cities, like women, could be told apart by their smell. The ports of French West Africa smelled strongly of onions fried in butter (so he said), a concoction which the young people would rub on their bodies like a perfume; Rio de Janeiro smells of ripe guavas, Lisbon of sardines, basil and Members of Parliament. As Arcénio de Carpo (the elder) recalled, in the south of Angola, among the *cuambatos*, women rub their hair with cow dung, which for them is considered one of the most delicate of fragrances. (1988, 132–33)

Why does it matter? (smell) *Knowledge systems*

From many perspectives in the world, global knowledge systems exist almost solely in English. The text makes explicit the impact not only of socialist/capitalist knowledge systems, but those of the Portuguese-speaking world, in which music, soap operas, gossip, fashion, Wikipedia, and academic publications continue to circulate among roughly 260 million speakers, along routes first charted by fifteenth-century navigation that left traces of many kinds, including the olfactory. It provokes us to ask not only "what is known" but also "*how* it is known," and the way such knowledge impacts on individual and collective understandings of self and community. This compels engagements with ontology (how we are) and epistemology (how we know) that go much, much deeper than a simple recognition of why, in the era of Internet freedom, we also have fake news. In recent times the contestation of such systems has taken place using the term "decoloniality." This book as a whole probes what decoloniality in this context might mean; this chapter does so through attention to the body's smells: their acceptance, disguise, messaging, and interpretation.

Recording Fieldwork: Notes, Objects, Structured Observations of Space

How do researchers record? Fieldnotes are intensely personal, and there are many ways to keep them. As I explained in the section on methodology in the Introduction, I used paper notebooks, my phone, and voice-notes as my primary means of recollection, complemented by thousands of photographs (largely taken on my phone but also with a camera) and material objects. Here, I share three methods by which I recorded the work that comprises this book: first notes—photographed as snapshots and a screen grab—the way one does in everyday life; second objects; and finally details about one specific space where I undertook research, that of the gym.

Notes

The photographs in Image 1.1 show the record of several different conversations. At the top is a photograph of details taken from notebook V, recording part of Interview #30, Benguela. During the interview the person with whom I was speaking pointed me to a particular edition of the "diary of the Republic"—a daily gazette produced by the government recording important proceedings and announcements (in this case to do with the national library system). On the right page is part of the person's life story, jotted by hand whilst I listened to him and typed up in detail immediately after, largely translated into English and coded for key words.

In the bottom left corner is the first page of my final fieldwork notebook, which I kept in December 2014. The notebook includes my name, Angolan telephone number, and graduate school email address on the left in case it was lost. Much more interesting is the drawing by a child named Chelsy. Writing in 2018, I have no recollection whatsoever of who Chelsy was or how and why she drew in my notebook. Usually in such cases I made a note of collaborative efforts—writing above the drawing to provide extra context—but in this case I did not. Nonetheless, her record of our relationship is very clear. A few pages later in the same notebook are questions pertaining to perfume, which were preparation for discussions I planned to have with perfume vendors.

Finally, I include a screen shot from my cell phone taken during my most recent trip to Angola in 2018. There I was much more consciously exploring not only fragrances but also stenches, and had several informative discussions on

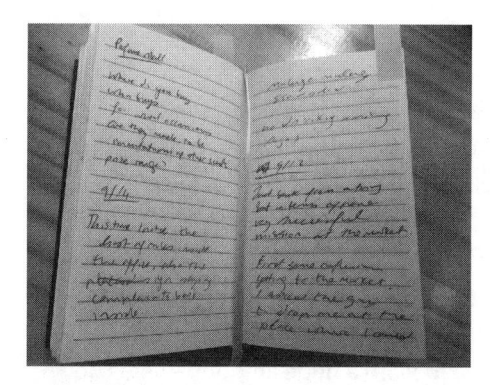

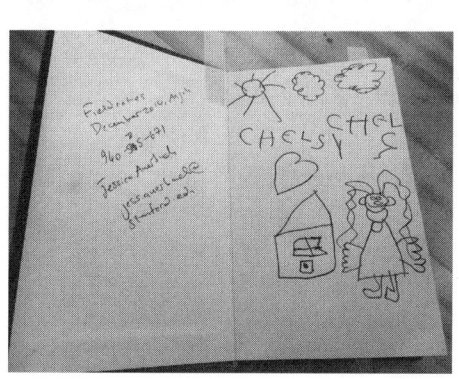

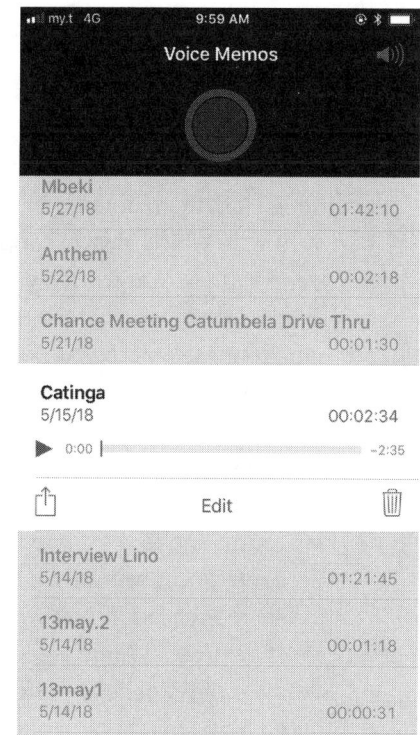

Image 1.1. *Top left*: Pages from notebook V. *Bottom left*: Final notebook from fieldwork. *Right*: Screenshot of voice memos.

the subject of *catinga*, or bad bodily odor. After one such discussion I paused for a moment on the street and spoke into my phone so that I did not forget the nuances of what had been said. I transcribed the notes later. In the screen shot, the anthem that is represented in the chapter on sound is also visible: often recording sounds as voice notes was an important tool for accurately capturing nuance, and it was less intrusive than video (though I had to be even more careful that I ensured I had relevant consent, as without the visual cues of video recording people around me sometimes forgot I was a researcher).

Objects

The social sciences typically give a lot of attention to what is called "material culture"—or sometimes "the stories of stuff" (I recommend the twenty-minute documentary on YouTube with that title: https://www.youtube

.com/watch?v=9GorqroigqM) (Fox 2007; K. Harvey 2009; Miller 2005). When I finished my fieldwork, I gave away most of the objects that I had accumulated in everyday life—pots, sheets, a plastic table, and so on. However, I chose to keep a shoebox full of things that represented important themes from fieldwork, and in December 2018, while writing this book in Mauritius, I laid them out upon my desk (Image 1.2). Immediately my skin began to itch, which always happened when I handled the "cobra" perfume, and this text was written with the strong scent of the objects in that box clinging to the wood of the table, my skin, and my computer. Through attention to these objects it is possible to learn a huge amount—here I go through them in brief:

1. The now-empty bottle of Nina Ricci perfume described in the chapter above. Whenever I smell it, I am transported back to my Angolan classrooms and to the company of the children I taught there.
2. Like conferences everywhere, those in Angola required presenters to wear identification. This was the conference where I presented my work to a broader Angolan public for the first time.
3. Slightly more expensive perfume—Pure Love—manufactured in the United Arab Emirates and purchased at the same time as I bought the Cobra perfume.
4. Zé was an Angolan student living in Rio de Janeiro whom I got to know very well. He did not wear perfume but was utterly obsessed with a particular cream produced by Revlon—Fire and Ice—which he felt complemented his unique skin smell in powerful ways. It had been discontinued, but as a thank-you for his help during my research, I was able to track down several samplers at the Revlon factory via Amazon.com, and I posted them to him in Rio. I kept one simply because it had been such a project to get hold of them, and it's an interesting example of one man's relationship with moisturizer.
5. Cloth badges made in Portugal and imported by the Angolan Scouts as part of their uniform.
6. At Christmas time 2013, these dolls appeared on the shelves of Angolan supermarkets. Many friends expressed happiness to finally see brown dolls in a space that for a long time only sold dolls with Caucasian skin tones. I found the box fascinating: the text, in English, reads "Happy Childhood" and the figure itself appears to be an Asian stereotype.

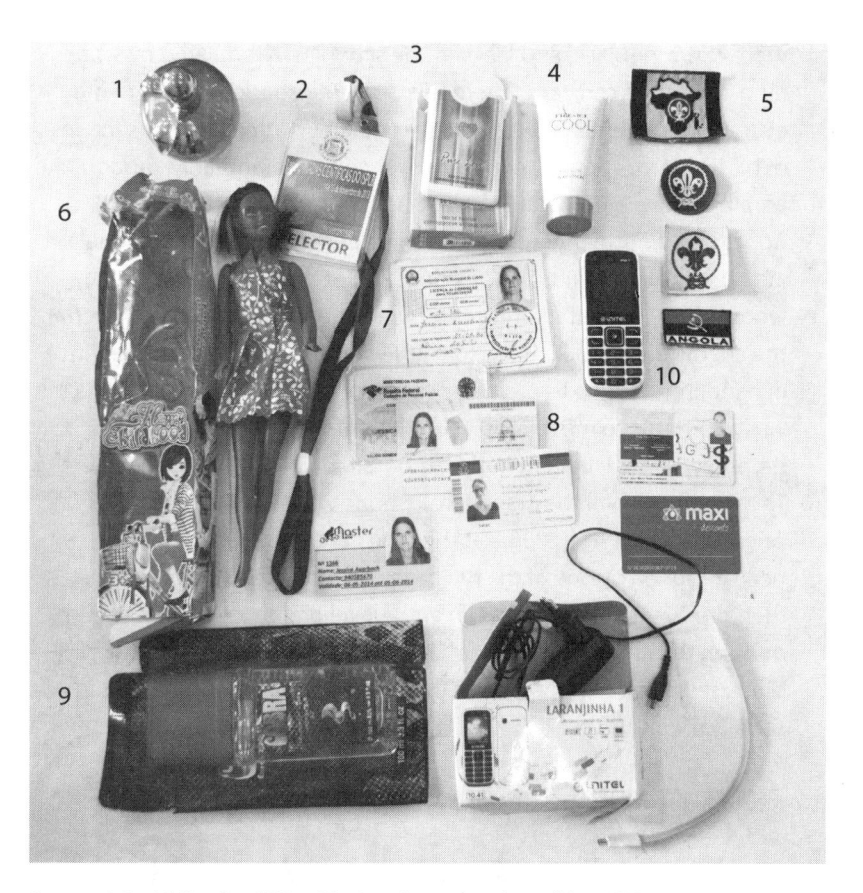

Image 1.2. (1) Bottle of Nina Ricci perfume purchased for AOK15,000. (2) Prelector: participation lanyard for conference at Lusíedas University. (3) Pure Love perfume purchased at market in Benguela for AOK150. (4) Cream for Zé: Revlon Fire & Ice. (5) Angola Scout badges to be sewn on uniform. (6) Plastic doll purchased in supermarket over Christmas period 2013. (7) Angolan motorcycle license. (8) Personal cards for supermarket, gym, school, and library in Angola, and foreign resident's card for Brazil. (9) Cobra perfume purchased at market in Benguela for AOK100. (10) Basic Angolan cellphone.

7   My Angolan motorcycle license was typed out by hand by a kind woman who had been working at the Lobito document center since the early 1960s. She explained that such licenses were impossible to forge because the police knew the nuances of her typewriter, which had nicks on particular letters (Fieldnotes 131122).
8   Loyalty card for the supermarket; access card to the gym; employment card for the school where I taught—barcodes were becoming much

more commonplace, and labor at the school was regulated by scanning in. I had to carry my Foreign Person's registration card with me everywhere I went in Brazil. Unlike Angolan documents, it was made of plastic and designed to make forgery difficult (arguably, though, the administrative typewriter in Lobito had precisely the same effect).

9 Cobra perfume, manufactured in China and purchased in Benguela at the outdoor market. The box does not say where precisely (or by whom) it was manufactured, and many interlocutors warned me that the chemicals were likely poisonous—something that my experience in handling it suggests is almost certainly true. At AOK100 (US$1.00), it was affordable to most people. Ingredients were not listed on the bottle, and without lab analysis it is impossible to know what is in there.

10 The *laranginha* or "little orange" cell phone was affordable for most Angolans (it cost AOK2000—at the time about US$20), and had been designed by one of the major cellular providers (owned by the then-president's daughter) as an entry-level phone to get almost everybody on the network. It did not have any smartphone functionality, but I used it as a back-up phone that was virtually indestructible and socially unobtrusive.

Structured Observations of Space

This topic concerns how one *does* ethnography: What is it like to observe a space? Here is one suggestion: construct a sensory grid so that scent, not sight, is prioritized. The one I constructed describes a gym in Lobito where I used to train regularly, and where I met and socialized with those who were making their bodies "fit for peace." These notes were written up from my paper notebooks, from the "notes" function of my phone, from voice-notes that I recorded to myself—as mentioned above—and from a series of photos that I took (with permission) at the gym. They later informed an interview I did with the owner, who came from a former Soviet Union country and had married an Angolan who was studying in now-Russia on a Soviet-era scholarship (Interview #37). I also interviewed the athletics instructor (Interview #106), who had taught himself the trade by watching YouTube, as well as several patrons of the gym—many of whom were also parents at the school where I taught. I have included it here to open up the process of spatial interrogation through the senses, and to provide a model of one tool that students might use to "make the familiar strange" (Myers 2011).

Recording Fieldwork

	Downstairs Space A	Downstairs Space B	Mezzanine
Ventilation	Two fans	Air-conditioning	One fan in the corner, one small window
What is the space?	Weights room	Machines room	Athletics room (during session); where people go to stretch and use Pilates balls
Who's in it?	Mostly men; most of them are probably 17–mid-30s	Mixed men and women; some people are a bit older here	All women except the instructor of the athletics class. Quite a wide range of dress and body type. 17 people in total—women in rows, instructor at front. When there's no session a mix of genders use it, but more women than men
Time of day?	6 a.m.	5:30 p.m.	6:30 p.m.
What does it smell like?	Reeks of sweat. Only some people seem to use towels. Also smells of sports drinks	Also intense sweat smell in some places. Plastic from machines. Spandex	Rubber from the matting on the floor. When class is going on, sweat smell is overpowering because only a tiny window and one small fan
What do I see?	Weight racks laid in clusters. Groups of people clustered around them. On one side dumbbells and skipping ropes. Mirrors on far wall. Television screening music videos on mute	Row of treadmills and two bicycle machines; one is broken. Open space for stretching, etc. Wooden racks on walls. Television screening music video on mute	Pile of blue Pilates balls in corner. Small (1 kg) dumbbells lined up and plastic steps in corner. Sweat dripping off everyone. Spandex pants reveal all curves (and some angles). From top of most spandex pants cling-film emerges (wrapping yourself that way is supposed to lead to faster weight loss). During push-ups I notice everyone else has artificial nail extensions
What can I hear?	People talking, weights being lifted and dropped onto metal	Rhythmic sound of feet on treadmill with hum of music in the background; music changed depending on time of day. Usually *kuduro* beats but not always—sometimes just regular MTV	Women grunting and sighing (sometimes grunts and sighs come from me). Instructor shouting at us to go faster. *Kuduro* music playing really loudly

(continued)

	Downstairs Space A	Downstairs Space B	Mezzanine
What am I touching?	Usually weights, or parts of the lifting machinery	Nothing with my hands. Leg machines	The rubber mats on the floor, which often leave bits of material on my hands. Other women because space is small and we often bump into each other
Anything to taste?	My own sweat	My own sweat	My own sweat plus gulps of water when given 3-minute breaks. Once I fell and got some rubber from the matting in my mouth. Ugh
What should I wear?	Most women in this space wear basketball shorts and tank tops. Some wear spandex pants	Spandex pants and tank top	Spandex pants and tank top
How do people communicate?	Lots of pair-work so people speak softly together. Occasional interventions from machine supervisors	More casual chat than in the first space. Quite often people use machines and text at the same time	Glances of solidarity between participants. Texting during (rare) longer breaks
Questions for later?	Where do the machines come from? How do they get maintained? When do most of the users start working out this way and why? What jobs do people using the gym do? What else do they do in their spare time?	Will the second bike machine ever get fixed? What jobs do people using the gym do? What else do they do in their spare time? Why don't they go running on the beach instead?	Why the cling film? What makes people choose group classes over working out downstairs? What is the aesthetic model that women are going for? Does that have a different source to that of men? (i.e., Brazilian soap operas versus He-Man or something?)

CHAPTER 2

Touch and the Tactile: The Textures of Scouting in *Capitalismo selvagem*

Seeing through the Skin

On 22 March 2014 a flash flood swept down the usually dry bed of a river near Lobito. The warning system that was supposed to be in place did not work, and a group of children who were playing between the two banks were in mortal danger of being washed away. Nearby, members of the Angolan Scouts Troop No. 44 were out on a hike.[1] Taking stock of the situation, they rushed to help. Though they saved the children's lives, five Scouts drowned, including their *chefe* (leader), a young man named Hipólito.[2]

The funeral was held in a church and attended by Scouts from across the country. Black ribbons were passed around and carefully attached to each Scout's uniform. The five coffins were laid out, draped with both the Angolan flag and that of Scouting, and a young man named Ruben, close friend of the dead *chefe*, stood guard over them and gently guided mourners as they paid their last respects. The impact of Ruben's own grief was visible in his straining neck muscles and the sheen of water on his eyes. During a ceremony that moved frequently between prayer, speech, and song, the dead were hailed as heroes for the new Angola. They were held up as young people who had made the ultimate sacrifice for others, and who had abided to the last by the laws of Scouting, God, and Citizenship that shaped the realities of a country at peace (Fieldnotes 140325).

This chapter is about touch, and it is also a chapter about Scouting. It is about touch in the physical sense, what scholars often call the haptic (Marks 2002), and it is about touch in the emotional sense, as in to be touched by something. It is also about texture and social class, and how the feeling of cloth and substance on a person's skin (which itself may vary in texture) locates an individual in social, economic, and material space. As many scholars before me have observed, in the post-Enlightenment era, the visual has become dominant in most parts of the world, often at the expense of other senses (cf. Stoler 1989). This is, I think, why the Finnish architect Juhani Pallasmaa (2005) titled one of his books *The Eyes of the Skin*. In that book, Pallasmaa writes about the body as being "truly the navel of [the] world, not in the sense of the viewing point of the central perspective, but as the very locus of reference, memory, imagination and integration" (11).

Pallasmaa calls touch "the mother of all senses" (11) because through touch one knows the world, and after all other senses have been dulled through age or "put out" through trauma, "touch is the last remaining means of guiding yourself"—according here to another philosopher, Michel Serres (2008, 18). Yet touch cannot be alone: one must touch something, or someone, or be touched (perhaps emotionally) by something. To put it another way, "sensation is not only an individual but also a social experience, one that connects the individual not only to others but also to their larger surroundings" (Ameeriar 2017, 14).

Here, the "seeing through the skin" that I hope readers will explore allows an understanding of Angola through the experiences of some of the young women and men who were involved in Scouting. This is a group that was sometimes referred to as a "mafia for good" (Interview #54) because of the ways that they worked to change Angolan society outside of governmental structures but still very much within an organized entity. Wearing the cotton uniform of the Scouts was a constant reminder to young men and women to live by the moral code of Scouting. It gave collective identity and individual comfort, and the sensations—often tactile—that came from time spent *in uniform*, for example out hiking or gathered around a camp fire, would support individuals in their personal quests to better their own lives and those of their communities.

Making the Mafia

Angolan Scouting is in some ways a recent phenomenon. In its current form the AEA (Associação de Escuteiros de Angola, Angolan Scouts Association) has existed only since 1991, making it one of the youngest Scout associations in the world. Scouting was founded by the Englishman Sir Robert Baden-Powell, who was an important figure in the Anglo-Boer War (1899–1902). It is arguably one of the first truly transnational and global organizations. During the Anglo-Boer war, which took place in South Africa between the Afrikaners and the British, Baden-Powell "liberated" the town of Mafeking, despite a much larger Boer army in opposition, after a siege that lasted 217 days (Edward Ross 1980; Hopkins and Dugmore 2000). Part of Baden-Powell's strategy during that conflict was to recruit young boys as "scouts" to help him. This was an intervention he later claimed was critical to British triumph, and which has subsequently become the origin story of a movement with some forty million members worldwide (www.scout.org).

Angolan Scouts existed under Portuguese colonization in small numbers, but were revived in the 1990s. By 2014, the AEA had approximately twenty thousand registered fully paid members across most of the country, though the real numbers were much higher. Scouts met weekly or biweekly in troops, each one associated with a particular church (e.g., the Church of St. Antony in Catumbela), and were divided by age bands: tumbling Cubs (ages six to ten), enthusiastic Junior and Senior Scouts (eleven to seventeen), and earnest *Caminheiros* (eighteen to twenty-five). Through friendships made at the school where I taught, I joined the *Caminheiros* of Troop No. 21—a group of young people of mixed socioeconomic status who all attended one of the biggest churches in the region, overlooking the river Catumbela. One of their leaders, *Chefe* Pedro, was friends with a colleague who taught with me at the College of Stars, and it was on his invitation that I formally joined that troop. By chance, my great-grandfather was one of the first Scouts in South Africa in the very early 1900s, founding one of Cape Town's first troops, and in childhood I had participated in the movement's programming. This fact was helpful in earning entry, and though the Portuguese translations of the prayers, songs, and stories were new to me, I was familiar with the broad theology of the movement and knew the tunes, if not the words, of all the songs.

Two of Angola's most senior Scout leaders referred to their movement as a "mafia for good" (Interview #54)—a nomenclature that was not uncommon. In this chapter, I show how Scouting has played, and continues to play, a very important role in the emergence of a "country at peace" in the context of *capitalismo selvagem*. In particular, the chapter demonstrates how Scouting is seen by many as one of the assurances of "quality personhood," or morality, that importantly comes *with* material benefits "of quality" as well. Scouts tread a delicate line from which they are both explicitly politically independent and operate transparently enough to remain both intelligible and trusted by the MPLA, the dominant political party of Angola.

It is the political independence of Scouting, as well as the explicit commitment to helping insiders within the group, that earns the organization the moniker "mafia." Yet how can one dislike a mafia that is so explicitly committed to social projects, singing around the campfire, and the training of wholesome, morally grounded individuals? Timothy Parsons (2004) has considered the evidence for and against Scouting as a movement that either upheld colonial regimes or undermined them. Parsons notes that few Scouts had difficulty seeing the benefits of the structure of Scouting while maintaining critical distance from the behaviors of British colonists. So, too, in Lobito, where many were deeply reflective about the irony of adopting a British military youth movement so soon after the end of the civil war, whilst also appreciating its tremendous ability to unify young people toward a common cause. Thus, Scouting has become a mafia for *good* that is acceptable to what is effectively a one-party state where a national youth movement with structures of command, mobilization, and response, and that does not answer to any political leader, might be seen as somewhat threatening.

Scouting claims to be the largest movement of any kind outside of the dominant political party structure maintained by the MPLA. Though it is much smaller than the MPLA's youth wing, Scouts are visible in almost every city and at most major events. Because it is non-partisan, Scouting includes those who are members of Angola's two other main political organizations (UNITA and CASA-CE) as well as those with no political affiliation at all—but its members are all religious. The organization's funding comes entirely from fees paid to the organization, and many of the Scout leaders contribute sometimes significant amounts from their own pockets. Most groups operate on shoestring budgets, and nobody is paid a salary. At a moment's notice, Scouts can mobilize one another and their communities, as they did in the lead-up to the funeral described above; taking care of the affected families, speaking with the media, organizing space, food, the funeral procession, and comforting one another in moments of deep grief: touching one another, both emotionally and with their presence.

The military-inspired structures of Scout hierarchy conform to the expectations of several generations of parents who came of age during war, and this is at least in part why the movement has been so successful. The idea of Scouts as "soldiers for peace" was occasionally mentioned, particularly by Scout *chefes* who had themselves been part of the Angolan armed forces, and who saw their work as to mobilize youth toward a vision of society that they felt many politicians had lost sight of. The curriculum that Scouting offered provided a helpful scaffold in the context of the transition from a socialist to capitalist market economy, combined with a much-vaunted "youth bulge" in which young people now outnumber their parents and their expectations of the world are vastly changed (Auerbach 2010; Durham 2011; Ferguson 2006, 2015).

Stitching *Pano* Pants

There are many other reasons that Scouting has done so well. The most obvious should not be discounted—Scouting is fun. Recreational activities aimed at youth are few and far between in Angola, and the movement provided structured activities, outings, "adventures," a ready-made group of friends, mentored pathways to expand one's horizons that were supervised by adults and also came with material markers of participation and prestige.

Camping and other excursions were part of the appeal, and were almost always commemorated through specially produced T-shirts and other materials. The day before I went with Troop No. 21 to a different province for the national Africa Scout Day celebrations, I met with Ruben and another Scout leader to prepare (Fieldnotes 140314). *Chefe* Ruben, mentioned at the beginning of this chapter, was the man who had held the flag for the deceased *Chefe* Hipólito, and was also the assistant director of the *Clã*, described below. Pedro, Ruben, and I went to several houses to collect supplies, the funds for which had come in part from participants' contributions but largely from Pedro's own pocket. We purchased T-shirts marked with the Scout logo and the date and name of the event, as well as twenty-five pairs of *pano* trousers, which, both Pedro and Ruben insisted, needed to be of a certain "quality."

"*Pano*" refers to a printed cotton cloth that is popular in Angola as well as many other parts of the continent. Like all textiles, it has a rich history (Mazuri Designs 2016; Nielson 1973; Sylvanus 2007). During the early colonial era, the Dutch learned the fabric-dying techniques of *batik* in their colony of Indonesia. They took back these techniques and mechanized them, and for a long time the majority of available wax-print cloth that became, and remains, associated with "African" fashion originated in Holland. Today, most of it is made in China.

In Angola, there is a very specific print of orange, red, yellow, white, and black that is known as *pano nacional* or *semakaka*. It is often used to celebrate the country, or to show belonging. *Semakaka* is quickly identifiable, but in general wearing any kind of *pano* is seen as a way to demonstrate national pride, and also cultural pride that is distinctly non-European in its referents. Once a week, on Fridays, children are encouraged to wear *pano* clothes to school to celebrate "African identity"—a change that has taken place only since the end of the civil war. Articles made of *pano* are also used to carry, wrap, and warm, and almost everybody from poorest to richest owns several. Like other commodities, they vary in cost and quality, and women in particular read *panos* for what thread, dye, and design reveal about social status (more is written on this in Chapter 3).

When *Chefe* Pedro went to buy *pano* pants for the young people in his Scout troop, he was doing three things. First, he was promoting an emergent national culture, in which people were unified by symbols—including, in this case, the wearing of *pano*. Second, he was strengthening the feeling of group belonging and membership, as our troop would be identifiable in part by their *pano* pants. Finally, he was providing participants with a tangible, tactile souvenir of their experience that they would take with them after the event.

Symbols, membership, and materiality were critical components of both Scouting and nation building. It is important to remember that the previous generation of Angolans had *also* had such symbols, membership, and materiality, but in many cases theirs were the symbols, membership, and materiality that came from being part of actual armies. In a delicate book devoted to understanding *pano* (which in francophone West Africa is referred to as *pagne*), Nina Sylvanus writes, "in the folds of wax cloth's dense materiality we see the historical and contemporary making, unmaking, and remaking of relations between people, things, and the institutions that govern them" (2016, 5). Wearing *pano* pants instead of military uniforms signified that these Scouts were being clothed to serve a different role in their society than those who had come before, and with new institutional allegiances—in this case to Scouting.

Chefe Pedro was adamant that the quality of the *pano* mattered, just like the quality of the Scout uniform, which was produced in Portugal "to EU standards." As with the example of Joyce in the previous chapter, the material circumstances of the body *in their entirety* were understood to reflect, to some extent, one's inner world. I stress *"in their entirety"* because I was also often warned not to trust people based on appearances alone, which could easily be "faked." That was in part why smell, texture of clothing, and *habitus* needed to align—with the Scouts through appropriate behavior that accorded with the Scout law. Much like Joyce with her gift of perfume for her sons, *Chefe* Pedro felt that good-quality *pano* pants could inspire his charges, and remind them of their moral and social identities and aspirations.

Catching Slipping Children

On another excursion, I spoke to Gabriella, an eighteen-year-old who, at the time, was finishing high school and hoped to find a way to university the following year. I asked her why she had joined the Scouts, and what she gained from membership. She responded:

> I like the Scouts because they are unified. I am from Lobito, and I was raised by my mom, and my adopted father. I have three siblings, all younger than me, and I was sent to Luanda to clean the house of a lady, so that with the money I could keep going to school. But then my step-father died, and I came back to help my

mother. While I was in Luanda, I looked for my biological dad—who never acknowledged I existed. I found out who he was, and his address, and I went to see him. He was so cruel—he shouted at me in front of everybody on the street, and said he never wanted to see me again. It was very hard. A man was watching from the side of the road. He called me afterward and he said, "*Filha* [daughter], everybody has troubles. Even rich people who have cars—you don't know what is in their hearts." It turned out he was a Scout *chefe*, and he invited me to join his *agrupamento* [troop] there in Luanda. He raised money for me to buy the scarf, and to make the Promise, and even though I am here now, he is like a father to me, and I speak to him almost every day on my cellphone. (Fieldnotes 140607)

Through the course of my engagement with the Scouts, I met many men and women who had devoted their energy to "catching" young people like Gabriella—*Chefe* Pedro being one of them. Most of the Scout leadership were also professional teachers, but were often frustrated by the limitations of schooling structures and assessment demands when it came to addressing the underlying social challenges of the communities in which they lived. They found in Scouting a way to offer not only intellectual but moral support and to provide youth with contacts who could care for them and provide mentorship and encouragement in the direction of what was understood to be right action.

Scouting created community. When the bus picked us up on the trip with Gabriella, we all piled in and sang non-stop for four hours until we reached our destination. We arrived in the dark at a hall where we were to camp, and we pitched our tents in the garden before gathering inside. Gabriella and the others greeted Scouts from different parts of the country with warmth and enthusiasm, and there was laughter that built as the evening progressed. We cooked and ate with representatives from some of the other thirty-plus troops attending the event, and in the evening competed in storytelling and performance, with Troop No. 21 distinguishing ourselves in part through the *pano* trousers that *Chefe* Pedro had handed out to whoops of enthusiasm on the journey. After food and storytelling inside, a bonfire was lit in the garden, and a more reflective and spiritual component of the night began. This also prepared the group for their role in the national celebration the next day, where *Caminheiros*, as the senior tier in Scouting, were expected to play an important role in both building and holding the national movement.

Through field trips such as the excursion to Lubango, young people were placed into a structure where they would meet others from different neighborhoods, cities, and sometimes even countries, and from those meetings came friendship and wider horizons. The movement stresses that any Scout in uniform is a "sibling" (*irmão*) regardless of his or her position in society outside Scouting. It is one of the very few spaces in the country where the children of governmental ministers and the children of brick-layers could—and did—mix as equals, at least at events like Africa Scout Day. Here, too, the texturing of uniforms served to flatten differences of economic status revealed by everyday clothing.

The "official" uniform of Scouting remains unchanged from the British colonial era. It comprises heavy canvas boots, long shorts, thick knee-length woolen socks with red woolen tassels, a belt with buckle embossed with the Scout logo of the *fleur de lis*, a khaki shirt with epaulettes on which were sewn badges and group markers, the Scout scarf (colored according to level, like the T-shirts described below), and a circular, wide-brimmed felt hat. This uniform was worn only on official occasions and in church. At most meetings, Scouts wore long socks, navy shorts, and T-shirts with the name of their *agrupamento* that were color coded: yellow for Cubs, blue and green for Junior and Senior Scouts respectively, and red for *Caminheiros*. Scout *chefes* usually wore purple T-shirts, and their scarves were dark green. *Caminheiros* were expected to always carry a forked stick, which represented both their "personal journey through life" and the choices they were to make between good and evil. All told, the full uniform cost more than US$200, which Scouts—the older they got—went to considerable lengths to obtain.

Interestingly, the flattening effect of the uniform worked best at the *Caminheiro* level. The market for second-hand clothes in Angola was often flooded with cast-off Canadian and US American uniforms for Cubs and Junior Scouts. Parents would buy these for their children in an effort to save money, but these efforts were usually gently reprimanded: we were the *Angolan* Scouts and should not be trying to imitate North Americans, we were told again and again despite the costs involved. About four hundred people attended Africa Scout

Day 2014, and the national head of Scouting addressed us all as we gathered in a Chinese-built stadium after a day of performances, prayers, and team-building activities. "Leave the world better than you found it," he said to us, "and remember that through Scouting we will find employment for one another, and teach you to be *moral citizens* building the New Angola" (Fieldnotes 140315, my emphasis).

Lighting the Fire as Service

When the national chief spoke about moral citizenship, he had very particular concerns in mind. One of the movement's local leaders—Rui Luís Falção Pinto de Andrade—has written extensively on Scouting in Angola, and in his most widely available book he writes:

> In a society such as ours, where principles, rules, and norms of social behaviour have been, over decades, profoundly undermined [*desvirtuados*], it is necessary that the Scout movement be more than a mere actor in civil society, and instead assume the role of a go-to organization in the environment of recuperation, as quickly as possible regaining the social values that have been much misapplied and even lost [in contemporary society]. (2010, 17, my translation)

He continues on the following page:

> Our only objective is to bring to society in general, and in particular to those who dedicate their lives to education, our knowledge of what can be lost if the state continues to pretend that it doesn't understand that some institutions, because of their intrinsic value, are much more than mere [*meras*] youth associations to engage young people in their spare time.... Rather than being seen as a youth association, Scouting should be recognized and accepted as a *socially useful organization* because of the method that distinguishes it from others. (19–20, my emphasis)

The "method," as de Andrade explains it, is one of self-directed education based on a curriculum that has been planned with the psychological needs of youth in mind (25). It is about lifelong education (45) based on symbols that are drawn upon for guidance, that have been adapted from a Christian frame of reference. Scouts learn *(aprender)* how to do *(fazer)*, as well as how to be, both in a given moment *(estar)* (54) and intrinsically—at the level of morality and/or the soul *(ser)*. They also study how to fulfill what Angolan Scout leaders see as a duty *(dever)* first to God and then to nation, *agrupamento*, family, and self (63). De Andrade defends the inclusion of women in all levels of Scouting, and emphasizes the need for all Scout leaders to be constantly improving themselves and their communities—that they must lead by example.

Service is paramount in the Scouts, and those who go through the curriculum have many opportunities to practice it. The movement is full of symbolism, and Scouts identify one another through uniform, handshake, greetings, and moral code. *Caminheiros* greet one another in both everyday life and at Scouts with a salute and the simple statement/instruction *"Servir!"* (serve, or to serve). Should a Scout be seen to stray from the Scout law, as well as from the moral values espoused by his or her church community, she or he faced sanction, usually in the form of not being allowed to wear the scarf until the situation had been made right. For example, one of my colleagues had had a child out of wedlock; until an appropriate ceremony had been arranged and undertaken and the child assured a respectable Christian upbringing, he was not permitted to wear the scarf (the rest of the uniform was considered acceptable). Due to the costs involved, this process could take many years, and he used to joke that by the time he got his own scarf back, he would be buying one for his little son, who he imagined by then would be in the Cubs (Fieldnotes 140211).

Unlike many other countries, Angola does not allow the existence of secular Scouts. As already stated, Scout membership hinges on church membership. The country has had a complicated relationship with Islam, and there are few visible Muslims (BBC 2016; de Morais 2014; K. Patel 2013). Of other religions, I was often told that the Jewish community left in 1975 (many synagogues are still visible but have since been repurposed), and since then there has been (supposedly) no religious diversity, though there is plenty of competition between different manifestations of Christianity. The regularity with which even the Angolan news itself reported the state's tearing down mosques suggested, however, that reality was slightly more complicated (Patel 2013). Many people I knew consulted regularly with so-called traditional healers, though the Scouts were particularly vociferous in their criticism of such practices, referring to individuals involved as witches (*bruxas*). Many churches also had several different youth organizations attached to them, Scouting being only one, albeit the one with the greatest recognition and national support. This was at least in part because the broadly conservative leanings of the movement as a whole made it appear controllable and unlikely to upset systems of power, as I will shortly elaborate.

Symbolism amongst the Scouts was extremely important. As Sherry Ortner (1973) wrote in the 1970s, symbols encode complex meanings and make them workable. She describes what she calls summarizing and elaborating symbols: summarizing symbols capture the broad meanings associated with them "in an emotionally powerful and broadly undifferentiated way" (1339); elaborating symbols, by contrast, help us to "sort out complex and undifferentiated feelings and ideas, making them comprehensible to oneself, communicable to others, and translatable into orderly action" (1340). For the Scouts, and specifically for the *Caminheiros*, fire, in the form of a bonfire, was a very important summarizing symbol, and at almost all gatherings was either physically used or invoked. Fire, according to the *Caminheiro* handbook, is a "symbol of the descent of the Holy Spirit, a dynamic force of love and strength that helps us to concretize the gospel into words and gestures, the darkness into light. It is the fire that lights the way for you, and warms you during your journey, that comforts both body and soul" (AEA 2013, 34, my translation). With the lighting of the bonfire, Scouts were encouraged to *feel* (both physically and emotionally) the "warmth" of service and to internalize a series of sensory experiences as a form of moral guidance. This was to serve the end of becoming, to use Ortner's terminology of an elaborating symbol, "a new [hu]man."

Building the New Man

O Pátria, nunca mais esqueceremos	O Fatherland, we shall not forget
Os heróis do quatro de Fevereiro.	The Heroes of February 4th.
O Pátria, nós saudamos os teus filhos	O Fatherland, we salute your sons

Tombados pela nossa Independência.	Who died for our independence.
Honramos o passado e a nossa História,	We honor the past and our history,
Construindo no Trabalho o Homem novo,	Building with work the new man,
Honramos o passado e a nossa História,	We honor the past and our history,
Construindo no Trabalho o Homem novo!	Building with work the new Man!

National anthem of Angola, verse 1, my translation

The national anthem of Angola, composed by Rui Alberto Viera Das Mingas and sung by school children every day, references the beginnings of the Independence War (4 February 1961) and then articulates a commitment to build "with work" the new man (*homem novo* is a gender-inclusive term). The "new man" was also an extremely important notion in Angolan Scouting, though the two usages, in the anthem and in Scouts, had very different origins and interpretations. Here it is useful to understand them both, as they capture the ideals that Scouts are expected to live by, and in the case of *Chefe* Hipólito, described at the beginning of this chapter, to die by as well.

The phrase "new man" is one that has two relevant points of origin: the socialist struggle for a transformed society, and the biblical transformation described when people encounter Christ. The notion appeared frequently in nationalist literature and propaganda from the 1960s to the early 2000s (Hatzky 2012; Marcum 1978; Mourier-Genoud 2012) as people sought a collective vision for the new country. During the civil war, thousands of young Angolans studied in Cuba, and there the new man was an idea that was presented to students from a host of different sources "from both side of the global ideological divide," according to Delinda Collier (2012, 187). She continues: "In Angola, the New Man was used to indicate the universalist notion of developmentalism, held in tension with the particulars of Africanity and Angolanity" (187). The "new man" was, from its inception, a way of describing both what was, because of independence, and what was desired and dreamed for the future. By the time I began my fieldwork, however, the new man as a notion was only rarely referred to with recognition of its socialist origins. Instead, it was more commonly referenced in terms of Ephesians 4:24, "And that you put on the new man, which after God is created in righteousness and Holiness" (Interviews #54 and #55).

In the *Caminheiro* guidebook, Scouts are told:

> "The Life of the New Man." The construction of the Church of Christ signals maturity and faith, it is a project of Man for the world. As a Christian, you are called to be the "salt of the earth," "light of the world," and "leaven in the dough," assuming an active place in the construction of "new skies for a new land."
>
> The Kingdom of God, whose law is manifest in Good-Adventures, and the life of Christ—"the New Man": this will therefore be the measure by which one becomes a *Caminheiro*.
>
> The ideal of *Caminheirismo* is the symbol of "the New Man," based on Good-Adventures, Fraternity, and Service. The New Man is free and responsible, [and] seeks to develop the world, based on the concept of peace and justice, helping everyone around him, trying to avoid the dependencies of the world, attempting to serve wherever possible. (AEA 2013, 27, my translation)

The "new man" of Scouting is modeled on Christ, as the guidebook makes clear, and Scouts are expected to follow His (unequivocally male) example at all times. In an interview conducted with two of Angola's most senior Scouting officials, I asked about the concept. Speaking together, they responded:

> *O homem novo* is part of the "mysticism" [*mística*] of the *Caminheiros*. It orientates the fundamental ideas in the final stage of Scouting. It is in the prayer, and it is about Christ's transformation. It is supposed to give youth a sense of how they themselves have the potential to transform. It also gives young people mechanisms to cope with change, and to find in themselves the ability to build solidarity with other people.
>
> It was a concept that became strong in Angola politically in the 1980s, when we had what was called the "politics of clemency" where people who were with FNLA [at one stage an opposition party that collapsed early in the war] opposition parties could

join the MPLA without risk, and ex-soldiers could be integrated into either the MPLA's army or civil society. *Homem novo* is a "mystery" that helps youth serve better, that gives them a sense of responsibility toward their friends, and can be a model to which they can aspire. It is an inclusive concept that also helps youth to think of their lives in the context of the world, and to be flexible with change. (Interview #54)

The two Scout leaders were well aware of the two different meanings of the term "new man," but for them it was still useful. "Thinking about one's life in the context of the world" was important for young people coming of age in a country undergoing such change, they felt, and the two points of origin of the term were valuable because Angola *had* been through a war, and most Angolans *were* Christian, and finding cohesion—not dissonance—in interpretations of the nationalist struggle and the Bible was very useful. The idea of the "new man" unified young people, and gave them a language with which to define adulthoods vastly different from those of their parents because of the absence of war. Through invocations of Jesus, it preserved a sense of care of community that was at least theoretically very strong during the socialist era alongside the personal-growth ethos of capitalism. The term opened up an imaginative space for creating and inhabiting a country recognizable but also fundamentally different from that of the past in terms not only of ideology but of the *textures* of everyday life that surrounded them. The textures of the "new man" were soft, clean, and pure: good-quality *pano* pants, air-conditioning in the vans that drove them to events such as Africa Scout Day, and the material feeling of camping and a fire under the stars.

Choosing Appropriate T-Shirts

Events such as Africa Day were highlights for many Scouts, and for some the primary reason that they joined the movement. But the real work of "practicing peace" took place during weekly gatherings of the troop, where the *caminheiros* went into a classroom at a local primary school and worked through the Scout curriculum. Each group of *caminheiros*, usually twenty-four to thirty people, was called a *clã*, meaning clan. The *clã* would be known to other Scouts not by a troop number (in this case, No. 21) but by a chosen name, bestowed only at the moment of *clã* formation and therefore of some significance. Ruben, the young man I described above, holding up the flag for his dead friend, was the assistant *chefe* of *clã* No. 21, responsible for managing the week-to-week activities of the group and bringing it from an informal gathering of young people into the formal structures of Scouting. In the session where the group was to choose a name, held shortly before Africa Scout Day, the dialogue showed both the possibilities and limitations of freedom of speech within Scouting and the New Angola, as well as the workings of the "mafia for good." It went roughly like this:

> CHEFE RUBEN: *Servir*! [to serve—the way Scouts greet one another]
> GROUP: *Servir*!
> CHEFE RUBEN: We need to choose a name for our *clã*. It needs to be a name that is inspiring; it should be after a great person in history.
> MAGDALENA: If that is the criteria, how come there are no *clãs* called Savimbi? Savimbi was a leader and he was inspiring. (Fieldnotes 140308)

The room went silent both at the mention of Jonas Savimbi's name and the statement that he had inspired. Jonas Savimbi was the former military leader of UNITA, whose death ended the civil war. He was rarely acknowledged and even more rarely even subtly praised, as to do so was seen as provoking the ruling MPLA government. Many Scouts were members of the MPLA's youth wing, the JMPLA, which was acceptable on the strict assumption that one's political and Scouting lives were to be kept separate (Interview #54).

Pausing for a moment, Ruben finally responded:

> To name a *clã* Savimbi would be against common sense! We all know that Savimbi was *not* an example for us to follow. It would be impossible to give that name, because we have to go with the values of our society, and the majority say that that is not okay.

"What is the majority?" somebody else asked, and the conversation quickly became heated. Ruben, however, would have none of it, and called for order repeatedly. He put a stop to the discussion and instead insisted that the group undertake a dictation of Angolan Scout Law, which the *Caminheiros* painstakingly transcribed into their notebooks, as few could afford the printed copies (Fieldnotes 140308). The moment was illustrative of both what Scouting enabled and what it foreclosed. It made possible discussions that in most Angolan contexts were simply unspeakable at that time. In 2014, many believed that even saying Savimbi's name could be read as an act of rebellion, and most people were too afraid to do so. The memory of a highly functioning secret police still loomed in much of Angolan society, and to publicly articulate critique was highly risky. Scouts was one of the few places where *some* discussion was possible, though as Ruben pointed out so quickly, Scouting "went with the values of society." In practice, that meant playing diligent lip service to the MPLA, which earned the movement sufficient space to flourish but closed off opportunities for genuine discussion and debate.

In a later conversation, Ruben spoke very differently to me about Savimbi. Whilst waiting to pick up the T-shirts to be given out at Africa Scout Day, he and I discussed both the civil war and the teaching event described before, and he commented:

> Savimbi never killed people, you know, it was his soldiers who killed. But we can't say that because in Angola freedom of speech is not really allowed. It's complicated here. I myself am not like other Angolans, because I think about it, you know, how strange it is we cannot speak…. I also refuse MPLA membership, because it's important to be neutral, and then to create space for opposition. My dad was in the MPLA, a military man, and I know it was not all good. I have this memory of growing up in the war, I was six, maybe seven years old. I grew up in [the interior city of] Huambo, where the war was bad. There was a day where my dad's friend was shot in front of us, I don't know why. Not once but ten or eleven times, they just wouldn't stop. Sometimes I wake up [after] dreaming of it. People here in Benguela province have no idea about how the war really was, even though they pretend they do. It was so hard. I was a chubby kid you know, just naturally chubby like some children are, and I was so hungry in that time. I also remember how the UN would come and they

would measure children's wrists and only give food to the thin ones. I carry that memory too, I was too fat, but so hungry. That was the war. (Fieldnotes 140314)

Ruben's two very different articulations of Savimbi's role in his life were typical of young people I knew, who toed the line in public but in private were often much more critical than they felt they could ever let on. The risks of critique in the context of *capitalismo selvagem* are better understood by turning to one of Ruben's "older brothers" and mentors, a man I call Bruno, one of the most senior Scouts in the region. The two men worked closely together and had known one another since Ruben moved to Benguela at the age of eleven.

Bruno came from an extremely poor family with no political connections. As a child he was entranced by young people whom he saw wearing the Scout uniform, which appealed to his orderly sense of fashion. He persuaded his parents to let him join a group of Cubs—one of the neighbors of *Agrupamento Z*. He worked his way through the ranks, and his dedication to Scouting quickly became a well-known aspect of his character. He took on as many leadership roles as he could, and the skills and contacts that he gained through Scouting enabled him to connect with several NGOs and also the local Junior MPLA branch. Being kind, sincere, intelligent, and boundlessly enthusiastic, Bruno became, in adolescence, one of the best-known young people in Benguela-Lobito and, by the time I met him, an influential youth leader whose presence and networks spanned several organizations. Scouting, however, as he told anyone who would listen, was his first love.

At the time when Bruno and I came to know each other, his family had just made a difficult decision: he was to take an official role within the MPLA structure. The decision was difficult because Bruno knew that it would compromise his ability to be critical of "the [political] party" and to some extent would limit his Scouting activities. He also knew that many people who looked up to him and were quietly very critical of the state would see him as selling out. "But that's exactly what I am doing, you see," he explained:

> I have no choice. The MPLA said I am getting too influential, and now I must either be with them, or they will say I am against them, and cut my water and my light. I called all the elders in my family together and asked them what I should do, and they

said, my son, you are a poor boy with nothing—you must join the party, it is the only way, or they will put you in jail. They said to me, Bruno, it is not about ideals, but this is just how it is in Angola. And so I have done it, I am with the party, and I no longer go to talk to the NGOs, though the people in them know that in my heart I am still there with them. (Fieldnotes 140310)

When Bruno was "only" a Scout leader, he had had some ability to be a little critical of the MPLA (as Ruben had been, at least in private), but now that he worked for them as his official day job, he couldn't do that (if he did, he would be accused of disloyalty and promptly dismissed). Because of the principle of Scout neutrality, Bruno explained, "I don't wear my MPLA T-shirt to Scouts, and I don't wear my Scout T-shirt to the MPLA, but the same heart beats underneath, and that heart is loyal to my Scout *irmãos* before the party" (Fieldnotes 140310).

Practicing Peace

In knowing what T-shirt to wear and when, or when to critique the Angolan state, both Bruno and Ruben demonstrate the lessons of the mafia for good for thriving under conditions of *capitalismo selvagem*. As an organization, Scouting structured and disciplined individuals' behaviors, but it also opened up spaces for dialogue that otherwise might not have existed. Both men were very aware of their own choices, as the interviews reveal, and moments such as that with Magdalena, described above, show how there is a constant testing of the boundaries and exploration of the limits of peace and conflict. What lay beneath the T-shirt and in the heart was known only with the "eyes of the skin" and in each case was deeply personal, but Scouting provided a structure and a community in which to consciously work toward a transformed Angolan society. Through blood drives, nutrition campaigns, public building maintenance, or participation in Africa Scout Day, young women and men in the Scouts assumed a public role as examples of citizenship in the postwar country, and their friendships, their mafia for good, sustained them.

Here it is useful to reflect on the materiality of not only building new homes, but building new people. Uniforms lie against the skin, hats shade the eyes, owning a belt or a whistle or a pair of boots marks one's belonging. Yet materiality alone was not enough to convince witnesses of "quality"—that needed to exist in the context of a moral and social structure. Building homes, going to school, or being part of the Scouts are all ways in which the New Angola can be negotiated, and the networks needed for thriving in conditions of *capitalismo selvagem* could be maintained.

Why does it matter? (touch)   *Learning peace*

For peace to become an expectation, it must be practiced again and again. The *Oxford English Dictionary* defines a practice as "the actual application or use of an idea, belief, or method, as opposed to the theory or principles of it." The application or use of peace in Angola as idea, belief, and method has not been straightforward: its arrival was sudden and unexpected, and after centuries of colonization and decades of civil war, being a citizen of a country at peace was a new experience for everybody. So too was (and is) raising children in peace, so too was (and is) engaging a generation of adolescents who have never known war. "Practice" is also a verb: "to pursue or be engaged in (a particular occupation, profession, skill, or art)" (ibid.). Peace must be practiced in this sense, too, and this process is also underway across the country. Thousands of everyday actions try, test, refine, and expand the practical understanding of what one interlocutor called "the peace that we have" (Interview #104) and, through everyday action and dialogue, the peace that people want.

    This book explores the practices of peace, as both noun and verb, practices that most readers will find resonate with their own everyday lived experience. Peace is also an image, or the lack of an image, of war. Liisa Malkki (1996) has written extensively on the impact of images of civil war on Africans' bodies; Jain (2013) has shown that the language of war wreaks the same effects as certain kinds of diseases. In an era of increasing pixilation, how do we now imagine a country at peace? What catches the eye—and the iPhone—of everyday people, and how do the portrayals of everyday life on Facebook, Instagram, or SnapChat complement or challenge the image of the world that readers themselves are making? How does that world feel?

Poems 1

Fatherhood

he tells me that his goal
is to earn enough
that his two daughters do not have to drink unfiltered water
he says that he
has already developed the parasites to resist illness
but he wishes that his little girls
never have such creatures in their bellies.
filtered water is more expensive than gasoline in this town
he observes. does the government
think that we should all just
drink fuel, instead?
he asks, enraged

Radio Building

on the beach, sand gnawing at the entrances
an egg-cup-castle-shaped building monitors the
going and coming of boats in the port of Lobito
this was the radio tower, from whence power fled
and as the fleeing happened so too did the arrivals—refugees—and
now women grow fields of maize next to its doors and
families sleep in the turntable centres. the paint
is faded but bright: pink, orange, green the building
is an astonishment of architecture and fantasy and it homes
fifty pairs of curious human eyes and cats and dogs
and even two goats and in the garden chickens which also
is a place where busses have been abandoned to rust, becoming
a playground of magnificent proportions for small
children and there is a basketball court, paved where
groups gather on saturdays with a ball and they play
laughing, as the sun sets. but the radio building is
next to the sports club and the sports club is
next to the expensive hotel and as the lightbulbs
on streetlamps are reinserted the city's administrators are
starting to clench their fists. it seems doubtful
that the eyes and ears and mouths inside the radio building
can stay for very long, so fear has now descended
with every switching on of central light.
(here they are thankful for the Crisis, change postponed, once again
the spiral stairway continues its slow disintegration)

Seven Women

there are seven old women, some barefoot, some in plastic sandals,
all slightly hunched under big plastic colorful buckets, all wrinkled from
years of sun
their t-shirts, mostly white, are tucked neatly into wraps of bright *pano*
and they run geriatrically across the road, such that all the traffic
holds it breath to see if they will pass
or a bucket will fall; that they succeed seems nothing less than miraculous.
seven old women, some barefoot, some in plastic sandals,
big plastic colorful buckets filled with vegetables
crossing the road.

Buying Cloth

enter the informal market.
fight through motorbikes and hanging
strips of meat. carefully keep the upper teeth
touching the lower lip to avoid the breathing in of flies.
after the meat is the section where charcoal is sold, after
charcoal, electronics. keep going, push past
men with wooden-wheel carts and quick step, quick
quick step to the spot
where three women sit with piles of patterned cloth. after
speaking for a while
you will realize that behind them is a place where
people pay to urinate and defecate against the
wall in privacy, your nose will observe this with interest.
the women will chat and chat and laugh and say look! this one is beautiful!
the patterns of birds, orange and yellow
flying over a teal blue sky and into the green blue trees.

Fátima's Mother, on Christmas Day 2013

The box contains perfume, it is Christmas day
(and she ululates with joy and throws her arms to the sky)
The food is well cooked, it is Christmas day
(and she ululates with unabashed joy, and blesses it)
The church is full, it is Christmas night
(and she ululates with unabashed reverie, and praises God)
The house is full, it is Christmas day,
(and she ululates with unabashed sincerity and tells stories of devotion to the children)
The heart is full, it is Christmas day,
(and she ululates with gratitude and we do too)
With thanks for being together, bellies full, smelling so good.

The Cuban Help

a woman has a daughter who suffers
and the country does not have the resources
they are told at every turn
to accommodate the child's needs
but there is a young man, a Cuban nurse
who shows her, quickly, in some stolen moments at the clinic
a technique to help the child walk one day
a few more moments, over weeks, of hurried conversation
and the Cuban nurse comes to the house where the child lives
and begins to carve her a brace from wood
and from within the brace, he kneads her legs
tells them with his fingers what they were built to do
she takes a step without falling over
her mother weeps
she pays him under the table
the little girl calls him Uncle Cuba.

The Driver

I have never seen a man so big, his muscles
the size of coconuts on his arms, each leg a drum pulled
tight flexing for battle.
He folds himself into his tiny car
or under the chair at the neat plaid-cloth-covered-table that his
wife has laid for him with delicate china
He unfolds on the beach, the visage
of every baywatch, bay-watching superhero
the yellow sand and steel-blue water framing him for Instagram.
He drives cars to make a living for a company
and lifts things for them too, because he can
and comes home tired with his body reined in; hours upon hours.
And then he sits on his love-red sofa
with a hairy carpet to massage his feet and sighs,
voicing every contentment in the world
:) ;)

CHAPTER 3

Changing Tastes: Palates and the Possible

This chapter begins with recipes, which readers may wish to make at home and digest whilst reading. It then shifts into an exploration of gustatory experiences before focusing on two men, a chef and a tailor. The chef's life story is soaked in flavors both literally and figuratively. The tailor's passionate commitment to "Angolan fashion" opens awareness of aesthetics and taste in a more inclusive sensory framework.

Recipes

Funge

Ingredients:

Two cups of *funge* (ground cassava meal), salt, water

Instructions:

Heat water in a pot. While the water is heating, beat the *funge* with cold water until it is a smooth consistency. Then add it to the hot water and stir regularly until the *funge* reaches a thick, gelatinous consistency. Add salt, and serve with other dishes rich in sauce.

Calulu (grilled fish)

Ingredients:

About a kilogram of dried fish, tomatoes, chili, one or two onions, okra if it is available, garlic, one cup of red palm oil, other vegetables, especially cassava or sweet potato leaves

Instructions:

Wash fish, then soak in boiling water and set aside. Make sure the fish is deboned and deskinned. Cover in boiling water again and leave to soften. Put layers of fish and vegetables into a saucepan and cook. Add the palm oil and the leaves last. Simmer until everything is very soft. Serve.

Bolo de Arroz (rice cake)

Ingredients:

Eggs, wheat flour, rice flower, sugar, butter, rising agent

Instructions:

Mix into batter, place in tubes made from paper, and bake in a hot oven until golden brown.

The Man Who Made Cake, Dona Maria, and the Sushi Chef

Before my arrival in Lobito, I had heard about "the magical Aurea's restaurant," which, it was whispered, made the best *pasteis de nata* in the province of Benguela. *Pasteis de nata* (literally cream pastries) are small tart-like confectionaries made of cream, eggs, vanilla, and sugar with a light dough base, typically burnt brown on top. They famously originated in Lisbon, when monks who had to sustain themselves after the Liberal Revolution of 1820 approached a nearby sugar refinery to sell their egg tarts. The results have become famous throughout the world, and are a staple of lusophone cuisine, including in Angola.

Aurea's was renowned for its confectionaries, but also because of the legendary status of its proprietor, whom I will refer to here as Dono Joaquim (*Dono* and *Dona* are the Portuguese words for *Mr.* and *Mrs.*). Dono Joaquim, I was told repeatedly, was nothing less than a social and civic genius. During the war, all thirty years of it, he never ceased baking cakes—he found sugar, eggs, and flour ("who knows where!") and produced sweetness for the people of Lobito. Originally from Portugal, he had arrived in Angola at age seventeen and never returned. "He is more Angolan than Angolans," I heard often—a rare compliment for one from the global north and former colonizing power.

For months, I would pass by Aurea's almost every day, for a sandwich and a *galão*, a milky coffee, to observe people flowing in and out, to write my notes, to speak to friends. I often conducted interviews there, and I learned a great deal about the dynamics of the town by simply watching. In anthropology, we call this "deep hanging out" (Geertz 1973) and it allows for the scents, textures, and flavors of a place to permeate the skin, and the sounds of ambient noise as well as dialogue to enter the mind.

Every day without fail, around ten in the morning, Dono Joaquim came down from the flat where he lived above the restaurant. Shrunken in his eighty-six-year-old body, he would stand behind the counter and respond hazily to the stream of greetings thrown at him by young and old alike. When I tried to interview him, I quickly realized that he could no longer see or hear very much at all, but a team of workers lead by his two sons gently guided him throughout the morning, and the affection that was shown to him seemed to be the reward for forty years of cakes baked at dawn.

One of the most striking things about Aurea's was that it served everybody. By that I mean that it was one of the few establishments in Lobito frequented by all tiers of Angolan society. From 6 to 8 a.m. it was typically filled with manual laborers—dock workers, builders, agriculturalists. Its tables were packed with mostly men, almost all wearing uniforms with reflective stripes, drinking large *galãos* laced with spoons of sugar and eating massive chunks of fried white bread. Children from the houses nearby ran in and out buying fresh breakfasts for their families.

After eight, it was quiet until midmorning, when professionals in high heels and polished shoes started entering and meetings over americanos and cappuccinos commenced, accompanied by delicate biscuits and note-taking on iPads. At lunch, again, a massive rush: now, mostly toasted cheese sandwiches with ham, thick croissants, and of course *pasteis de nata*. In the afternoon, parents with children in private-school uniforms appeared, sitting in deep discussion, the mothers drinking tea, the children, with their legs swinging above the floor, usually drinking milkshakes. And before closing, another rush: bread, unsold pastries, fruit, and cakes: the beautiful cakes that lined the shelves of the confectionary section and were sought out for every occasion by the wealthiest and the poorest of the city alike.

Aurea's was central: people flowed past on their way to work, to government offices, to buy groceries at the recently opened South African supermarket chain Shoprite. It lay at the intersection of residential, bureaucratic, and commercial spaces that almost everyone had to visit eventually, in the concrete old city of the *zona baixa*, near the entry and exit point of many roads. Above the *zona baixa* was the *zona alta*, leading up to Victoria's house, and beyond them both, as the crow flew, was the *Restinga*. The *Restinga* is a narrow strip of land that pointed out into the ocean, forming the natural harbor that made Lobito so important as a port. The *Restinga* was where the city's wealthiest people had historically lived: the houses were huge, the pavements both existed (this was not to be taken for granted!) and were wide and cobbled. The sea lapped the shores on both sides of three blocks, and right at the point was a boat in the middle of a roundabout. The boat was the vessel that Eduardo dos Santos (president, 1979–2017) had once fled in to save his life during the anti-colonial war. It now stands as a national monument just across from a very expensive restaurant run by South Africans, called Zulu.

Zulu was a bar for the truly elite, where a glass of orange juice cost more than many Angolans earned in a full day's work, but along the coast were many other options. In one, Dona Maria held court with an iron fist. A black (see Introduction, note 1 on race) Angolan married to a white man—also Portuguese by birth, also nationalized—she counted the restaurant as her seventh or eighth career, the first of which had been as a soldier. Given the location of her establishment, her clients were largely expatriates and very wealthy Angolans. Though the space was simple (a concrete slab that extended out onto the beach, plastic tables branded with the emblem of the local brewery), the social dynamic was very, very different from that of Aurea's: it was much less crowded, and the visitors were exclusively people with means. Dona Maria ran the kitchen, and four young women served and supported her. The women looked unhappy and uncomfortable and usually down at the floor while Dona Maria hurled insults at them daily: Lazy! Dirty! Stupid! At times the tirade was relentless.

There were few places in Lobito that made anything a vegetarian could eat, and vegetarianism was an almost lifelong habit that I found I could not shake off. So, despite my discomfort with the ambience at times, I found myself returning to Dona Maria's, and slowly I got to know her. Her life had not been easy. Her family had been "almost *assimilado*" (almost assimilated) before the war, but had never been granted Portuguese citizenship. ("*Assimilado*" was a category used by the Portuguese colonial power to grant citizenship and social privilege to Angolans and others in their colonies who had assimilated culturally to the values, religion, practices, and comportment of Portuguese society writ large [Corrado 2008; Ferreira Rosa 1936; Soares de Oliveira 2015]). When the regime in Lisbon fell in 1975, families such as Maria's were socially and economically stranded. Some found ways to go to Portugal, but in many cases—including this one—they quickly committed to the idea of an independent Angola.

Dona Maria signed up to join the armed forces, and there she had many profound but difficult experiences. She raised five children, three of whom lived to adulthood, and her life, she would tell me each time I came, deserved to be written as a book. I volunteered occasionally to help her do that book, but she was busy with the restaurant and with her grandchildren. Snippets of the many layers of sacrifice that she had made along the way emerged occasionally in casual conversation. By the time I left the country I recognized in her many of the subtle markers of a veteran of that particular generation: posture, tone of voice, a resolute will, an impatience with those who were younger who had not played so active a role in the unfolding of history. She was deeply committed to a version of *"Angolanidade,"* Angolan-ness (Soares de Oliveira 2016), articulated in the language of the MPLA's nationalizing project of the 1970s and 1980s designed to unify Angolans around a set of core beliefs and cultural practices at a national level. National cuisine was integral to that process, and so for Dona Maria, at this moment of her career, *Angolanidade* was manifest in plates of *funge* and fresh fried fish with peanut sauce.

Another world away (though in this case, about two hundred meters) was the Pizza Shack. The Pizza Shack had opened only a few weeks before my arrival in Lobito, and it was considered one of the classiest restaurants in town. People dressed in their best to go there—nobody was admitted wearing flip flops or jeans, and the cost of a Coca Cola was about triple what one paid on the street. Once a week, on Tuesday nights, the Pizza Shack transformed: it became the only restaurant in the province to offer sushi, and it burst at the seams with the population of the city who had, in most cases, spent time abroad and desired intensely to reconnect to the cosmopolitan experiences they had had there.

The chef who made the sushi, Xavier, was from Luanda. He was young, visibly strong, and very charming. He was always immaculately dressed in a white button-down shirt, blue dress pants, and a blue striped apron. He stood behind the bar brandishing knives, expertly dissecting fish and layering the pieces in complex patterns on rolls of sticky rice whilst bantering with clients and deftly transforming fish, fruits, and vegetables into masterly arrangements of sushi. The restaurant flew him down from the capital city once a week, and the owners assured me that his presence generated enough to cover the ticket and far, far more.

Xavier had trained to make sushi in Brazil after a chance encounter with it when he was pursuing a bachelor's degree in São Paulo. Falling in love with the food, he decided to change his life direction, and bring it home. He relished his customers' responses to the strange textures and flavors of his creations, and experimented constantly. For Xavier, his work was both about exposing Angolans to new flavors and new culinary experiences and about bringing his own unique flair to the techniques he had learned studying under a master chef who himself was a fourth-generation Japanese Brazilian.

The genre of food writing is vast and very rich. Much of it is practical and manifest in the form of recipe books. Some is political. Judith

Farquhar (2002) is an anthropologist who has written a book called *Appetites: Food and Sex in Post-Socialist China* in which she quotes *Red Flag*, a magazine produced during China's "great leap forward" from 1958 to 1962 when Mao Zedong was pushing radically for industrialization: "Is eating and drinking a mere trifle? No. Class struggle exists even at the tips of your chopsticks," the text proclaims (79). In the narratives of Dono Joaquim, Dona Maria, and Xavier there is indeed much that is political, from citizenship through struggle in the war to educational opportunities in contemporary Brazil.

Food can also be about commodities, and there are excellent examples that trace the complex histories of humanity from the perspective of particular foods, such as sugar (Mintz 1986), coffee (Pendergrast 2010), and bread (Jacob 1997). Food is a rich subject for those of us in the social sciences, because from the perspective of food we can trace entire histories of the ingredients, how they were produced and by whom, and the meanings associated with that food, the status that it reveals about its eater (think undergraduates and free pizza), the journeys that individual ingredients of the food have had to make in order to end up on the table. Sometimes we even learn a great deal by looking at the table itself (Schielke 2011).

In Angola, the staple carbohydrate is *funge* (pronounced *foonj*), a glutinous, dense, and relatively bland white substance made from cassava roots or, sometimes, corn meal. *Funge* is eaten with fish, chicken, or vegetables and needs sauce to give it flavor. The cassava is locally grown, and the roots are pounded in drum-sized wooden mortars until a fine white powder forms. This powder is added to boiling water, with some salt and sometimes a little oil, and it is stirred over heat until it thickens. It is cheap and relatively nutritious. The plant is native to Brazil—it was Portuguese slave traders who originally introduced it to Angola. Now it is the third-most-consumed carbohydrate in the tropics, after wheat and rice, and the biggest state producer is Nigeria. It is used in biofuel, animal feed, laundry starch, and to make tapioca—including the balls that are found in bubble tea.

The flavors that Xavier, Dono Joaquim, and Dona Maria brought to life with each meal evoked travel, struggle, and aspiration. Through the foods that they prepared, the experiences in their own lives and the lives of those around them were mirrored and elaborated. When Xavier made sushi with raw fish caught that day in the Atlantic and delicate strips of mango, he built upon a tradition that had long since outgrown Japan. When Dona Maria prepared *funge* and *calulu* (dried fish with beans in palm oil sauce and sizzling sweet potato leaves) she blended ingredients from around the world in a way that has become recognizable as "Angolan," adding her own spices and flavors in a gustatory signature that many of her clients would know anywhere. Dono Joaquim did much the same with his cakes and his *pasteis de nata*—when I asked for a recipe for the latter, my request was politely and firmly declined: "his recipe is his secret, Jéssica," I was told (Fieldnotes 180516).

Understanding what people eat, how they eat, and the judgments others make about them because of what and how they eat is essential to understanding class, health, politics, and food distribution in the world we live in. In the previous chapter, *Chefe* Ruben, of the Scouts, spoke movingly about his memory of United Nations peacekeepers providing food during the civil war. It is worth reflecting that in 2018, when this text was being written, about 150 thousand tons of food are thrown away every day in the United States, according to a recent report (Milman 2018). Simultaneously famine pushes millions toward starvation in Yemen—an inequality mirrored in less stark terms in almost every major city in the world, where some parts of the population feast and others go hungry, or fill themselves with the empty carbohydrates of fast foods or processed foods.

The issue is not a lack of food in the world but challenges of distribution, and every piece of food that one consumes is imbued with history. One can see that point beautifully laid out in the book *Hungry Planet* by Peter Menzel and Faith D'Aluisio (2007), which shows what a week of groceries looks like in families in fifty countries around the world. I also recommend keeping and comparing food diaries, where each person writes down what he or she has eaten each day for a week, and then all as a group compare their diaries to see taste, culture, history, and economics laid bare on the table. At the end of this chapter a visual essay makes this easier to imagine in the context of this book, where people with disposable income were beginning to eat out for the first time, and where new tastes—including that for sushi—were being cultivated. First, though, let me share two oral histories of "taste-makers" in Lobito: Mr. Oniko and Lino, whose life stories show the ways in which tastes are learned, refined, and shaped.

Oral Histories: The Stories of Two Lives

At the time of writing, more than eighteen million people around the world have "liked" the Facebook page "Humans of New York." The website's author/photographer, Brandon Stanton, became internationally famous after he set out to photograph ten thousand "humans" in New York City, and then realized that by publishing fragments of the conversations he had with the people concerned, he could capture something of their life story and communicate it effectively. Most importantly, he realized that other people actually cared (Stanton 2015). Part of what has made Stanton's work so powerful is that social media enables public commentary and can inspire action, and in many cases the "stories" shared on the platform have gone viral, leading to the donation of money or resources, or offers of support and intervention that are far beyond what appeals on conventional platforms could achieve. Stanton now often works in partnership with the United Nations and other humanitarian entities, trying to increase awareness, empathy, and action for those who might otherwise fall "beyond the lens" of humanitarian intervention (Malkki 1996).

Telling stories of wider significance through the lives of individuals is not new in the social sciences. Stanton found a magical formula to do so, understanding the workings of social media and the increasing visuality of our contemporary world. Historians, anthropologists, classicists, archaeologists, and others have used "life histories" or "oral histories" for centuries, though, in order to demonstrate how one individual's experience might come to represent themes of relevance to the society as a whole, or those beyond it (Biehl 2013; Peacock and Holland 1993; Portelli 2003; Vansina 1985).

In this section, I tell the "life stories" of two men, Dono Oniko and Lino Espelanga. With Lino, I use his real name, because he hopes that readers will reach out to him on Facebook (Lino Espelanga Estilista [stylist]); Dono Oniko will be easily identifiable to people who live in Lobito, should they desire to speak to him, because they will recognize the cinema where he works. He is okay with that, but has chosen a pseudonym anyway, as he is a more private man when it comes to outsiders and strangers. His only request was that the pseudonym allocated be an African name because, in his words, "names are powerful, they reach our truth" (Fieldnotes 180520). From 2011 to 2018, I came to know both of them very well. Lino and I chat regularly on

Facebook, but Dono Oniko does not own a smartphone or use the Internet, so very occasionally I call him on his phone.

I have written these life histories in the first person, keeping to the words of our interviews and conversations but at times rearranging the sequencing to suit the logical flow required of reading. Lino has been through his, and given me the thumbs up—at least to the Portuguese version, as his English is not very fluent. My friend Victoria took a printed copy of Dono Oniko's story to him to read at Cinema Flamingo, and he told her he liked it, that he was glad I focused on his life, because that was the one thing he could recount for sure after so many years (email, 14 January 2019).

Anthropology and other disciplines have long been aware of dynamics of power, language, and voice that validate specific kinds of narrative, but the digital revolution has dramatically changed the speed and intensity of collaboration both in academic and public dialogue. It is less the self and the "other," as it used to be understood, and more the selfie and the other now (see Chapter 5). In these oral histories, Dono Oniko's life gives insight into food as something that sustains, nourishes, and mirrors social change. Since he is a chef and a farmer, it is easy to read "taste" into his experiences. Lino's story, however, is that of a taste-maker, where taste refers to preferences of fashion and style. It connects to the tactility of the previous chapter, and the changing aspirational desires of people in Lino's generation, for whom food was often less of a preoccupation.

Dono Oniko

Source: Various in-person discussions during 2013, 2014, and 2018, but the majority were elicited during Interview #25 and updated in May 2018 over three visits.

"[May 2018:] I remember when you first came here, I didn't want to tell you about my life, but I changed my mind. I am going to share this with you because it is important that people know how things really are. In 2013, 2014, when we were talking before, it was so much better. Now, after the economic crisis, it has been very hard. I will tell you about my life, and you will see how hard things are again. Perhaps it will change, if God wills it, but now sometimes I lose hope. I am very angry, but you cannot live with so much anger, it makes you bitter. So I carry on, every day, and do what I can. Perhaps God understands it, I do not know.

Image 3.1. Dono Oniko at the bar of the Joker restaurant at Cinema Flamingo.

"The war stole my youth. I grew up in the colonial times, here in Benguela province, in a suburb of Benguela city itself. I trained as a chef when I was fourteen, and started working for the Portuguese. I got married, young, but then it was normal, I married for the first time at nineteen, I had a son. Then I had to go to the army—there was no choice—and I stayed there until I was thirty-five. When the army disarmed in the nineties, the younger soldiers were incorporated into the new army, but those of us who were older, we were just discarded, like we didn't matter at all. Generally, the government in Angola is not so worried about the people. Now you see a lot of roads and bridges, and that's good, but it's not enough. How can a state be a state if it only invests in infrastructure, not in people? Anyway. Young people now are passive, so it is partly their fault.

"When I left the army, I didn't know what to do. Because before the war, I was a cook, I decided I should try again. I learned to speak a lot of languages while I was in the war—French, Spanish, and so many national languages of Angola, so I was lucky. Because I could speak to foreigners I got a job at the national oil company as a chef. They paid me well! And I could learn a lot from the people who were working there. There was one French man, and it turned out he was a vegetarian. They had been trying to kill him! I swear, they gave this man just chips and salad for an entire year. So I learned how to cook for him, and now I take care of all the vegetarians. He was so grateful.

"I worked for all the oil companies at different times, Chevron, Total, Sanangol. I learned to cook so many foods—there was even a man from Korea who said if he could, he would have taken me home with him because he appreciated so much the food I made for him. I learned Korean food just from his descriptions, it was fun! I cooked for French, English, Germans, even some people from the Soviet Union! I was able to get an apartment in the *Restinga* that was abandoned, I got it through a contact in the port. Now I rent that out, but I still don't have the money to maintain it.

"About five years after the war, the oil company where I was cooking was expanding, and they wanted to send me to Nigeria. They were willing to double my salary, but I would have had to leave Angola, and by then I had five of my six children, I had found another wife. After the war, I did not want to sacrifice my family again, and so I left the oil company—I decided to go. I had three thousand kwanzas in my pocket, and I wondered, what will I do now?

"This space that we are in, this old cinema—when I was a child the whole city used to come here to watch movies, and it was fantastic! I knew that nobody was in it, so I spoke to my wife, and through a friend of a friend we found the contact of the Portuguese man who owns it. It was never nationalized so it still belonged to him. During the war he paid for security, so the building never got occupied either. The security was good, because this section of the city used to be a fun park: it had rides, carousals and dodgem cars, and people selling popcorn, you know, with the beach so close. It was one of the open parts of the city, so when the refugees came from the interior they made a camp there, and they live there still. Today it is still dangerous because the refugees really had nothing then and they have almost as little now, thirty years later.

"The Portuguese man responded to me. His lawyer came down twice from Luanda, and we agreed that I could open this restaurant. I paid him US$500 a month in rent, even though I did all the work and he wasn't using it. I painted, I cleaned, I restored everything I could. I had vegetables growing in the old park, and I put fish back into the ponds. I worked in the office, and the old bar, now that is the Joker restaurant. My wife cooked, and we served maybe fifty or sixty people every day and on the weekends we rented the space for weddings and did the catering. I would love to buy and restore it, but I asked the man, he said he wants eight million dollars for it. *Eight million dollars!* If I had even three million, trust me, I would not be working here! The owner is a very old man, he thinks the cinema is frozen in time, just as he left it. He does not understand what the war did to us, to the city.

"We started the restaurant, it was hard work, but very slowly we made a name for us, and I fixed the building. Every time I had money, it went into this place, or to the house that I am building in Catumbela. My youngest daughter is very, very smart. I want her to have a different life, so I am sending her to a private school. It's expensive, but it is good, and I was saving money to buy her a computer, because I can see that is the future. Once a month I drove to Lubango to buy chickens and other supplies, because they are cheaper there.

"Until the economic crisis, the one that happened at the end of 2014, things were going well. Then it started to fall apart with onions. Suddenly there was a blight and onions got really expensive, so many of us started to plant them a lot. But then the market flooded and nobody was buying. I had thousands and thousands of onions, and I got no money for them. Then the price of oil came down, and the government had no money either. People were not getting paid, most of the foreigners left, it was like the end of the world again. Suddenly, all these new sicknesses appeared, and there were no medicines in the shops just like before. Many shops closed.

"Here in Angola, life is like that. It has always been like that. You cannot think so much about tomorrow, you just have to find a way to survive today. With all these challenges, people don't work very well, and often they are not committed. It's a real problem, but it's not surprising, with our history, with what is happening now. We have a lot of corruption, but that's also not surprising—just look at our history. During the war, there were three kinds of shops, for three kinds of people, and poor people, well, the only way they could get beer was to trade it illegally, so now we have the same logic in action again, and again, there is not enough of anything to go around.

"I had another son in 2016, he is now two. But his mother—my wife, who used to cook, you remember her? She died last year, she just got up one day, and then she died. It's difficult to raise the children, to do all this without her. Especially at my age. That little son is actually in the hospital right now, I need to go to visit him today. I hope he does not die as well, because how can you trust the doctors? And they might tell me now that they need money that I do not have. Not even the landlord asks for money any more, he's there in Portugal, I think that he is still alive.

"It's very difficult here now. Nobody has money any more, they don't come to eat at restaurants. You know, though, a cook and a doctor are very similar people. *O cozinheiro trabalha com carnes mortas para salvar, e o médico trabalha com carnes vivas para salva-las da morte.* This means a chef works with dead meat to keep life, and a doctor works with live meat to keep it from death. Before the crisis, Angolans began to taste good food—things that were healthy, things that sustained them, nourished them, but after the crisis it has become so bad again. If people can't afford to eat, they will be going to doctors, but it's sad because if they came to me I could keep them healthy—that would be so much better. I don't trust the government at all, I trust only in work. You work hard, very hard, and your life continues, until your time is done. That is all."

Lino Espelanga

Source: Various documented discussions in person in 2013 and 2014, regular social media dialogue from 2014 to 2019, and a formal interview, #107.

"My life has been about falling and getting up, falling and getting up again. It has not been easy, but everything is in the hands of God. It is only God who knows our future, and if something happens, it is because of God's will, because of his plan.

Image 3.2. Lino at his stall at the Compão Market.

"I was born in 1990, in the province of Huambo. It was the war then, things were not easy. My family was not wealthy, not wealthy at all. I only ever met my father once, just before he died. My mother raised us but she is nearly blind, so she never worked. People helped us, and we did what we could for food. Sometimes my mother got some disability from the state, but usually it had no money. We were five children—I am in the middle. Now we are four.

"My older brother did some small trade, before then he was also a soldier, and a doctor in the military, and then a catechist. He supported us until he died—mostly it was him who brought money into the house, so I went to primary school with his support. Then, in 2005, he left the house, we thought he was going to preach. It was a Friday. He didn't come home. On Saturday we started asking around, then on Sunday at church, but nobody had seen him. On Monday my cousin, who is a nurse, said she thought we should come to the hospital. He was there, he had been attacked, so badly beaten. His body—I can't begin to tell you what had happened to his body. He had been made to drink petrol. He died about two hours after we got there. That was so hard. To this day we do not know why.

"So now we are four, two sisters are in Huambo still, and I live with my third sister and our mother and my brother's three children and my son, here in Lobito. We came to Lobito because my mother has relatives here and in childhood we visited it once. I thought it would be better than Huambo, Huambo has too many memories, we needed to begin again. My brother's wife did not want to come, so it has been years now since she saw her children. The oldest is now twelve, the other two are six and eight, and my own little boy is two.

"But let me go backward, to childhood. I finished primary school, but the school was not so good. Sometimes the teachers came, sometimes they didn't, and we had very little money. I could not continue school because the family needed money for food. I tried so many things: I worked as a security guard, but my boss there was terrible—so angry. I had to sit outside all night, and I got malaria so many times. I left that job when I was very, very sick, I had to go to hospital and I was too weak. So I got better, then I was a bricklayer, but it is boring work, and your body gets so tired, and I tried so many different jobs, but I didn't like any of them. My destiny just wasn't in the things I was trying, and I kept thinking no, there must be a better way.

"Becoming a tailor happened by chance, by lucky chance. I have always loved fashion! I was that child who was not so interested in soccer, but always looking at beautiful clothes. One day, I was walking in Huambo, there where I used to live, and I saw a man making clothes. He was working at his machine and he had people helping him, and the things he was making were so beautiful. I became curious about this: how are our clothes made? What about special clothes, for weddings, for other events? Eventually I got brave enough to talk to him, and persuaded him to teach me. I stopped just wearing fashion, I started learning how to make it! That was such an important thing in my life.

"I worked with this man for maybe four months, he taught me a lot. I remember the first pair of trousers that I made. Wow, those trousers took me four days! Now I make trousers in half an hour, they are so easy—but I didn't know anything then. I was lucky, because it turns out my grandfather had an old, old sewing machine in Kwanza Sul, and I had been to visit him. He wasn't using it so he said take it, and suddenly I found myself with the beginnings of a career in fashion, which I love so much.

"I started to believe in myself. The man I apprenticed for didn't have much time, so after four months I left him, and learned on my own. People started to hear about me so then slowly, slowly they started asking me to do things for them, and I was improving as I went. I experimented, I made many mistakes, but I paid a lot of attention to all the different kinds of clothing that I saw, and slowly got better.

"In 2006, when my brother died, like I said, we moved to Lobito. I took the sewing machine with me and I got my space here at the *praça* [outdoor market] and began to work. At the time, not many people were working with *pano Africano* but it was beginning to become popular, and the government helped a lot because they were trying to make sure everyone had national pride. The government was saying, why always do what the Europeans and Asians and Brazilians do—why not be Angolan, be African? It is about black pride, you know.

"Suddenly people were wearing much more *pano* on TV, and then they began to in life as well, and that was good for me because you know, I am a proud Angolan, and I like working with the cloth. Now I have made everything: formal clothes for weddings, for every occasion, for the bride, for the groom, for children. I like to make clothes with *pano* most, but if a client wants something, I can do it, whatever it is. If I don't know I will just learn right then. There is an agency of models in Huambo, sometimes I also work for them, if they need local cloth. They trust in my designs and they know I sew well.

"A few months into 2009, just when I had some customers and things were good here in Lobito, the storage building for the *praça* was robbed at night. I lost everything! My sewing machine, the clothes for many clients, all my supplies. That was hard. Thanks be to God, most of my clients were understanding, but it was a very difficult time and

I did not know what to do. Then one of my brother's friends told me he had a sewing machine that he wasn't using, so I borrowed it, and I began again, and things were good. I had my Facebook page and some clients from Brazil, Spain, Portugal. They would place orders on Facebook and then I would send them things with the post, and I started to make some good money.

"I bought a tiny piece of land to build a house of my own on in the *Zona Alta* and I was preparing to move my business to the center of Lobito, the commercial zone, into a real shop, which is my dream. I was so close, and then the floods came. The floods were in March 2015, and they washed away the house I was living in—luckily nobody was at home when it happened. But in the house were all my documents, everything! Birth certificate, ID card, MPLA card, because you know how we have to be part of the party here, *everything*. For my sister and my mother as well. We lost so much. Also, many things from the *praça* were damaged, so my business really suffered, and we were closed for a long time. It was another moment that was so difficult, I can't describe it. Fall down, get up again though, you understand, so I had no choice but to get up.

"Since 2015, I have been rebuilding. It's going quite well now; people's taste has changed and they like what I do—they like *pano Africano*. Most of my customers are women, to be honest. Sometimes they force their husbands to come here and I measure them for a shirt, if there is a wedding or something, but mostly it is a woman and now they see how good it is to dress in *pano*, especially the *semakaka*. I am nearly ready to get my business formalized, I am just waiting for the last of the documents and some more money. Replacing all the documents took a long, long time, I still need one last one, and it is very expensive for all the fees. To move into the center of the city is not easy as well, because you need money, but it would be much better for business, as people would trust me even more if I was not working in the open air.

"Once I have my documents, I will complete the registration process of my business in Luanda. That's also difficult, but once it is done then you can do so much. I have applied for a permit for the "Lino Esplanada Group"—not just tailoring, but I want to have a model agency as well, where we can do fashion shows of my designs, and also related services: many kinds of sewing, a beauty parlor, also a petrol station so people can fill up their car while they wait, I will register all twenty-eight and see what happens. It's expensive though, each stamp is 5,500 kwanzas, and there are twenty pages that need stamping. Then you have to get to Luanda, transport is maybe 10,000 kwanzas, and you have to spend at least 2,000 kwanzas to sleep in the city at a hotel. Also, you can't just be there for two days because you will never manage to do everything, so it has to be at least a week. It becomes a lot of money. If anyone ever thought about the money properly, they would never register a business! But you need it, because when the business is approved, then you can get a loan from the bank, and then everything is possible that was not possible before.

"For now, I don't want to get married. My child lives with me, I love him, and I love his mother, but for right now my business is everything. Later on, I think I would like to be married, it's just not so important at the moment, and I already have so many responsibilities. They say that God helps those who run. Let me tell you, I have been running a lot! Right now, I only have two employees, but my dream is to become a great employer. I would like to have the model agency, like I said, to show my clothes, and a factory to produce them. I would like people to buy my clothes in Brazil, Portugal, US America, Cuba. I want people to know that it is me, Lino Espelanga, stylist. I want them to like what I do.

"First I know I need to study. I am finishing high school now, at night. After work I go for three hours every evening, and I like it, I am learning. When I have that certificate then I want to study design in Portugal. I know it will be difficult, and only God knows how I will pay for it and keep giving food to all the children, but I need to get more skills, so that I can be part of the global market. I am always looking for partners. Angola is hard, but it is also a good country, and I am proud. Little by little we are moving in the right direction, and I am only twenty-eight years old, so I am young...."

> **Why does it matter? (taste)** *Mobility*
>
> Human beings are mobile, but mobile in many different ways. This is not new. Angola and its relationship with Brazil complicates narratives of south-north migration and reminds us that the globe has been traversed for centuries. Amongst English speakers, there is little general awareness that far more slaves were taken to South America and the Caribbean than to the United States, for example (Eltis and Tullos 2013). The mobility of cuisine, geography, social class, lifestyle, religion, and Scouting, within ideological systems of Cold War–era scholarships, and circulated by contemporary media, reminds us of the desire that so many human beings have to change themselves, to explore new horizons, and to quite literally open new doors for their families.
>
> "Journeys" are now frequently mapped on Google or Waze, but the word has the same root as "day," and the verb "to journal" means "to record and to write." In older literature, a "journey" is usually spiritual as well as physical, and requires overcoming of obstacles that are both external and more personal (Calvino 1972; Ingold 2007b; Narayan 2012). Empathy with the journeys of others is critical to success in a globalized workforce, and attention to the mobility, the journeys, of those in Angola may open new imaginative doors for readers themselves. Empathetic feeling alone, however, is not enough: it might lead to petition clicks for causes far away, but without clear political agendas and actions, very little of the status quo is likely to change.
>
> Many people in the world today live multisited lives, meaning that their loyalties, love, money, and dreams extend among several different countries at the same time (Glick-Schiller and Fouron 2001; Holmes 2013; Vertovec 2009). This in turn complicates ideas of nationalism that have dominated international discourse in the last three centuries, and points to the need for new tools that comprehend how changing technologies have also led to shifting allegiances that are often far less "grounded" than before, are often emotionally driven, instead of being based in coherent political change likely to lead to structural adjustment (in the literal sense of the term) (Gusterson 2016; Välaiho 2014).

Photo Essays

Photo Essay 1: The Flavors of Peace

In the evening, neighbors in Bela Vista enjoy beers from a shipping-container shop at an informal restaurant. Living in an apartment building allows one to look down at social life in the city. I took this photograph from Victoria's balcony.

Diners at an exclusive restaurant in Luanda enjoy cocktails and fresh shrimp; in a modest home, ingredients for a typical meal are laid out before cooking begins.

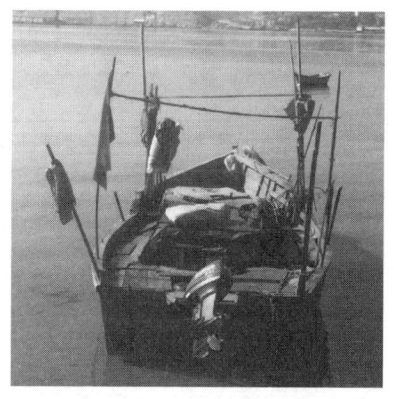

Sweets and cakes are on display at Aurea's restaurant; a fishing boat is docked in the harbor at the edge of Lobito.

Much of Angola is still agricultural land. In the past, this region was known for coffee and cotton. Now there are mostly vegetable plots. For decades there was a risk of land-mine accidents when working agricultural land in many places. Years of hard and dangerous work have made the soil safe again for planting. It is fed by rivers such as this one—the Catumbela, once a conduit for slaves captured inland and taken to the coast.

Photo Essay 2: Choices and Consumption

This is the market place in Catumbela, from which slaves were sold to Brazil, Europe, and the rest of the Americas. Few local people know its history, and at the time of writing, there was not even a plaque.

Shopping today means going to many kinds of places. In the *praças*, or outdoor markets, one can buy used clothes from the global north, or cheap new clothes from China. All of this is underpinned by the activities of the port, which make Lobito one of Angola's most important cities. Here, its infrastructure slowly appears above nearby houses at dawn.

Billboards advertise new things to buy, such as a South African creamy alcohol made with berries from the marula tree. A spate of good will in the US in 2012 led to a sudden abundance at the *praça* of T-shirts with the name of a Ugandan war lord.

During the civil war, supermarkets struggled to keep stock on the shelves, and most of the population's food came from ration stores. Now, free-market capitalism sees a proliferation of supermarkets, which are almost always air-conditioned but where produce is rarely as fresh or as cheap as that available at the markets.

~ Sound ~

CHAPTER 4

Music, *Fofoca*, and the News: Sound, Space, and Orientation

Sound Readings: Spectrographs, Annotation, Language

How do we think of, or in, sound? The images presented in Image 4.1 are spectrographs of MP3 recordings made on my iPhone during fieldwork. I imported them into GarageBand on my laptop and took screenshots of the autogenerated spectrographs that are made to help sound workers mix, modify, and accentuate sound. Spectrographs were once unusual, but today they are all but passé, and many people can "hear" spectrographs the way musicians trained in Western notation can look at notes on a stave[1] and "hear" the notes (Ingold 2007b).

In this chapter I emphasize sound in society—not only music, which has been richly explored in terms of Angolan nationalism by Marissa Moorman (2004, 2019), but language and ambient noise, and the way all of this comes together in a sensory experience that shapes not only what we know, but how we know it and what we do as a result. My hope is that readers will absorb this chapter whilst turning on YouTube or Spotify or almost any sound service, and listening to some of the rich and varied music of Angola. The list is long; my personal favorites include Paulo Flores, Erika Nelumba, Celma Ribas, Yannick Afroman, MC Kappa, Mathias de Másio, Nelo Paím, and Neide Vanduném.

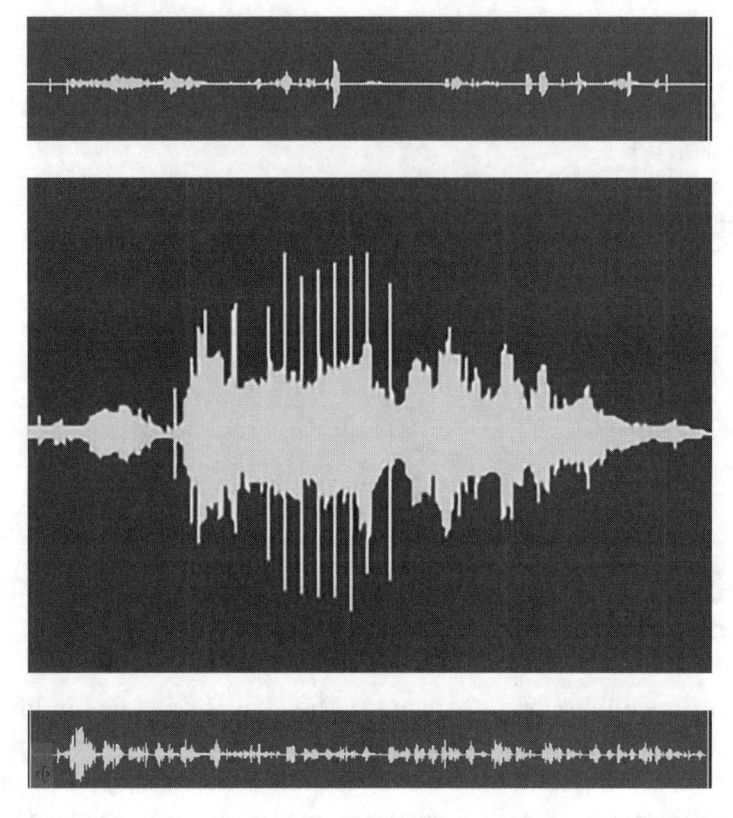

Image 4.1. *Top*: Ambient noise recorded from Victoria's house, 10 May 2018, Lobito. *Middle*: Detail of ambient noise, 10 May 2018, Lobito. *Bottom*: Children singing the Angolan national anthem, 22 May 2018, Lobito.

Zumba, which has now become popular across the world, comes from the term *kizomba*, a type of dance that originated in Angola. The Brazilian martial art form capoeira also traces its origins to Angola, and many of the instruments that are used in capoeira today are still commonly played there. Those who have a particular fascination with music should research the Angolan composer/artist/instrument builder Victor Gama, who specializes in the development of new musical instruments and who has performed alongside some of the most well-known musicians in the world, bringing into their repertoire the sounds of his home country.

In this chapter, I use the emergence of the Angolan higher education sector as a site with which to think through sound, and the ways sound can shape us. First, however, it is helpful to ensure a certain shared vocabulary is in place. To that end, I share here ten key words pertaining to sounds in the social sciences. As a list it is far from comprehensive, and has been included largely so that the following section makes more sense. Complex ideas sometimes also require an expansion of vocabulary, as words are the tools we have to "hear" sounds, and when sounds are not yet known, we need to find ways to scaffold them in our imaginations.

Sound

Sound is a wave of pressure that reaches our ears, and that we interpret. Physicists, linguists, psychologists, musicians, and so many more have studied and written and experimented with sound, and there is even an entire branch of anthropology that has emerged around the subject (Cox 2018). It is so basic, so uniform, and *also* so subjective as to be almost silenced in our everyday lives, and often we experience sound more as vibration. In this chapter, it will be helpful to retune (instead of refocus) with sound in mind, in order to pay full attention to sounds, both ambient and otherwise (for example, the sound of traffic in Lobito, which has woven into it the undertones of street vendors calling out in Umbundu or Portuguese, of children laughing, of kizomba and kuduro beats, of engines not always perfectly tuned).

Soundscape

"Soundscape" is a term that was coined in the 1970s by the Canadian musicologist/composer R. Murray Schafer (1977) in a book called *The Tuning of the World*. A little like landscape, a soundscape is supposed to capture the "totality of sounds perceived by an individual in a given spatial setting and environment" (Eisenlohr 2018, 12), and the term has become popular in contemporary art, where soundscapes are now frequently installed in museums. Not everybody likes the term: Tim Ingold (2007a) feels very strongly that "soundscapes," like artistic "landscapes," remove the listener from the *experience* of sound, and should therefore be abandoned. Whether or not one likes the word, an example is captured in Image 4.1 above, where the ambient noise surrounding Victoria's balcony was recorded.

Sound Blindness

"Sound blindness" is another famous term, coined in 1889 by Franz Boas. Boas used it to describe his observation that many people placed in a new aural environment could not "hear" what others perceived as basic distinctions in sound, leading to tremendous confusion in terms of meaning, pronunciation, and assumed intent. Anyone who has learned a new language is likely to have an appreciation of how at first everything is like noise, but slowly, with practice, one begins to "see" through sound, understanding and identifying the different units of speech at hand. For example, I had a close friend in Angola who was Portuguese, but it took me six months to learn to understand her Portuguese. The accent of people from her region of Portugal was so different from the way I had learned the language that for months I simply couldn't distinguish words in the stream of sound. I was very embarrassed that we had to speak in English, but she was kind, and patient with me. Language is almost always learned in context, and common vocabulary and grammar structure are sometimes not enough for communication.

Music and Noise

What is the distinction between music and noise, and is one person's music another's noise? (During my heavy metal period in high school my mother certainly thought so.) How do we identify and move to rhythms? What do we think of as harmonious? How do we expect music to progress and develop and conclude? This, too, is culturally and socially determined. Some scholars have suggested that music is about power and how power is organized in society, and it has everything to do with channeling order, disorder, and violence (Attali 1977; Cox 2018). Others say taste in music (as with taste in everything else) is a product of socialization and class positioning (Bourdieu 1984). Few would argue that a recognition of and appreciation for music is often learned very young, and later in life is usually a question of aural exposure. Noise, according to R. Murray Schafer, is that which blocks communication (Schafer 1977; see also Serres 2008).

I once went to Copenhagen to do some political work for a Pan-African youth body that I was affiliated with at the time. I remember persuading a Cameroonian colleague to sneak into the back of the Danish symphony hall to listen to a classical orchestra, which he had never heard before. He lasted about seven minutes before he walked out, clutching his ears—he told me it was the worst thing he had ever heard, and looked at the price of tickets in astonishment (I was relieved we hadn't paid!). For my colleague, the harmonies and form produced by the stringed instruments did not blend, did not follow a flow that he could make sense of: the violins were too high pitched, the wind instruments sounded to him like water, and what was most striking to me was his reaction to the musicians themselves. I did not write down what he said, but it was something to the effect of "How can they be musicians if they sit so rigidly with their instruments, if not even they themselves can move with the sound?" For him, music was also movement, was almost dance.

Voice

"It's not just that voices *sound* different," writes Matt Rahaim, "voices *are* different" (email to author, 31 October 2018). Rahaim helps us to think about how the words "voice" or "the voice" can mean many, many different things depending on the context—from the physical voices of children singing mapped, for example, on one of the spectrographs of Image 4.1, to the "voice of the people" who "spoke" in the 2017 elections and replaced one president of Angola with another. Voices—human ones—are accented, and those accents often give clues to origin (e.g., my Portuguese friend, mentioned above), social class, education, or global exposure, but animals have accents too: a cat purrs in English but *ronronars* in Portuguese. That I spoke Portuguese with a Brazilian accent but then proved to be South African confused many of my interlocutors in Angola, and also freed me from some of the negative associations of white South Africans there. That I spoke Kreol in Mauritius with an accent tinged by South Africa, Angola, and the United States did exactly the same, and since returning home to Cape Town after a decade away I am struck by how often, on greeting, somebody asks me, "Which country are you from?" There is also an extensive literature on this topic, some of which I have included in the Indicative Bibliography.

Listening

Writing this section from Mauritius, far away from the fifteen-million-plus items in the university library where I used to go to read, I wanted to get a copy of a book called *On Listening* (Lane and Carlyle 2015). Pulled down an Internet black hole, I found myself googling "how to listen," and was astonished to see more than *one billion and thirty million* pages in English alone. Apparently, listening is something people have issues with! A quick glance through a few of the first pages, however, suggests that "the people" to whom the Internet is speaking are generally (but not exclusively) WEIRD. "WEIRD" is short-hand for Western, Educated, Industrialized, Rich, and Democratic. These are also largely (but again not exclusively, and there are many excellent initiatives to bring change) the people who write the algorithms on which the Internet is based (Rudder 2014).

Of the many, many entries on the subject, the first to appear was a wikiHow page entitled "How to Listen," which began:

> Taking an active, engaged approach to listening will improve your relationships and enrich your experience of the world. If you want to learn how to listen with undivided attention and respond in a way that keeps people talking, keep reading. (wikiHow 2019)

As is so often the case with WEIRD communication, the "you" here is assumed to be one kind of reader: a WEIRD reader, just like the WEIRD writer of the post. That wikiHow writer did not, and perhaps could not, acknowledge that this form of communication is culturally conscribed, and largely informed by the mind-blowing success of a single book and the industry that emerged around it: Dale Carnegie's (2004) *How To Win Friends and Influence People,* which was first published in 1936. Susan Cain (2013), amongst others, has demonstrated how this book consolidated an extroverted, hyperactive form of WEIRD communication that can be enormously challenging for introverts within the WEIRD context, never mind those who live outside it. In the context of *capitalismo selvagem*, people in Angola listened deeply, not only to the words but to all that was revealed in the unsaid, where both were shaped by the social and political moment (there as elsewhere). These revealed clues regarding education, influence, and, as the section below explores, also ideology.

Translation

If, like many people, you speak more than one language, you will already know that translation is not an exact science. Many words are difficult to translate, because they capture broader cultural experiences or reference points. Numerous films, books, plays, and even physical art explore the challenges of translation, which of course were also the challenges of writing this book in English. It is important to remember that almost everything described in this text was actually said, heard, and experienced in Portuguese, or perhaps in Umbundu or Chockwe or Spanish—but that often I experienced sound blindness and perhaps did not even hear some details that could have been highly relevant. Arguably, we all experience sound blindness in different moments, not only with language, but with regard to gender, age, and broader context, and that is one of the challenges of translation. How do we translate that which we simply do not hear?

Iracema Dulley (2015a, 2015b) has written powerfully about the way that language and (mis)translation served the interests of various power groups in Angola. I have already written about the difficulties of translating *capitalismo selvagem* as a term itself, but here let me give the example of *fixe*. The first time I wrote it in my notes, I transcribed it as *fish*, and only learned to spell it properly after Victoria nearly fell off her chair laughing at me. *Fixe* was the Angolan equivalent of the Brazilian word *legal*, which comes from the English "legal" meaning legitimate. *Fixe* also means cool, excellent, okay, and more besides. "How are you?" *Fixe*. "How was the weekend?" *Fixe*. "How do you feel about translation?" *Fixe*.

Body Language/Gesture

When people interact, it is very rare indeed for them to stay still, and often body language provides critical clues for how a phrase should be interpreted. Scholars sometimes refer to this process as gesturing (Rahaim 2012). Body language can be difficult to capture in written text, and gestures are sometimes left out of notes and texts altogether, so in what follows I have deliberately included the gestures made by interlocutors that helped me to interpret what they were saying. As the text that follows demonstrates, some gestures are deeply steeped in history. In our interview, when Dr. Nascimento felt strongly about a point he would slam his fist down on the table, subtly referring to the gavel of a judge; when Dr. Tchimboto taught from a lectern, he was "channeling" priestly discourse. If it is possible to think in multiple dimensions when reading, the experience will be greatly enriched.

Silence

Amidst all of these words, it is critical that we do not lose attention to silence (F. Ross 2001). Silences provide the pauses in which we gather our thoughts, are fully present with that which is unfolding, perhaps recognize the limitations to our knowledge. Without silence, there can be no sound, and like sound, silence is infinitely variable. Like sound, the silences must also be heard.

Cold War Echoes: Higher Education, Ideology, and Contested Duties

Universities Out of the Dust

On a hot afternoon, I sat with Dr. Tchimboto, then-head of the Instituto Superior Jean Piaget de Benguela (hereafter Jean Piaget) just outside Benguela. We were outside, in the campus garden, where the sound of water squirting from a sprinkler system gave a rhythmic undertone to our conversation. The water landed on finger-thick blades of grass, and a pair of small white birds searched for food under a tropical palm, occasionally chirruping. In the buildings around us, preparations were underway for the institution's tenth birthday celebrations: desks and chairs scraped on the concrete floors, instructions were given in loud voices and enacted in softer ones. Dr. Tchimboto was both quietly proud of the journey that the university had taken thus far, and all too aware of how difficult it would be to continue to thrive in the challenging social and political climate. "We are beginning the tradition of the university, here in Angola," he said thoughtfully, "and everything that will come later depends on what we do now" (Interview #36).

Here, I explore these beginnings. I consider the emerging university sector as a space in which both social mobility and the transition from socialism to capitalism have particular relevance, and where the practices of peace have powerful traction. I lever Raymond William's (1977) notion of "structures of feeling" to argue for attention to how individual faculty members' views of the world are shared through language and communicated to the next generation. These biographies were shaped by the ideological contestations at play in the Cold War and manifest in the slogans, songs, and ways of expressing oneself that supported both socialist and capitalist doctrine. These doctrines (defined in the Introduction and understood here as the collective of ideas that a particular group subscribes to) were apparent in institutions of higher education. In this chapter I focus on two of them, the state university in Benguela, Universidade Katyavala Bwila (hereafter UKB), and Jean Piaget, a private Catholic university that is part of a chain based in Portugal but extending throughout the lusophone world. Note that this analysis reflects how things were in 2013 and 2014—by 2018, there had been certain shifts that I reflect on at the end of the chapter.

At UKB, faculty were mostly trained in Cuba and the former Soviet Union, or were Cuban professors on short-term contracts. Socialism was the ideology that had shaped most of their lives, and to which they were expected to subscribe. At Jean Piaget, by contrast, teaching was done largely by people who had studied in Brazil, Portugal, South Africa, and Europe, where capitalism was far more entrenched. Many of them were foreign nationals, too, but there were no Cubans amongst the teaching staff, and the institution's head was emphatic that he would not hire any because of "differences in ways of thinking" (Interview #36).

Through the ethnography that follows, I will illustrate how and why these differences comes to have significance. For now, let me say simply that when Jonas Savimbi—leader of the long-term opposition party UNITA—was killed on 22 February 2002, bringing to a close the long civil war, intellectuals trained under socialism did not simply go to bed and wake up Trumpian capitalists. Rather, as with those in other sectors of Angolan society, university professors found themselves grappling with the new rules at play in *capitalismo selvagem*, whilst remaining guided by the training that they had received. Networks, needs, and the "traffic of influence" (see previous chapter) determined who was hired where and to do what, and of course individuals were drawn to places where they felt familiar with intellectual and social mores—both explicit and implicit.

The argument made here is that the Cold War continues to shape Angolan intellectual landscapes largely by what is said (or not said) and to whom. It probes how thinking came to be structured during the Cold War era and how that plays out in peace. I explore the utility of university education in the context of *capitalismo selvagem* before taking up the notion of "scientific journeys," or conferences. On one level, "scientific journeys" is simply one of the available literal translations of the Portuguese *jornadas científicas,* and describes the gatherings of academics in the nascent higher education sector. In its more poetic form, *jornadas científicas* is a helpful term for making sense of the country's attempt to create what then-minister for higher education Dr. Adão Nascimento (may he rest in peace) referred to as a "scientific identity" for the country at peace (Interview #55).

When I sat with Dr. Tchimboto in the garden of Jean Piaget, he pointed to the newly painted building that stood to our right, and to the plants, and the birds. "We have to build the universities from nothing, out of the dust," he said (Interview #36). What Dr. Tchimboto described here was the construction of the infrastructure necessary for learning to take place; the building of institutions one brick at a time. Equally significant is the development of infrastructures of knowledge that is taking place in Angolan higher education today, in which universities are but one part of an aural environment that includes religious institutions, the media, popular culture, the state, storytelling and, of course, simple, everyday *fofoca,* or gossip.

The Angolan Higher Education Sector

Angola's flagship university, Universidade Agostinho Neto, was founded in Luanda in 1962. It was originally called the General University of Angola, and its history and functionality have been well documented in the comprehensive study of the institution by Angolan sociologist Maria C.B. Mendes (2013). Until relatively recently, Agostinho Neto was the only university in the country, maintaining small satellite campuses in provincial capitals, including Benguela. The satellite in Benguela offered teacher training and psychology until 2009, when government policy changed and mandated that Agostinho Neto be split into several independent institutions. At the time of writing there were twelve of these, spread throughout Angola's eighteen provinces, and the plan was for national expansion until all regions are served (INEE 2006).

These newly constituted universities are known as *publicas*, or "public" universities, and they are free to attend, unlike the *privadas* (private universities), which were usually several hundred US dollars a month. At the *publicas*, admission is secured via an entrance exam that is open to anybody who chooses, but access is enormously competitive. I was unable to obtain hard numbers on entrance examinations, but anecdotal evidence at UKB suggested matriculation into certain courses may well be more competitive than admission to US Tier One universities such as Harvard and Stanford (supposedly the most difficult to get into in "the world").[2] At UKB, in some cases hundreds of students compete for only twenty spots in a given subject class, and the process is further complicated by bribes being accepted in some faculties but not others, or by spaces being "reserved" for the relatives of powerful individuals (though legacy admissions are hardly a challenge unique to Angola [Friedman 2019]).

Unlike at the private universities (described below), the majority of students at the *publicas* were in their early twenties. Most still lived at home, and the majority also worked to finance the expenses of their education. Though tuition was free, the state did not (and does not) provide a living allowance. Christiano was an extremely talented nineteen-year-old whom I came to know well. He grew up in precarious circumstances, and was drawn to a US American Christian missionary station because of the music that was offered at its church. He had rapidly mastered all the instruments available, and his dream was to study music in Brazil. However, he took the entrance exam to UKB *"por acaso"* (by chance, or just in case) and was admitted to study computer science in 2014.

When I gave up my position at the school where I taught music in order to travel to Brazil for further research, Christiano took over from me (doing a far, far better job than I had). He worked full time at the school, constantly juggling the schedule of his university classes with the school's timetabling requirements, and traveling frantically on public transport on the thirty-kilometer road that separated the institutions. He wanted to either study full time or teach full time, but without his work he could not afford to live nor make the expected contribution to his family's household income. He was also very well aware that in the context of *capitalismo selvagem* a university degree would at least partly compensate for what he lacked in terms of social and economic capital, and as the country tried to regulate itself, increasingly qualifications were being insisted upon. Many jobs required university degrees, though often they did not specify the discipline. As such, it was common to hear people describe the motivation for their studies as *"por o papel, não por interesse"*—for the paper (degree), not for interest.

As a result, like most Angolans I knew, he worked ferociously hard to both study and earn. This, I was told, was expected in *capitalismo selvagem*. When I returned in 2018 Christiano had nearly completed his studies, though he had convinced UKB to let him change to pedagogy. He had also successfully established an orchestra in the school, where nobody had previously known how to read music, and I was astonished to see the music room filled with children whom I had struggled to teach the recorder at age six, now ten-year-olds playing violins!

The limitations on places at public universities created what is effectively a seller's market in the field of higher education. Multiple institutions rapidly opened, and they had no shortage of students—at least until the financial crash. One sociology student at Jean Piaget who I guessed to be in her late seventies explained it as follows: "The war stole our education, and now we want it back" (Fieldnotes 140510). The Angolan government was well aware of the challenges it faced (and continues to confront) and was working enormously hard to support the emergence of a functional higher education sector. The *Plano Nacional de Formação dos Quadros* (literally, National Plan for the Training of Cadres) addressed the need to prepare the country for the postwar baby boom that already sees a large youth bulge of people from all sectors of society who need to be educated. In the 2012 plan, the government estimated that by 2015, 200,000 young people would be enrolled in tertiary education,[3] though the financial crisis dampened those numbers considerably (Angola 2012).

At the time of my fieldwork, there were six private universities and one public (UKB) serving the two cities in which I worked, and students at private universities would pay US$200–$350 per month to attend classes, with extra fees being levied for materials and ceremonies. Admissions at these institutions were generally not competitive at all; what mattered was simply one's ability to pay the fees. Many students studied for a few months or perhaps one to two years, then would take a break to earn more money before continuing. Lusíadas, at US$350 per month, was by far the most expensive of the private universities, and did have some students who did not work and were instead supported by their parents. This was rare overall, however, as the majority of families who already had the resources to pay for university education chose to send their children abroad: to Brazil, to Namibia, to South Africa, or—in the case of the most wealthy—to Portugal or the United States. They did this because of a general perception that overseas institutions offered a higher quality of education that was more rigorous and supported by better material infrastructure than that available in Angola. Providing in-depth analyses of each of the universities in Lobito-Benguela is beyond the scope of this chapter, but my argument relies on a more nuanced understanding of both UKB and the Benguela campus of Jean Piaget. In the following section I therefore provide a brief portrait of each institution.

Universidade Katyavala Bwila

At the time of my research, UKB was housed almost entirely in prefabricated buildings not far from the Benguela military airport. Classrooms seated around forty students, and each was equipped with a projector, though there was no Internet except on the cluster of computers in the IT center and about six more in the library—which also housed around four hundred books that could only be read on-site. The majority of individuals who worked at UKB were trained in either Cuba or the former Soviet Union. A few had done their undergraduate degrees at the University of Agostinho Neto in Luanda and left the country for graduate school if their disciplines required it. Only two individuals that I knew personally, including Dr. Daniella, who features prominently elsewhere in this book, had been trained in Brazil, though I heard that there were others.

The teaching faculty also included several professors from Cuba, all of whom lived together in a house very close to the university, and who taught on contracts of between one and four years. In 2014, the image of then-president Eduardo dos Santos was on display in most rooms, and I quickly learned that the size of the portrait of dos Santos in a given faculty member's office was a helpful guide to the kinds of questions that I could comfortably pose: the larger the portrait, the more careful I needed to be not to imply any concern or criticism with regard to the state of the nation.

UKB was a government institution, and as such loyalty to the state (which meant, in practice, to the MPLA) was viewed by those who worked there, and the government workers who oversaw their appointment, as crucial. When I began a short series of lectures on research methods in May 2014 at UKB, I was repeatedly warned against any overt or covert criticism of the state/MPLA in my lectures. I was told the classrooms were "full of spies" and repeatedly heard about a history professor who had been fired for teaching a version of Angolan war narrative that was sympathetic to the opposition party UNITA.

Freedom of speech was understood to be desirable under conditions of "peace," but many people were still in the process of learning what that meant in everyday life, and in the interim maintaining an accepted and familiar tune was expected. Both faculty and students relied directly on the state at UKB—faculty for their salaries and retirement benefits and students for their free educations. Most were willing to at least appear to toe the line, and I never heard any political debate on that campus, nor saw signs of protest action. Noticeably, when Abel Chivukuvuku, leader of a significant opposition party, came to Benguela province in 2014, he made visits to private universities but explicitly avoided UKB, where it was made very clear that he would not be welcomed (Fieldnotes 140327).

Instituto Superior Jean Piaget de Benguela

One of the places where Abel Chivukuvuku was indeed welcomed was Jean Piaget, where Dr. Tchimboto said with a smile, "We had some good debate" (Interview #36; all quotes from Dr. Tchimboto below are from this interview). Jean Piaget was also where the "dissident" historian mentioned above "sought refuge" after being reported, bringing his family to the university until they were able to move to a different province for safety. The Benguela campus of Jean Piaget was the second from the same broad institutional network to open in Angola—the first, and larger, being in Luanda and a third opening in Lubango after my fieldwork was completed. Established in 1979, it also has campuses in Portugal, Mozambique, Cape Verde, Brazil, and Guinea Bissau. Instituto Piaget is based on a curriculum that is shared across campuses and is broadly humanist in nature. Its founder is a Portuguese man, who would periodically visit the individual campuses.

"This university is a university of the poor," Dr. Tchimboto explained, saying that the majority of students took their classes at night because they had to work during the day, and that many of them struggled to pay their fees at the end of the month. Of the faculty, the majority were Angolan, though many trained outside the country, in Portugal, Brazil, and elsewhere. At the time, Jean Piaget had a large number of Portuguese on the staff owing to the economic downturn in Europe, and many people who were Italian or trained there due to Piaget's theological links with Italy, but as mentioned above, there was not a single Cuban employed by the university. "Cubans are very difficult to work with," Dr. Tchimboto explained, "because the ideology of Marxism is almost entirely incompatible with the ideology of the church." He went on to explain that the other "problem" with Cubans was that they didn't "come from a democracy." Angola needed people who had *lived* in a democracy already to help usher it into being, and Cubans simply couldn't do that. "They are just for the government, that's all," he said shaking his head.

Dr. Tchimboto said that the faculty knew the classrooms were infiltrated (*infiltrado*) by MPLA party loyalists, but the institution's commitment to religion allowed them to speak and act with much more freedom (in the guise of religious education) than if their public standpoint was secular. This space of freedom had a huge impact at Jean Piaget, where students were actively encouraged to engage in debate and to formulate their own opinions, and where Wifi was available for anybody anywhere on the campus. "Having the Internet does make a difference, it's a subterranean [*subterrâneo*, underground] difference, but it matters," he explained, "but in general it's hard because most of the students are just getting their degree for the qualification, they don't really care about the content. We don't yet have a tradition of learning, so we still have to make everything from scratch. Remember that before we just had dust here"—when he said "here," the implication was that the dust was not only on the ground but in people's heads as well, but his eyes smiled gently.

On Voice

Dr. Tchimboto was well aware that to some degree the power that Jean Piaget had in the public domain came from its affiliation with Christian religious structures. Though in political terms Angola was nominally secular, the church had wielded enormous influence in the colonial era (Péclard 1998) and continued to do so to the present. "The party [MPLA] wants to be part of everything," he said, "but I am a priest, and I can say no, you see. Most people do not have that power, just the priests in the Catholic Church, and that allows us to have a space that is a little bit different."

Being able to say no is in many places and many contexts a tremendous privilege, and indeed choice is arguably one of the greatest assets of those who are middle or upper class (often older, often male) across the world. To have one's voice heard—whether dissenting, agreeing, negotiating, or even joking—is to have access to certain kinds of power. Scholars have been thinking about voice for a long time. Often judgments about what kind of person is speaking are based on sound, accent, vocabulary, and choice of words (Fischer 2016; Ondjaki 2014). Not only did Dr. Tchimboto have an actual pulpit, and also a lectern (remember that universities emerged from Christian monastic practices of learning via preaching), he also spoke in a way that demonstrated a high level of education. In Portuguese, that meant conjugating verbs correctly, knowing when to use formal versus informal language, but also, importantly, being able to change registers from formal to informal, Portuguese to Umbundu (or Italian) depending on what would connect him most quickly to his listeners. Linguists call this "code-switching," and it is an important tool of communication that is received as authentic by listeners.

I experienced this powerfully one day with my closest friend in Angola, Victoria. Victoria and I had lived, worked, shopped, studied, and traveled together extensively, and by the end of my fieldwork I thought I knew her very well. Her father, with whom she was very close, had been a low-level civil servant who had purchased the apartment in which she lived in the 1990s, after the period of nationalization and then liberalization of fixed property (Gastrow 2015). He had supported her through school and her first two years of university, allowing her to intern in her spare time with a local NGO, at which she acquired both skills and social capital, and where she and I originally met. His death in 2012 was a significant blow, and placed major financial responsibilities upon her—not only for herself, in terms of sustenance and university fees, but also in terms of contributing to the care of her eight younger siblings. Her mother was a teacher, and Victoria had a complicated relationship with her.

On one particular day, Victoria and I sat together on her bed, both of us preparing to travel. The phone rang, she answered, and I found myself staring at her in shock—it was like listening to a completely different person. Gone was the internationally traveled consultant placing high heels and perfume into a suitcase; instead the aural tone suggested a fierce woman at the market bargaining for a decent deal, refusing to back down. Her tone, accent, vocabulary, and pitch completely shifted, as she glided between Umbundu and Portuguese and back again in a way that was completely impossible for me to follow. The discussion concluded and she hung up, muttering bitterly about the expectations at play and the limits of maternal authority. Her voice returned to what I recognized, and she delicately selected a blouse and folded it into her suitcase (Fieldnotes 141211).

Listening, Speaking, and Thinking through the Cold War

Anne Pitcher and Kelly Askew have written about the post-socialist period in Africa. They observe that despite the prevalence of socialism on the African continent from the 1950s to late 1990s, relatively little has been written about the processes of its demise. Pitcher and Askew note:

> Instead of "postsocialism," the language of "neo-liberalism," "democratic transition" and "civil society" dominates discussions of Africa's recent transformations. It looks forward to a presumed rosy and successful future, rather than looking backward to a failed socialist past. And it prevails because its many advocates—development experts, multinational representatives, foreign consultants, NGOs and the current African elite—dictate its terms. They assume and assert that the collapse of socialism has left a "blank slate" on which the story of "free market democracy" can be written. In so doing, they devalue and ignore the interpenetration and interweaving of the old with the new order in the

> formulation of national policies as well as local responses to the enormous challenges that have taken place. (2006, 3)

Angola is unusual in its history for many reasons, not least the fact that during the first phase of the civil war (1975–91) over 430,000 Spanish-speaking Cubans served there both in the military and in the health, education, and civil service sectors (George 2005). This service was part of an ideological commitment to the spread of socialism worldwide made by Cuban leaders, who trained hundreds of thousands of young people from across Africa and other parts of the developing world. Soldiers remained relatively distant from the majority of the population, but teachers, nurses, and civil servants of various kinds were to have a profound impact—particularly on those who were children during the war (Hatzky 2012). Both Benguela and Lobito hosted Cuban teachers during the war, and both cities also sent many young people to Cuba's Isla de la Juventud (Island of Youth), a small island off the coast of Cuba on which some sixty schools were established hosting approximately eighteen thousand students from Asia, Africa, and the Americas. Students received travel, board, and education in return for seasonal work on the island's citrus plantations (George 2005, 159), and many stayed on in Cuba afterward to complete university education. The impact that this training was to have can perhaps best be understood through a case study. Here, let me share parts of the biography of a man I call Dr. Marcos, who served in the senior leadership of UKB. I interviewed him on the university campus, his modest office dominated by an enormous poster of President dos Santos in a crisp wooden frame (Interview #14).

When Dr. Marcos was twelve years old, he and his classmates at a school in Moxico province—the easternmost and by many measures poorest of Angola's regions—wrote a national test. The top students from this test were to be sent for education abroad in either Cuba or the countries of the former Soviet Union. In 1985 he embarked for the Island of Youth, where he was to stay until he left Cuba some thirteen years later. That was in 1999, and the civil war was still underway, so he went to Portugal and then to Spain where he completed a master's degree, moving back to Angola only in 2006. At the time of writing, he was planning to return to Cuba to undertake a PhD.

Dr. Marcos felt he owed everything he had to the Angolan and Cuban governments, who paid for his education and facilitated his career trajectory. He said the time on "the island" was hard, of course, he missed his family. When he left he had eight siblings, when he returned twenty-two! Being away for so long was challenging "but I had to fulfill my mission, there was no question of that. My mission was to complete my studies, this gave me focus. Everybody had to do their part for the development of Angola, and that was mine. So it was okay to suffer a little." In that time, Dr. Marcos's father died—but he only heard of the death four years after it happened. He received three letters from home over thirteen years, and the bonds of blood family were gradually superseded by relationships with those whom Kath Westin (1997) calls "fictive kin"—people with whom one forms life-sustaining relationships that in some ways can substitute for family.

On return, those educated in Cuba were expected to accept without question postings from the Angolan state—regardless of where. One woman I knew had loved engineering, but had been compelled to study veterinary science because that year veterinary science was what government policy had determined was needed. She was then sent to the most rural province of the country, and for three years helped cows give birth, daydreaming about the urban infrastructure she would so much rather have been building, but accepting the role that she had been given in history and only much later becoming a science teacher and then school administrator (Interview #41).

Closeness and solidarity in the fulfillment of duty were common themes amongst those educated in Cuba and the former USSR, most of whom had made what they understood to be great sacrifices and acts of selflessness in order to gain skills needed for the advancement of the country. They followed instructions without question, and spoke often about duty and service. They shared songs, sounds, and language (Spanish or Russian, as well as the languages shared between them from different regions of Angola), and the words and experiences that went with them created bonds, social networks, and shared experiences that played out in the everyday of a country at peace.

Overall, Angolans trained in Cuba were supportive of the Angolan state's more repressive policies when it came to managing dissent and progress, accepting the narrative that those in power had the right and responsibility to determine the future of others. Those, like

Dr. Tchimboto, whose life experiences had been driven by immersion in democratic capitalist states, tended to have a view of the world that was based far more on an expectation of individual freedom. These two perspectives existed in tension with one another, and often also in tension with the state as well as cross-generationally. These perspectives informed what was said, what was heard, and the types of people that students were being taught to be.

Critical Thinking in *Capitalismo selvagem*

"Critical thinking" (*pensamento crítico*) was a term that susurrated throughout my fieldwork—whispered, but very rarely discussed upfront. Here, I quote at length from an interview with one individual, whose details I withhold due to the sensitivity of the content.

> Critical thought is a question of politics [*questão política*]. You have to use intelligence when dealing with this. For example, if they [the government] found out that I was thinking about it [critical thinking] too much, I'd lose my job. Because in practice this is a socialist state, democracy is "just a photograph" [*so é uma foto*] that is used to control, a representation. Critical thinking is not allowed because if it happens there will be a revolution. That's partly why the higher education sector is so poorly developed, and education so profoundly underfunded. The country needs skills, but why doesn't the government put money into education? The government won't allow it. Professors earn much, much less than people of their equivalent rank [*o posto equivalente*] in the military for example, or in finances, and so people in academia don't earn and can't be recognized.
>
> They [the government] prefer people who study in Russia and in Cuba because those countries don't teach critical thinking, it really is a different story for those who went to Brazil or the USA. And there are a lot of Angolans who are studying in Brazil but paying themselves, because the government won't fund them. It's partly because the protests [*manifestações*] that happened in 2003 in Luanda, and there were lots of them, were mostly managed by people who had studied outside the country, they were led by people who had been to Brazil, and the government became afraid.

People who trained in Russia and Cuba don't come back and protest, and the government wants those kinds of people. Those who study in Portugal don't either. Why not? I'm not sure, the context is different in Portugal but the high school preparation doesn't treat critical thinking in the same way, so they don't question so much. But in Brazil and the US there is a core training [*formação integral*] that teaches students to *be* researchers, to be critical people.

As professors, though, we have to be careful. To influence our students we have to use our intelligence, because we don't know who amongst them are spies, and we could be put in jail. Not jail in the literal sense, because the state won't get away with that, but jail in other terms. They will just close all the doors; all the opportunities to be promoted or to make something of your life will disappear. There are a few who are committed [to freedom of speech and freedom of thinking], who do it anyway, but they are a very, very small number, most just accept and stay silent.

This commentary highlights the complexities of critical thinking in the context of Angolan higher education. Many in the government felt that if people in Angola actually started to *think*, they would have no option but to rise up against the corruption and incompetence of the state, a perspective that was echoed by many interlocutors, including the then-minister of higher education himself (Interview #55). Critical thinking, in this worldview, implied critique, and critique, in the past, had been what led to war. Thus if feeling, too, were to become "too critical" the logical outcome would be revolution, and the logical outcome of revolution was another civil war, and that evoked a great deal of fear—albeit much less so for the younger generation, who were increasingly distant from knowledge and memories of the past.

The individual speaking in the interview above knew of many people who had studied in Brazil on a scholarship from then-president Eduardo dos Santos's private foundation, FESA. At the time we spoke, the foundation had dramatically reduced the number of young people it sponsored to go to Brazil, which, it was claimed, was largely because of the "trouble" caused when these people returned home. On return, they were viewed as having radically different perspectives on and expectations of the state that came out of a *"formação integral,"* or core training, that demanded criticality from students. This was something most of my informants in Brazil remarked upon: there, they were expected to have opinions, whereas in Angolan structures of traditional education, successful memorization in accordance with the teacher's perspective was what was valorized. Nonetheless, as the individual argued, a great many people *wanted* those perspectives and so were finding ways to self-finance their university education in Brazil. They wanted them precisely because what such perspectives enabled were alternative paths of action and relationships that did not require the "trafficking of influence" in *capitalismo selvagem*. If, it was hoped, enough people started operating differently, *capitalismo selvagem* might give way to something more regulated and predictable, and easier to manage.

Searching for a Scientific Identity

"Angolans are trained in all countries that want them," said Adão Nascimento, then minister of higher education, in an interview in May 2014 (#55; all quotes from Dr. Nascimento below are from this interview).

> The government is open to any support and any influence that will help us to create Angolan knowledge [*conhecimento Angolano*], which the country does not yet have. We do not have our own brand of science, we don't have our own technology. At this time, we are searching for an identity that is our own, that is more advanced.

I met with His Excellency Professor Dr. Nascimento at the offices of the Ministry for Higher Education in Luanda. Located in a colonial-era government building, the offices were not exactly drab, but certainly not lavish. Traffic vibrated outside, an air-conditioning unit hummed in the corner, and an old-looking TV showed national news at a low volume. A worn red rug covered the floor, two big leather sofas hugged the walls, and an empty water dispenser stood in the corner next to a tropical plant. In the minister's office, an Angolan flag flanked the president's image, and the table was polished wood covered with papers. Dr. Nascimento himself was trained in Leningrad (now St. Petersburg), in Russia, completing undergraduate and master's degrees there on a government scholarship. He later went to Montreal, where he did another master's degree and also got a doctorate in education. Dr. Nascimento described himself as an "MPLA militant" (*"eu sou militante de MPLA!"*) and was at pains in our discussion to describe how far the country had come since the colonial era.

For Dr. Nascimento, limiting freedom of expression at universities—and indeed limiting the sonic exposure to ideas circulating in general—was a necessary step in the "maturation" process of a very young nation. He understood the present generation to be laying the foundations of higher education in the country, where future generations would be the ones to "develop" it. "We don't yet have mature institutions, and we have to nurture a lot in terms of the quantity and quality of what we offer, to have higher education that is reasonable," he explained, well aware of the many shortcomings of not only universities but the entire educational sector, where what we might think of as "knowledge infrastructures" were extremely limited (Edwards et al. 2013). In the case of the universities that I explore in this chapter, the buildings themselves are new—layered on land that has had many uses in the past.

Yet the faculty teaching in those universities have, as I have shown, their own "structures of thinking" already in place that have been informed by their experiences of their own education: the specific time and the specific context, be that in Brazil, in Cuba, or elsewhere. Faculty reproduced what they had learned, whilst at the same time trying to prepare students for the new realities of the country at peace. Some were able to think flexibly, and adapt both their material and mode of delivery, but for others that was more challenging, and so they relied on rote learning as if the broader context of 1980s Cuba or even early 2000s Brazil was echoed in the classrooms in Lobito. In the university classroom, where structure of thinking meets knowledge infrastructure, the "scientific identity" that Dr. Nascimento described was being created on a daily basis. During the time of my fieldwork I was fortunate to be able to participate in two significant moments where such sharing and co-creation occurred: through the first and second *jornadas científicas*, literally "scientific journeys," held both at Jean Piaget and at another of Lobito's universities.

The content of both "scientific journeys" that I attended was wide ranging, and the purpose as I understood it was less to engage one another as experts than to *initiate a practice of listening* in which expertise could be engaged. The events were covered on national television and taken extremely seriously by all concerned, as they marked a concerted effort to bring front and center the "new scientific identity" that Dr. Nascimento articulated. Later in the same month I spoke at length with the minister himself. The *Jornada* at Jean Piaget was a helpful shared reference point, for him, an example of *Angola Faz*.

Angola Faz—Angola does—has been one of the most significant slogans in the postwar period. The verb *fazer* is difficult to translate, as it can mean "doing," "making," "creating," "succeeding." For the sake of consistency, I will use "do" here in translating Dr. Nascimento's words about the state of higher education in the country at that time. It is not as elegant as it would be in Portuguese, but I hope the meaning of "do" in the continuous sense is nonetheless communicated.

> Institutions are doing, higher education is doing. In our context, higher education is fundamental to the country. We need to do a lot more, because we still lack so much. Higher education is a factor in the development of the Angolan person, the Angolan citizen, the Angolan professional, the scientific Angolan, the researching Angolan. Our Ministry of Higher Education will help to create institutions that make up [*compoeam*] society, and for that reason each one has to be inserted into the Angolan system.

To the minister, being "inserted" into the Angolan system meant something quite clear. Drawing a square on a napkin in front of him, he then drew arrows pointing at it. "Jess, you have your space," he explained,

> you have your way of being [*maneira de estar*]. If everything [showing the arrows] that comes at you agrees with your way of being, that is good, but if it doesn't, if it hurts you, you won't like it. This happens with all countries. Angola just wants what everybody wants, to be a state with its own orientation, its own space, its true way of being. In America, if the image of the state is damaged, you go to jail and get tortured. It's the same here. The USA has a tradition of government that goes back centuries. We have only a few years here. It's very recent, it needs to mature. Just remember, until 1970 in America the black people *did not have* [his emphasis] freedom of expression. The lack of freedom of expression should not frighten us here, because it will get better

with time. There is a certain freedom already, people can say what they want *in the correct places* [my emphasis].

What the minister described was a context in which the people inhabiting the physical infrastructures of knowledge that the government allowed to emerge (by licensing institutions) had to cohere with a framework of speaking and presentation that did not damage the reputation of the state. One could say what one wanted "in the correct place," but that place was explicitly *not* the university, according to Nascimento. Peace, again, demanded pacification. Physical infrastructure enabled knowledge infrastructure—some of which was beyond the control of the state (as in whether or not a private university provided free Wifi), but knowledge infrastructure was also created by people, as in the case of the *jornadas científicas*. Each person brought with them an already-existing "structure of thinking" informed by social, political, economic, religious, generational, and technological experiences. Yet the wonder and hope of that moment in Angolan history was that there were so many points of disconnection. In order to bridge these disconnections, everybody had to think outside the frameworks they arrived with, and this was ultimately the great success that the university enabled.

Sound, Structure, and Imagination

Sound, like smell, touch, and taste, is also inflected by class. Generally, the more money one has the more one can control the sound around oneself—the "soundscapes," to use one of the words from the beginning of this chapter. That might involve being inside a private car versus on public transportation, or have to do with the closeness of housemates or neighbors, or the ability of the state to enter one's home through national radio and television versus the private choice that comes with streaming from the Internet—and the headphones that tailor and individualize aural experiences—linking one either to the very local or the explicitly transnational. Writing this chapter, I have found it helpful to at moments stream Rádio Ecclésia (https://streema.com/radios/Radio_Ecclesia) through the Internet, listening to the news from the perspective of Luanda, reminding myself of the accents and phrases of Portuguese (like the private universities, religious radio stations have far more freedom of expression than do state alternatives). At other moments I listened to MC Kappa on YouTube, and at others paid careful attention to the sounds around me at my desk in Mauritius.

I have been interested here in how what one thinks is effectively shaped by what one hears, the noises of everyday life at different registers from the mundane to the political, from the spiritual to the familial. Musicians, as Marissa Moorman (2004) has so beautifully demonstrated, have played a formative role in bringing the "new Angola" into being, and they continue to do so today, but so too have children singing the national anthem, as described previously, and so too do the sounds made by the opening and closing of doors that literally did not exist in the country a decade ago, or the muezzins in mosques that are constructed and periodically destroyed by the Angolan state. The Cold War echoes in Angola—more there than in many other places—but new speakers also bring new sounds and new imaginations. Even *fofoca*, the gossip, has slowly shifted as mobile phones have transformed not only what is heard, but the platforms on which aurality takes place, defined now far more by the constant pinging of incoming WhatsApps than anything the state can dream.

> **Why does it matter? (sound)**   *Ideological contestation*
>
> As I write this text in 2019, it seems that today neoliberalism is so dominant that it is often difficult to imagine any other option was ever seriously on the table. Through the impacts of ideological contestation that this ethnography explores, readers are reminded that in the recent past, the logics of capitalist expansion that currently dominate the world were far from given. Exploring expectations toward a state in socialist-capitalist transition draws attention to how different groups navigate between the structures around them: governance, social life, financial markets, education systems, religions, fashion, and what might be considered the diverse "sound tracks" of everyday life in different places. Reading about people who "traffic in influence" or who thrive in *capitalismo selvagem* compels questions regarding similarity and difference, as well as choice and imposition. In the same circumstances, what would I do? If I were here, what choices would I make in both the long and the short term? Decisions of action are after all based on personal and collective beliefs not only of what the world *is*, but what it could *become*.

Poems 2

Estrelinha *(Little Star)*

quick eyes quick wide eyes watching watching knowing who is here
and who is not and who is kind and who is not and who
kisses whom in the corridor and where the stray cat has hidden her
    kittens
quick eyes quick wide eyes and a belly button that extends like a fist
marking a birth where scissors must have been in scant supply
but where kisses were not, were not because look at her hugging her
    mother
clasping her neck whispering secrets into her ears
quick eyes quick wide eyes watching and commenting on the children
    with fancy uniforms
the unfathomable distance between their flats up above with barbies
    and the
converted garage with no window where she sleeps while her stepfather
    drinks and drinks in the building Quick eyes
she knows where he keeps the extra beer cans and the notes secreted
    away for whisky
and she looks and looks and looks, dressed in her white public-school
    coat like a physicist
holding a crayon
looks and looks for an escape route and for a place to play and for
    somebody to dance with
and a place to draw uninterrupted. Quick eyes, the little girl is always
    watching. The women
upstairs tell me that they pray for her.

Birds on Campus

three white egrets on long green blades of grass like knives from the earth this is a strong grass, thick enough to hold them to resist their scratches and to give back small ecosystems of sustenance. there are three white egrets on the long green blades of grass that grow at the university that grow with the university a university that is growing out of depleted soils. out of the soils of war the poets have said and they are right because when there is destruction there is dust and after that distraction the grass needs time to grow to root itself in the dust before the egrets may come. Egrets under a tree at a university that is now one decade old, egrets doing normal egret things while some students sit in nearby shade cursing calculus and another reads a book of philosophy and a woman who is seventy and had her education stolen by uniformed men walks painfully to the registration desk in the hallway and states that she is there to learn. Having come back the egrets are watching now with a degree of curiosity.

João, Collapsing

João has collapsed
on the stairway
frothing at the mouth
his epilepsy
attacked.
João has collapsed
on the stairway
drooling with drunkeness
his options for
entertainment limited.
João is asleep
on a piece of cardboard
outside the building
where
he is counted by the nice
young lady with a clip board
conducting the national
census.
João has enraged
the rich ladies upstairs
his conduct deemed
Inappropriate.
João has refused to carry
that heavy weight
for less money than
enough to buy beer
the ladies are disgusted
with him, illiterate
epileptic drunk
no sympathy here
the concrete of the stairs
is deemed appropriate
medication
and hopefully that
nice young lady
from the census bureau will
do something to
remove him.

Dona Maria Serving Soup

i should write a book about my life
says the old woman serving soup in flat blue plastic sandals.
in the war i carried guns for the troops and once when i had
   to shoot i did so
and my mother, poor thing, has a problem with her head and oh it can be
   very tiring sometimes.
here is soup, good soup, the vegetables i used are fresh.
i should write a book about the people who come to this place
(this open balcony on the beach warmed by soft scent
and cut by her acid voice speaking to the waitresses if they dare to be
   slower than quicksand.)
most of them who eat were born here, then they left, now they are back
but i stayed, you know, because we did not have a choice here my family
was noble, but not so noble to flee. and this is our place
i should write a book about my life and the time i swam through the water
   because my son was
drowning and how i pulled
him out, sweet boy, with the strength of a mad wolf
—carrying guns was nothing in comparison—and he is strong today.
in this book, there will be so many words but now, my daughter, eat
   your soup i am
too tired
to tell you them,
eat and go home.
good night

Dona Inês

bitter and cracked occasionally a flashed smile mirrors what might once could
have been, it is confusing to be so much caught
between the light and the dark of memory and the present of the city
as it was and now, as it is desired and as it is restricted it is hard
to watch bitterness drip in on itself and anger seethe amidst frustrated
memories, and it is difficult to navigate this during stairway encounters
and continue
unscathed into the day, unmarked by such fierce, dry rage.
Yes girl! she shouts
before the war this was
my house my place
it was beautiful and now
it is broken and i am broken
and my sons are broken
and the mother of my
grandchild who snorts coke
on fridays is broken and the
economy in portugal is broken
and oh my heart it has
imploded and splashed itself
onto a passport clawed back
for terra natal when terra paternal is
collapsing and oh girl it was
beautiful and now it has
crumbled and i, i am ang
gry ach
ing bit
ter
ter ...
o que eu tenho agora, filha?
ó lembranças. aqui é todo
destruida.

Two Photographers

(i)
Here is his camera.
We are at a wedding negotiation and two little girls wear
white satin and soft shoes
and there are china dogs on the dresser
and the room is painted orange and has linoleum on the floor
and is filled with people who bring preassigned gifts.
These the lady of the house will inspect: a golden dress
a suit, and tie (but the shoes and the belt do not match which is cause for
grave concern). And he photographs: click click, click click, smile now
    little girls, this is an
Important day
click click, click click click
he tells me his name and that this is his trade, and also that
he teaches at a primary school too
so we meet a few times, until his romantic interest
wanes after many rejections
But I remain, with the background soundtrack to his life, the 1960s
    instant-development camera: Click click click click click,
the 1980s generation man, click click click click click click
artistic stubble spread across the chin
head at an angle finding the correct frame.

(ii)
Here is her camera: it is bright and bold and big
and contrasts with her slender bodily frame
which she drapes artistically in flowing cloth,
now representing the river, tomorrow wind, perhaps tonight flame.
her camera knocks on the door to record, instead of clicking, it
knocks on memory and begs to be allowed in. her lips
are glossed and promise kisses and her eyes kohl-rimmed say
Ask Me to Help You Paint Your Life.

Cinema Church

A fire burns in the middle of the building
in an open space, where cement dust
rises into the air with each footstep.
Some distance away a concrete cinema screen
arches from the podium like the sea approaching Moses
and behind us the open-air seats cower under the new metallic roof
The church has engulfed the colonial cinema
and made it its own. Closed in the tools
of sinful imagery, and lit the fire of God.
Where once lights flickered onto the wall telling of
other countries, now one light—spotlight—is on
the priest, who guides us to the next world, true world he says
Each week bricks are added and the new cement is
stamped down into the floor. The collection tin is poured
into the walls and ceiling and new made altar.
The cinema is both abandoned and wrapped in adoration
space of humming sound generated deep in the bellies
the congregation, enraptured, join hands and look upward through the
　　new tin roof
and into the invisible.

Yoga Teacher

when she came
she planned to teach them
yoga and how to
ride bicycles;
she came to change and
civilize them she came to
practice ayurveda and play
singing bowls she came
to salve them to heal them;
she came with her curled hair
and her free spirit she came
with a force to bring universal
love; she curled in a ball on her
bed when it slowly dawned
that this was nothingness to passions
here dissipated like a pinch
of salt in the ocean spread
into meaningless as precious
dandelion seeds in the air after
a wind she lies curled on
her bed waiting for change
in universal love.

Photo Essays

Photo Essay 3: Childhoods

Children play on an urban roof in Huambo.

Around Christmas 2013, handcrafted reindeer appear at the College of Stars in Lobito. Just down the road, a young mother stands with her baby and her brand-new car, bought with bank financing, outside the house that she and her husband have recently restored.

Dolls hang out to dry in an apartment block in Lobito; a little girl stretches out her hand at Carnival.

In the Bela Vista neighborhood of Lobito, a concrete elephant is the only leftover from a park built in colonial times. Children still play on it, and motor-taxi drivers seek refuge in the shade.

Photo Essay 4: Leisure

The once-famous outdoor venue Cinema Kalunga at times hosts movie screenings, but more often at night is lit up for live shows. Here, it rests during the day.

Basketball is a very popular sport and hoops are everywhere. The Angolan national team is one of Africa's best. Many young people are involved in Scouting. Sometimes they bring their laptops to the meetings, always their phones.

A fisherman's boat (home-made) rests on the beach after the evening's catch, not far from the saltwater swimming pool of the Lobito Sports Club.

A concert featuring a local musician fills up Cinema Kalunga at night.

CHAPTER 5

National Rebranding

The Selfie and the Other

When I think back on my fieldwork, I still don't understand what compelled Sebastião to take the photo of my cupboard on his chipped Samsung phone. That said, when I look at my records, it's those strange images of everyday objects that make the place and people real to me: dolls hanging out to dry on the washing line, rusted weights covered in thick white paint, suitcases stacked against the eaves of an apartment building, sections of bright orange walls that linked themselves in my mind wherever they occurred: Angolan houses in Rio de Janeiro, Curitiba, São Paulo, and "at home" in Lobito, Benguela, Luanda. "Why do Angolans like orange walls so much?" I once asked Sebastião (Interview #62). He didn't know. He said that he suspected there was an oversupply of that color of paint during the civil war. Slowly, it must have become "normal" and seeped across what Miguel Vale de Almeida (2004) refers to as the "brown Atlantic,"[1] entering into the living spaces of the diaspora and the various lenses of graduate-student field photography.

The brown Atlantic; orange walls; the red, black, and yellow of the Angolan flag; white school shirts; a blue, high sky. Like many of my generation of what some scholars call almost-digital natives to describe our relationship with technology (Prensky 2001), my memories of space and place are visually proscribed, encoded, and archived in images that are frequently stored on social media and embedded by referents such as number of likes and whether or not my father made bold, if affectionate, comments in the public feed attached to them. The Internet has been a part of my world since childhood, and though I was alive at a time when my first camera was a pink plastic Kodak whose film consumed my pocket money in exchange for blurry photographs of the household cats, my world had gone digital, and quickly also online, by the start of my undergraduate training in Cape Town in 2005.

As a graduate student, I remember debating social media usage with my classmates during a methodology seminar. At the time, we were only a few kilometers from Facebook's headquarters, and our department had recently trialed a study on the use of the iPhone in fieldwork methodology (Ames 2013). Our class was divided as to whether or not it was a good idea to continue the use of the so-called fetishized paper notebook or switch over to technologies such as the iPad ("but what if you drop it in a river?" "your notebook would disintegrate there too"), and even more unsure when it came to the use of Facebook and other social media platforms in the field.

If one *was* to use Facebook in the field, what would the acceptable ethical parameters of such use be? Would it enable or hinder fieldwork? Should one have a "personal" account and a "professional" account that are separate (Walton and Hassreiter 2015)? What were the limits on what could be shared on the online platform with friends, with professional networks, or with interlocutors themselves? Should we add our interlocutors as friends, or not? If we had a fake/professional profile (and what did that even mean?), and interlocutors became "real" friends, would we then add them and blow our digital cover? What about WhatsApp and Instagram, which at the time were emergent technologies? Like many conversations during my postgraduate training, this one served to complicate everything and resolve nothing—but in a helpful way.

My own decision, then, was to be as honest and as natural as possible. I planned to continue using Facebook, but sparingly, to never show the faces of people in the field if I wanted to share details of my life in Angola with friends and family (unless I had their permission or they had posted the image in the first place), to add or accept as "friends" only those I knew in person, and to carefully consider the consequences of any posting or status update, much as I would in my everyday life. Never having been a huge user of social media in the first place, I was unconcerned about the shadow my digital life could cast on fieldwork until I found myself in the midst of a complex chain of events that unfolded as a result of my affiliation and genuine friendships with people the then-government did not approve of.

In this chapter, my goal is to explore what happens when "the self and the other" of ethnographic research[2] instead becomes "the selfie and the other."[3] It quickly emerged that my pre-field preparation had fallen short in a fundamental way, as I had not sufficiently considered how my interlocutors' use of social media could and would affect my research at every level. I discovered in no short order that full immersion into the field meant immersion within not only the physical but also the digital world of my interlocutors, and that that immersion had tremendous consequences in terms of access, trust, and practical, everyday information.

In recent years, many researchers have begun to explore the impact of social media usage on everyday life in a variety of different social and cultural contexts. Daniel Miller and his students, amongst others, have demonstrated that social media is used differently, and to do different things, in different parts of the world (Costa 2016; Horst and Miller 2012; Miller 2016). This should not be surprising. Rather, what was compelling in the Angolan context was that the processes and practices of social media use were taking place in a context that I develop here as one of national rebranding, in the sense of reconstituting a world through nationalist images and propaganda that highlighted changes that were real but had rarely "trickled down" to average Angolans. This process of rebranding was manifest in both print photography and digital worlds, and was one in which my participation was actively demanded.

In the first section of this chapter I explore that process, beginning with recollections of an image of a rock concert. Perhaps surprisingly, I do not include the images themselves, because I did not take them with the intention of reproduction—they were the visual equivalent of scribbled notes, and in the editorial process it emerged they could not be printed. It was an important lesson: one can rewrite a fieldnote, but not retake a snapshot from far away. In the second section, I draw on contemporary theory to argue that the biopolitical life of screens should be taken into account in today's ethnography and research, and in the third section I argue for the extension of participant observation into the digital worlds that reflect and shape the material worlds they document.

As of late 2019, visual literacy increasingly trumps the need to read text, and smartphone technologies combined with platforms such as Instagram allow all to become authors with millions of followers. I often wonder whether, had Instagram been in 2013 what it is now, I might have created a page reflecting the fascinating architecture of Benguela province, and if I had, what that process might have done for my research. The reality is that through photographs, both researchers and researched are increasingly engaging in the mutual sighting of culture,[4] but learning how to sift fact from fiction has now assumed a new level of importance and generated many unresolved questions. For example, is using a filter the same as editing an interview transcript? Can we blur or edit faces to avoid getting informed consent? How do we address visual privacy when photographing a house means revealing, within a community, the identity of interlocutors?

National Rebranding: Guarantee Your Children a Better Past

One of my earliest fieldwork experiences was going with friends to watch their daughter perform in a school play (Fieldnotes 131026). We drove to the rented hall where the event took place, and I watched with curiosity both the performance and the intensity with which it was documented: a small film company was making the "official DVD," which I was told all families present would purchase, and almost without exception each member of the audience recorded what unfolded on iPads and other tablet devices, giving the impression from my position in the back of the hall of a phosphorescent sea of flickering screens with the stage resembling a ship at a distance.

I was to witness "iPad seas" again and again during fieldwork: at Scout rallies, in schools, at concerts, and at Carnival. Images would be placed on social media and YouTube and shared with friends. People tagged one another and their children, bragged, laughed ("kkkkkk" is how one laughs online in Portuguese); often they shared the news, but much more often it was things that they found humorous. Unsurprisingly, and in line with what has been documented of social media usage in a variety of cultural contexts (Bolton, Parasuraman, and Hoefnagels 2013; Costa 2016; Miller 2016), content was almost entirely positive: the goal was to tell stories of success and happiness and to share these with as wide a world as possible. Many of these photographs remained on cell phones and in the cloud, but some were also printed, and in Lobito several small shops—largely run by Vietnamese immigrants—did a thriving business making material the digital imprints brought in from electronic devices. These would be exchanged as gifts, turned into calendars, inserted in family albums, or displayed on the walls (Strassler 2011).[5]

I was often surprised at how "known" my own presence at certain events was: one night I attended a concert of the Angolan musician Yannick Afroman, which took place in Benguela's Cinema Kalunga, an outdoor amphitheater turned concert venue. My friend Victoria and I carefully navigated the sloped terrain in our all-but-mandatory high heels, balancing plastic cups of beer in one hand, phones conspicuously in the other, purses dangling from our wrists. We posed for selfies and group photos what felt like hundreds of times throughout the night, and indeed, the next day at work (I was a primary school music teacher), with the Scouts (with whom I volunteered), and throughout my movements around town, people commented on my dress, the concert as a whole, and Afroman's music. My presence at the concert had been documented, observed, and incorporated into the social life of the town and those around me, and whether or not the other individual had attended, it was a starting point for discussions pertaining to music, fashion, race, Africanity, and identity.

The kind of witnessing that I found myself experiencing—both as seer and as the seen—stood apart from much of the literature that I had previously engaged with around photography. Angola, like so many other postwar countries, has been marked (some would say scarred) by a history of imagery in which the "lens" of international interest and often national knowledge as well has been focused primarily on that which is painful. Indeed, during my early reading on the country I was shocked to discover the existence of a beauty pageant entitled "Miss Landmine Angola," which had landmine victims competing for a beauty queen title in an attempt, amongst other things, to "question established concepts of physical perfection," "replace the passive term 'victim' with the active term 'survivor,'" and "have a good time" (MacKinnon 2008).

During my first trip to Angola in 2011, I met with a man who had recently edited Angola's first postwar national photo book with accompanying text in Portuguese and English: 186 pages of everyday people, landscapes, and infrastructure entitled *Angola, um País a Renascer*—Angola, a Country Reborn (Cerqueira and Schul 2008). Produced by the then-president's own non-profit organization, FESA, the book proclaims that "peace is here to stay (*"pax veio para ficar"*) (8). Its purpose, according to its preface, was "to show the world that Angolans are now fully able to contribute to the improvement of humankind" (8), and it was explicitly intended to offer to a global community a different way of "seeing" Angola.

Angola, um País a Renascer was quickly followed by a second publication, this time in Portuguese, English, and Mandarin, called *Cities and People of Angola* (Abrantes and Martins 2010). The latter was produced just in time to be displayed in Angola's stand at the Shanghai World Exposition of 2010. According to its editor (the same individual who produced the earlier text), they almost missed the print deadline because the president refused to allow publication until the book included an image of a man riding a Jet Ski. Why did the president care so much about a Jet Ski? The editor could not tell me precisely, but the purpose of both books was to provide a counterperspective on Angola—one that emphasized infrastructure and everyday peace. It was also, of course, to attract investment from outsiders, and the texts were produced parallel to the media campaign *Angola Faz!* (Angola does) that I have described above, and that was aimed at an internal audience. Together the books and campaign can be read cynically (if one does not believe them to represent a version of truth) as propaganda, pragmatically as a national rebranding that is necessary to the emergence of the neoliberal state. Rebranding is further essential if the national intention is to move out of *capitalismo selvagem* and into an economic structure that is slightly more internationally respectable, or, as I suggest here, as part of a process of national re-membering.

By "re-member," I do not mean anything to do with memory, but instead a process of nation building explicitly designed to change how Angola was known—both to Angolans themselves and to outsiders. This, in certain respects, was not dissimilar from how the US author Toni Morrison (2007) describes trying to reimagine or rework a body that others perceived as "ugly" into something that could be recognized as "beautiful." Above I quoted from Angolan author José Eduardo Agualusa's novel *Creole*. In another book, translated into English as *The Book of Chameleons*, Agualusa (2006) provides a powerful narrative of why personal histories and memories matter, and how they are achieved in a fiction that is perhaps less far from reality than one might think. Set in postwar Angola, the novel unfolds in the house of Felix Ventura, a man whose business card reads "Guarantee your children a better past" (23). Ventura lives surrounded by photographs and newspaper clippings, and his job is to recreate the past for clients who are "a whole new bourgeoisie": as the the text explains, Ventura's clients are

> businessmen, ministers, landowners, diamond smugglers, generals—people, in other words, whose futures are secure. But what these people lack is a good past, a distinguished ancestry, diplomas. In sum, a name that resonates with nobility and culture. He sells them a brand-new past. He draws up their family tree. He provides them with photographs of their grandparents and great-grandparents, gentlemen of elegant bearing and old-fashioned ladies. The businessmen, the ministers, would like to have women like that as their aunts, he went on, pointing to the portraits on the walls—old ladies swathed in fabrics, authentic bourgeois *bessanganas*—they'd like to have a grandfather with the distinguished bearing of a Machado de Assis, of a Cruz e Souza, of an Alexandre Dumas. And he sells them this simple dream. (23)

Ventura's work is similar to the ex-president's insistence on the Jet Ski in the process of national reimagination, and is an example of national re-membering. The iPad seas of the concert in Benguela and the children's play in Luanda are not dissimilar either: in all these cases, what is at stake is the visual imagination of who one is. If identity is framed by representations only of suffering, suffering becomes difficult to transcend, but if identity is framed by Jet Skis, "bourgeois *bessanganas*," and rock concerts under the stars, alternative futures become much easier to imagine—though no less difficult to achieve (and perhaps, as a result of that imagination, more disappointing when they remain a distant hope). In the following section, I consider the process of making such alternative futures through screens, of the power that such technologies increasingly have in real-world terms, and the implications of those alternative futures for fieldwork when they are not given due respect.

Biopolitical Screens: Frames of Vision

During the time that I lived in Lobito, one of the most important relationships I built was with a well-known NGO whose work focused on human rights and democratization. I visited their premises almost every day, and the director, employees, and participants became both extremely important enablers of my work and much-loved friends. These friendships were significant both in everyday life and on social media; in everyday life for conversations, laughter, introductions, and knowledge about Lobito, and online because the articles, blogs, videos, and networks that these individuals drew to my attention might have otherwise remained invisible to me. Relatively early on in my fieldwork, a group based in Luanda who had loose connections to them produced a DVD entitled *Geração da Mudança: O despertar de uma geração anestesiada: 32 é muito* (Generation of change: The awakening of an anesthetized generation: 32 is a lot) (Chipilica 2014). The numeral "32" here refers to the years in power of the country's then president, José Eduardo dos Santos, who had assumed office in 1979. *Geração da Mudança* contributed to a growing anti-president discourse promulgated in part by a group of young people known as the *revus* (Pearce, Péclard, and Soares De Oliveira 2018). Like many others, I was very interested in the DVD and asked to buy a copy. This was duly arranged at the NGO, and I agreed to participate in their social media advertising campaign, allowing them to photograph me with the DVD in hand.

I watched the film with interest, but thought nothing of the photo until several months later. Continuing my fieldwork in Rio de Janeiro, Brazil, I had an unexpected discussion with another interlocutor. In Rio, I worked closely with the Angolan consulate, as it formed the hub of Angolan social life, especially its cultural center. I had befriended a young man from Benguela who I call Xavier, whose experiences as a university student in Brazil were to form a core part of my doctoral dissertation. One afternoon, whilst watching the weekly inter-Angolan soccer match that took place not far from the consulate, he took me aside. The ensuing dialogue went roughly like this.

> "Jess, we have a problem."
> "We do? What is it?"
> "The problem is that you are friends with revolutionaries, and because of that, the consulate wants to stop your research."
> "Friends of revolutionaries?"
> "Yes. On Facebook we see it all the time. We think you must be CIA and trying to topple the regime." (Fieldnotes 140830)

Being mistaken for a CIA agent is neither a new experience in anthropology nor an unreasonable suggestion given the long imbrication of the discipline with security apparatuses of various states (Gordon 1987; Max 2008; Price 2016). Quickly realizing that this was serious, I did my best to assure Xavier of how incompetent I would be as a spy (in retrospect, a fairly lame move), and I revealed that I was there on funding from the Brazilian state, not the US National Science Foundation or the South African equivalent body—a fact he quickly checked online using his phone.

After some discussion, it emerged that the trigger had been the photograph of me holding the above-mentioned DVD. Without my knowledge, it had been blogged and re-blogged, and an employee of the consulate had seen it and recognized me. This in turn had led to a thorough investigation of my social media profiles, and despite a reasonable security setting on my profile, evidence of friendships with particular individuals already known to the government for their anti-state views was deemed enormously problematic and enough of a threat to put a stop to my research.

When I got home that evening, I decided to write to the director of the NGO via Facebook, who to my surprise was online despite it being about 3 a.m. in Angola at the time. I also wrote to some of the most prolific social media users amongst my friends, reasoning that if I could simply get them to not actively tag me in their posts, my attempts to bridge different worlds—the government and an element of civil society that at the time was somewhat in opposition to it—would be less visible. I wrote a simple message to all of them, saying how much I appreciated their posts but explaining that some of my current work involved interviews with government officials, and I therefore asked not to be tagged. To my surprise, the director responded immediately: her tone was furious. She accused me of being anti–free speech, supportive of the dictator, against democracy, a sell-out, and a traitor. I sat at my computer feeling kicked in the chest, and suspecting very much that she felt just the same. Trust is critical in ethnographic research, and so is trying to understand reality from as many perspectives as possible. In this case, at the time, it felt that those two needs were fundamentally incompatible with one another—the debate was far too polarized to bridge.

As it turned out, I was able to complete the research in practical terms (my visa was not revoked), but I often wonder what was lost through those interactions—ironically with both those who served the regime and those who critiqued it. My attempts at friendly neutrality had been compromised by social media, which also of course reflected a certain truth: I *was* friends with people who were critical of the state, and I myself was not in fact neutral in my views, even if I was diplomatic enough to usually keep that to myself. Neutrality, I was reminded yet again, was not possible (Hammersley 1999), and my mistake was to think that just because my interest in the Angolan consulate's perspective was *also* sincere, I would somehow transcend the rules of "with us or against us" that were fundamental to how the Angolan state apparatus operated at the time.

In the era of big data, fieldwork itself is rapidly changing, and after this experience I began to read new media scholarship much more seriously. Two ideas, in particular, stood out to me. In an article entitled "The New Visibility," John B. Thompson reflects on the torture of Iraqi prisoners in Abu Ghraib, a US-run detention facility located in Baghdad. In 2004, images of torture and abuse entered the public domain, becoming "iconic symbol[s] of abuse by an occupying power in the wake of a deeply divisive war" (2005, 35). Thompson reflects on what he calls a "new world of mediated visibility" (35) in which, he argues, individuals and organizations use images as explicit parts of their strategies in everyday struggles—a point made only more apt by the use of social media platforms, imagery, and video by contemporary groups such as ISIL (Farwell 2014; Klausen 2015). In very different circumstances, US anthropologist Danny Hoffman writes of images of nature in Sierra Leone as "icons of social context" (2007, 104), which provoke questions not only about the image itself, but about the broader circumstances of production and circulation. Putting the finishing touches to the proofs of this book in late 2019, I see already how dated some of this material might feel—that too is a new challenge of contemporary ethnography.

Norwegian art historian Pasi Väliaho has taken this point much further. In *Biopolitical Screens: Image, Power, and the Neoliberal Brain* (2014) he explores the effects of the technologies behind image production, most notably screens, on how the world is both made and experienced. "Screens and the images they materialize echo and evoke both psychic and somatic events," he writes, "weaving us and our inner visions into social fabrics of affectivity, desire, meaning, and behavior that we share with one another and as collective beings" (1). Väliaho reads screen technologies from video gaming to drone control, alongside works by social theorist Michel Foucault, to consider how interactions with screens (and, through new virtual reality technology, also projections) have consequences for the ways people interact, play, care, and sometimes kill one another—the latter an experience explored in poignant depth in Hugh Gusterson's (2016) ethnography of drone warfare.

Human interactions, Väliaho explains, are increasingly informed by pixelated imaginings of human beings that are far from any senses beyond sight: there is no smell of blood when one kills with a drone, no sound of a bomb falling or sensory stimulus to live and relive as part of ethical review—at most now, the experience of pressing a button or clicking on a screen, perhaps a little sweat. However, as a documentary film on the use of social scientists in modern warfare, *Human Terrain*, has demonstrated (Udris, Udris, and Der Derian 2010), that too can be overcome with training. In all these examples what emerges is not only that images reflect the world around us, but that they actively *make* it too, influencing "the movies running in our brains ... [to] bring forth the 'emergent present,' a moment of imagination and thinking that can picture what is not yet but could be" (Väliaho 2014, 129).

What could Angola be, and what is it possible to be in Angola? The answer to the latter is certainly "much more than a war victim," which may be in part why former Angolan opposition leader Jonas Savimbi's children have sued the makers of the video game *Call of Duty: Black Ops III*, which portrayed their father as a "barbarian" (Stuart 2016). That a real human being, Jonas Savimbi, even appeared in such a game in the first place says a great deal about how game making itself reflects stereotypes and tropes of contemporary world systems. That the makers thought they could get away with such a production suggests an incorrect assumption of asymmetrical connection. In all the examples given so far in these pages, it is possible to "see" the life-making properties of screens: in an image captured of a cupboard in Rio de Janeiro, a concert in Benguela, a Jet Ski in a photo book, a video game, and in the processes of ethnographic production. In the contemporary world, "the movies running in our heads" are more than lenses that inform how we see the world—they actively shape our decisions of where to go, whom to interact with, and how to respond when we meet in the flesh.

Laughing on the Internet

On 29 August 2014 a joke appeared on the Facebook page of the Angolan Scouts. The text read as follows:

> The president of the Republic [of Angola] travelled to Brazil with the vice president. On the journey, Vice President Manuel Vincente said, "I could throw one hundred five-thousand kwanza notes out the window and make one hundred people happy." [President] José Eduardo responded, "You like to compete with me! I am rich, so know that I could throw enough money out the window to make a whole province happy." Manuel replied, "I know, chill out, the only poor person amongst us is the pilot." The pilot then concluded: "It's you guys who should be thinking. I could toss the plane out of the sky and that way make the whole country happy." (my translation)

The joke was astonishing less because of its content than because of its context in surrounding years. In 2016 Angola was ranked 125th out of 180 countries by Reporters Without Borders (in 2018 it was 121, and the most recent rankings can be seen at https://rsf.org/en/angola)—and criticism of the state can and did result in punishment, as this book has already explored. Much like the DVD described above, however, the joke reflected a changing mood amongst Angola's younger population, a group who for the first time in almost forty years were coming of age without childhoods marked by war. A lot of people laughed publicly in the comments ("kkkkkkkkk!!!! ☺"), some praised the joke for its general accuracy. Many others expressed shock that individuals could take the liberty of critique—a shock proven justified in 2016 when fifteen young people were arrested simply for holding a reading group and engaging with US political scientist Gene Sharp's text *From Dictatorship to Democracy* (Marques 2015; Moorman 2015).

Whilst I was conducting my fieldwork, US photographer Brandon Stanton's Facebook page and blog *Humans of New York*[6] was at its height—including in Angola—and almost daily it came up in conversation. At the same time another American, Pharrell Williams (2013), had released a hit single entitled "Happy" that rapidly inspired "tribute videos" from around the world, including from my grade 6 music students at the school where I taught in Lobito. Inspired by what they were seeing online, my students successfully negotiated making a YouTube video instead of writing a final exam in order to "participate in the world" and "show [that world] Lobito" (Auerbach and Colégio 2014).

Though by no means representative of the entire country, these twelve-year-olds, and also the Scouts who posted the joke on Facebook, are part of a group that US educationalist Marc Prensky (2001) has famously referred to as "digital natives," those who have grown up, alongside class-equivalent peers across the world, connected through technology and conversant in how to use it. This is also the audience for whom this book has largely been written. Prensky does not engage "the world" writ large, nor the uneven impacts of globalization (Ferguson 2006) and access to technology (Piot 1999; Skuse and Cousins 2008), but the questions he raises about how one generation might think and act radically differently from another are certainly relevant to Angola, and to anyone interested in contemporary fieldwork methodologies.

There is an interesting paradox at play between the local and the global in the case of media imagery. The languages of the Internet still matter (increasingly less as translation technologies become more sophisticated), but geographic boundaries are less and less significant in the creation and maintenance of very real imagined communities, and the nationalism described so well by Benedict Anderson (1990) is increasingly ruptured by co-creation of global knowledge in which images play a fundamental role. Nonetheless, individuals are still geographically located, and "subversive" activities such as the posting of the joke described above might have radically different consequences depending on where and how the authors are actually grounded. The year 2018 was rocked by revelations of the ways in which Facebook data can be and had been sold, with the platform manipulated and used to influence not only individuals but the outcomes of elections (Cambridge Analytica, etc.). Moving forward, it is unclear whether the Internet will continue to function in the way it did in the first part of the twenty-first century or become monetized, securitized, and bordered much like the physical world it represents.

In the anglophone media, the focus of many news stories pertaining to Cambridge Analytica and beyond was the United States, which has both the financial resources to explore what was happening and a well-trained, well-resourced independent press determined to uncover at least a more coherent version of the truth. What the US seemed to be missing was the political will to act on it. Another meme that circulated in 2018, just before the Brazilian national election, commented wryly, *"Nunca imaginei que o futuro da democracia brasileira fosse depender do PT aprender a usar o Whatsapp"* (I never imagined that the future of Brazilian democracy would depend on whether the Workers Party could learn to use WhatsApp). Whether or not the Workers Party learned to use WhatsApp, they lost the election, at least in part because of messages circulating in social media, which are difficult to fact-check. The same has been argued in the case of Brexit (Cadwalladr 2019) and also claimed of Facebook as an instigator of ethnic cleansing in Myanmar (see John Oliver's comments, https://www.youtube.com/watch?v=OjPYmEZxACM). Who makes the Internet, and who (or, in the age of AI, what) determines what is seen and by whom?

Insta Lies or Insta Truths?

How do we make sense not only of partial truths, but of partial visions? The term "Insta lie" is probably familiar to any reader under the age of twenty-five, but perhaps less so to others. In a popular YouTube video entitled "Are you living an Insta lie?"(https://www.youtube.com/watch?v=0EFHbruKEmw), people are filmed applying make-up before going to bed to photograph themselves on their pillows, carrying bicycles up hills for "workouts," and posting buoyant photos of relationships that seem troubled—all for the satisfaction of social media "likes" and "loves." Most users of Instagram are well aware of the limitations of the reality that it reflects, but that does not change their desire to narrate a personal truth that is in some way aspirational. What happens when that takes place at a national level as well?

Visual truths are hotly contested, and there are usually many perspectives. Movements such as #TheAfricaTheyDon'tShowYou or #SomeoneTellCNN are examples of the power of social media to change global narratives in important ways, in these cases people from Africa speaking "back" to the lens of the global north. Most people choose to share beauty much more than they portray the ugly, knowing full well that images have the power to make worlds, to bring them into being, but visual imaginations are shaped by the same geopolitical forces that inform other domains of everyday life. Increasingly scholars have to make sense not only of what is said or written, but also what is shown. This is made all the more complex when we take into account the racial and social biases of algorithms (Buolamwini and Gebru 2018), and the ways in which connectivity itself is often uneven and unpredictable.

The Internet has changed the way that many people live, and arguably research methods and ethics are only beginning to catch up. We cannot separate our online and our embodied selves in the processes of engaging others, as this risks duplicity in an already duplicitous space. That in itself is not new: our offline selves are also carefully managed, and we certainly do not share everything with everybody—human history includes millions of examples of one bit of information being given to somebody and then metamorphosing into a different "truth." Given the emergence of "fake news" and the increasing complexity of trust as a basis for human communication, researchers now have to grapple with there being less and less coherent "truth" available, at least in the way that truth was understood in the twentieth century, and have to accept that their own bodies will be read and interpreted through both metaphoric and camera-based filters.

Finally, it is important to remember that knowledge is always embodied. The eyes are only one small part of the tool that our bodies represent, and though we might increasingly feel at ease in a twenty-first-century version of armchair anthropology[7]—effectively the mass consumption of "Insta lies"—the gaze alone will not teach us how to feel, or whether or not others are staring straight back at us, or editing our perspective through Wikipedia. If the objective is compassion, feeling with one another, making the world "safe for human difference" in the ways that our ethnographic ancestors suggested, it is still necessary to immerse ourselves in offline worlds: to smell, to taste, to touch, and to listen even, or perhaps especially, when the topic of conversation is how many likes a given post got on Instagram.

Fieldwork Ethics: Seven Afterimages

An afterimage is that which remains after one has ceased looking at a given image, picture, or space; this section is about some of the afterimages that have lingered in my mind since I completed the research that lead to this book. During my last years of primary school, the Truth and Reconciliation Commission (TRC) began its work in South Africa. From 1996 to 1999, from when I was eleven to when I was thirteen, the news carried almost daily updates of a process that both wrenched opened and tried to heal tremendous wounds from one of the most violent political regimes in history. The subject of the South African TRC is beyond the scope of this book, though it is worth noting that Angola has not yet had anything similar; its relevance here has to do with the processes of translation and ethics. I vividly remember watching sections of the TRC hearings on television, and reading about them later in the newspapers around our home. I remember that they were broadcast with live translation, and at times the cameras would pan to the translation booths where men and women who spoke all of South Africa's eleven official languages channeled the narratives that were being shared so that all of the country could hear them.

Some twenty years later, I was asked to review a film for an academic journal. *A Snake Gives Birth to a Snake* (Lessac 2014) is a documentary about those translators, and I have no problem admitting it made me weep. I cried so much watching it that it took me six hours to get through because I had to keep hitting pause. I wept both because of the content, and because the film reminded me of how frightened I was to grow up as a white South African just on the edge of apartheid. I always wondered who I would have been if I were born just fifteen years earlier. Would I have had the courage to go to jail, or exile, or face torture, or would I have cut my losses, closed my eyes, and made good for myself at the expense of other human beings? The film asks three very important questions, and they are useful here. First, "Must we forgive the past to survive the future?" Second, "Can we be unscathed?" And third, "What do you have to do to change a face?" (see Auerbach 2019).

The third question is the most important one, because it concerns the narrative one shares of others. In the film, the translators recognize that their choice of words might determine whether an individual is seen as a villain or a hero—a person worthy of curiosity, of empathy, or an inhuman monster. They realized this whilst simultaneously processing their own deep emotions based on being personally affected both by the hearings and by apartheid itself. In certain ways, this is a little bit like the process of ethnography, where researchers go and absorb themselves in a given social context, and then reflect it back for other people to read about, as you are doing here. For a long time, anthropology and other disciplines have recognized the ethical complexity of this process, and very little work is undertaken today that does not abide by carefully considered codes and charters, with the broad but very clear overarching maxim of "Do no harm." Yet the reality is often so much more complicated.

Very few ethnographies require the researcher to explicitly grapple with the ethical challenges and choices that their undertaking requires. Anthropologists and others commit to "doing no harm," yet almost all researchers can remember moments that haunt them—much as the translators for the TRC found themselves haunted in their lives by the narratives they had heard. These continue to live as afterimages in our minds and memories. There is tremendous fear that if we admit that perhaps, after all, we did do harm in some way, to some people, our work might be restricted, our discipline might be ashamed—perhaps nobody will hire us or the government won't fund us any more, perhaps our friends will think us terrible human beings or we will negatively evaluate ourselves. More likely, we won't get visas to go back or, if we are writing at "home," our friends and families might bear the consequences of our words.

But in my experience teaching, I have come to believe it is important to speak about these things. "Doing no harm" is far too simplistic a suggestion—it makes it appear that researchers are somehow angelic beings above the messy complexity of life. It makes it appear possible that we do not go into the field of everyday life as humans, who make mistakes but keep trying anyway, who work toward doing good but often respond out of fear instead, who cannot predict the future and so make the best decision possible with limited facts, but often realize in hindsight that our actions triggered reactions that hurt others in ways we could not have imagined, or sometimes helped others beyond their hopes. Here, I share some of the complex moments that continue to live with me.

My goal in sharing seven of them is to deepen the dialogue around research and ethics, to show just a little of the process that goes into knowing certain parts of the world and writing about them, to point out that we as researchers are ourselves deeply implicated and that in many cases we carry the impact of our fieldwork with us for the rest of our lives (see also Posel and Ross 2015). That isn't a problem at all, in my view. It's just how it is. It *would* be a problem if we were somehow so removed from it all that we never experienced the full spectrum of human life. The challenge is that we get credit for doing the dramatic, or for visible "acts of good," or even just solid social science research—this book reflects that. But it is much, much harder to write about the things that didn't work well, where we weren't sure if we made the right choice, where perhaps we got hurt and then have had to spend years healing. Just because it is difficult doesn't mean it isn't worth doing, though, or that others can't learn from our experience, from knowledge of the messy, complicated reality of the work we do. Here, on the request of one of my student readers, I would also like to add a trigger warning: what follows has the potential to disturb equanimity and to stir memory and emotion. Fieldwork itself does that, though, often in an instant, and certainly without warning. Engaging such memories and emotions in text may perhaps be helpful practice for at the very least becoming aware of one's own triggers—and therefore being better able to manage the reactions when they come.

1. Mercury

I was with some colleagues and we went for a tour of a very exclusive high school in one of the country's major cities. The facilities were impressive, and as we were being shown around a science lab, the enthusiastic teacher took out a vial of mercury. He gesticulated dramatically, explaining a point about pedagogy. The mercury fell out of the vial and onto a student's desk (there weren't any students in the classroom at the time). It slipped into the cracks and disappeared. Nobody said anything, and the teacher put the now-empty vial back in its stand (Fieldnotes 180509).

2. Dinner

I moved into my own apartment two weeks into my fieldwork. One of the downstairs neighbors was also a foreigner in Angola. We met a few times on the stairs, he was perfectly pleasant, and I didn't yet have any friends my age. He asked if he could come to my apartment for dinner, and explained that he lived with his mom, otherwise he'd invite me to his place. I said sure, no problem, come at 6 p.m. He came late, around 9. I'd given up on him and eaten long ago, but I said sure, come in and have some tea. He wanted wine, and had it with him, so we drank together. When the conversation turned to colonialism, he suddenly became very violent. I was injured, though not seriously enough for hospital. He stormed out of my apartment in a rage. I avoided him in the corridors of the building from then onward. He never apologized. I didn't drink alcohol for the next two years.

3. Photograph of a Little Girl

This experience is narrated in the Introduction as well....

When I first arrived in Lobito I used to take motorbike taxis a lot—riding as a passenger for a small fee. I got chatting to Abrão and he helped me buy my own, which felt a lot safer. I went to meet Abrão's family in one of the poorest suburbs of Lobito. Seven people lived in a two-roomed blockhouse full of mosquitos. I took photographs of his nieces because his mother asked me to. I drank some juice and ate some cookies, and when I prepared to leave his mother gave me two pink satin pillowcases and a sheet, as a welcome to the country. I still have them.

I printed the photos and called Abrão to give them to him, but he had lost his phone so never answered. For months they stayed by my bed. When it was nearing time to leave the country for a period of research in Brazil, I rode to the place where I knew he lived, and asked around. The neighbors helped me find his house in the labyrinth of narrow pathways. I brought with me a mosquito net, some other sheets, and the pictures. I gave them to his mother and she began to weep uncontrollably. I didn't understand what was going on. Abrão looked at the photographs and sighed deeply—the little girl in an orange dress had died, he said. Shocked, I asked him why. "Children just die sometimes," he responded, shrugging. His mother lit a stub of candle. It was the first and only photograph they had of her (Fieldnotes 140611).

4. Helping Strangers

From the window in my flat I could see a road that joined one section of Lobito to another. One day, I decided to explore it. On my motorbike I rode to where I thought it began, but I couldn't see an obvious point of entry. I asked a pedestrian where it was. He said, "just over there," and offered to show me, as he was heading home from work and took that road anyway. I often gave people lifts on the motorbike, and so agreed. We passed what looked like an entry point to a cement factory. I stopped and asked him if he was sure—he was very confident, pointing around the corner. I carried on slowly. Suddenly we were surrounded by five angry men. They shouted at us for trespassing. I was genuinely puzzled, stopped the motorbike, and calmly explained the misunderstanding. "Ask my passenger," I said, "he's just showing me directions."

One of the men, who proved to be security guards, then grabbed my passenger and pulled him off the bike. "You're trying to kill this woman!" they roared, "You wanted to steal her motorbike!" They started to beat him, and I screamed, saying it was a great misunderstanding. One of the guards found a pole with some concrete on it and hit the man in his ribs—I thought I heard them crack. I screamed more loudly, and one of the security men tried to grab my motorbike keys. At that moment a foreigner drove past, a white man. He stopped to see what was happening. He proved to be a manager from Texas who didn't speak any Portuguese, but while I was begging him to intervene anyway, my former passenger pulled loose and ran away. The guards did not give chase in his presence. I never saw any of them again (Fieldnotes 140118).

5. Being Helped by a Stranger

During my early fieldwork, in 2012, I was in Brazil doing preliminary interviews and language training. I had flown to Belo Horizonte for some meetings, and got to the airport for my flight back to Rio de Janeiro only to find it had been moved to the next day. I didn't have much money at the time, so chose to spend the night at the airport, something I'd done many times before in different parts of the world. I chose a spot to settle in, chatted to my parents on Skype, wrote up notes. I went to the same toilet four times over several hours. On the fourth entry, the janitor and I spoke. She asked me why I'd been at the airport so long. I explained my situation and asked if she knew any warm spots in the airport to sleep, as it was getting late. She paused for a moment, and said to me, "Child, if my own daughter were in a foreign country, I would not want her sleeping at an airport. Come to my home—it is humble, but we have a bed for you."

I stopped in my tracks and considered the suggestion. Emerelda was in her early fifties, streaks of gray in her hair. She told me her next shift was early morning, so she was taking the bus back anyway at 5 a.m. I said okay, thanked her, and got my bags. After an hour on a dark bus where her colleagues celebrated a five-euro tip left in the lavatory by a Swede and divided amongst them, we alighted in a neighborhood that, even with my significant global exposure to inequality, wrenched me inside. A child was dispatched to buy an egg for me to complement the beans and rice; we ate. The neighbors came, and soon we were all laughing. I showed them photographs of South Africa on my laptop—nobody there had seen a real Apple Mac before.

Emerelda told me she was saving to buy a laptop for her daughter, and I thought of Dono Oniko in Angola who was doing the same. I slept deeply that night, in a narrow twin bed, and woke up before dawn to take the bus, refreshed. I left the money that I had on me under the pillow with a note saying "laptop fund," because I knew that Emerelda would not accept it otherwise. When I went to board my flight I waved at her. She came and hugged me and said, "Safe travels, daughter." Emerelda didn't own a phone, so I have never heard from her again, though she gave me her address, and I did send a postcard to thank her (Fieldnotes 120829).

6. Travel and Privilege

As I finished writing this book, I did an extremely rough calculation of my work-related inter-regional travel (not including everyday movement) since the end of my undergraduate degree, and it came to roughly 580,957 kilometers. The calculation included return flights from South Africa, the US, the UK, Brazil, Angola, and Mauritius, as well as some circular movement within each of those spaces and visits to other countries for workshops, conferences, and in the case of Cuba deliberate tourism to understand the Cold War. The point of the exercise was more metaphoric power than accuracy about geography and kilometers flown, but the calculated total is literally a journey from the earth to the moon and back (calculated when the moon is reasonably close to our planet). That is a lot of carbon pumped into the atmosphere on my behalf.

Was it worth it? How do I grapple with being the recipient of an education that cost the earth so much? Is what I learned significant enough? How can I pay it forward? Most days I am calm on these subjects. I both worked very hard and was extremely lucky—neither stands alone—and I benefited from being in elite, extremely privileged institutions that compounded the privileges I already had. I took more than my share of the planet's resources during this time, for sure, but I also opened a great number of doors for others, and in my teaching work I try to do that still. Nonetheless, I often think about the very difficult scholarship interview that in many ways opened up this path. During the interview, South African constitutional court judge Edwin Cameron asked me what humankind was currently doing that would be viewed with the same moral horror that we see slavery today. Without hesitation I answered "flying," because of climate change. A decade later, and 580,957 kilometers ... ?

7. Malaria

I got malaria early on in fieldwork, and never fully recovered. My body was drained and weak, and my dreams were feverish for months from the illness. Brazil was great—I blended in more easily there, and importantly, the food was nourishing for me—but I battled in Angola, which is notoriously difficult for vegetarians. That said, I was glad I did get malaria, because it gave me first-hand sensory experience of an illness that affects almost the entire population at different times and informs the way people move, socialize, relax, and sleep at night. When I think back to being sick, the two weeks where I was genuinely ill were relatively easy to deal with: rest and medication. Recovery was much more complicated. How do you collect data—let alone rebuild a country—when your body feels like even its blood has lost the energy to run through your veins, and instead moves at a sluggish crawl?

What does one take from this? For myself, everything and nothing. These experiences have now folded into the longer fabric of my life, which has been just as richly filled with mostly kindness, and upholds my general faith that usually people are good, trustworthy, inclined to treat a stranger like a daughter. Some people are not, though, and I acknowledge that. My own judgment has certainly been flawed at times—for that, I willingly accept the consequences—but one learns from these experiences, and I would rather approach the world with openness and curiosity than default to fear. Years later, I still sometimes have flashbacks to that dinner, layered onto other experiences of violence unfortunately all too common, and I never gave an unknown man a lift on my motorbike again. I had lots of people over to my flat to eat though—men and women, alone and in groups—and I still love to interact with strangers and learn from them.

Looked at from a little ways away, my fieldwork was not particularly dangerous—it was something that I had to do, and I did it as well as I could, approaching it with quirks of personality, my ethics grounded in my idiosyncratic beliefs about right and wrong that thankfully accorded with the law. I think of Angola with only tremendous gratitude and appreciation. My friends tell me I still have a high tolerance for risk, but we are older now, so all of us are making different choices, including me. When my mom suggested my guardian angels were probably getting tired I laughed, but on my last trip to Angola, hurtling un-helmeted on the back of a motorbike taxi up a hill with an overloaded lorry in front of me, I started to think that perhaps she had a point. When my partner very gently asked if I'd consider staying in a hotel instead of on the floor of a friend, I suddenly realized that's now a possibility—financially as well psychologically. It's a privilege I have been fortunate to grow into.

The point is that life accretes for all of us, and we have to do our best to make good choices with the limited information we have, in line with where we are in our own development, or on our own path. "Do no harm" is an excellent point of departure, but when it comes to ethics, it is the beginning and not the destination, which, like life, is almost certainly much more complicated than it first appears, and even more so if it's been posted on Instagram.

> **Why does it matter? (sight)** **Which Africa rising?**
>
> Around 2013 there was a huge buzz, driven by *The Economist*, about "Africa rising," but what does that even mean (Bunce, Franks, and Paterson 2017; Company 2010)? Africa is not a country, and this book is not about the continent. It is about one nation-state in Africa, Angola, whose history has made visible patterns that mirror much of the world. Looking closely at one place makes it possible to interrogate broad claims, and test them, to see if they work. Reality is much more nuanced than media headlines about rising and falling, and the networks that link those who thrive and those who struggle often exist far beyond geopolitical boundaries.
>
> Rather than imagining a continent emerging out of the sea, or a beautiful (but mythic) Wakanda (Coogler 2018), it is helpful to look at individual people in one real place, and the socially mediated systems that guide their actions. Paying attention to what they are doing and, importantly, who they are helping (and who is helping them) gives insight into how trade, political policy, religious doctrine, aid, and more manifest in the reality of human worlds. Such knowledge is currently in fashion under the heading of "big data," which looks at patterns from people and raises very interesting questions about ethics, individuality, and generalizability that seem to make studying the micro, how things *actually* unfold at the level of ordinary people, even more important. It is worth remembering that when it comes to a continent of, in 2018, some 1.256 *billion* people in fifty-four different countries, accuracy is very important, and stereotypes will simply not suffice.

Photo Essays

Photo Essay 5: Art

Artwork opens to music at the former Ethnography Museum in Benguela, in May 2018.

Artist Bella White stands with her exhibition in May 2018, Benguela.

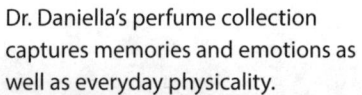

Dr. Daniella's perfume collection captures memories and emotions as well as everyday physicality.

At Cinema Flamingo, tiled origami birds welcome visitors through the entrance. At the entry point to the city of Lobito itself, a mural has been painted on the wall by a local NGO.

In an artisan's studio in Lobito, the figure of a man emerges from the wood in May 2018.

Photo Essay 6: Architecture

Cinema Flamingo in Lobito.

A church under construction in Lobito, May 2018. Women chat in a newly built apartment block in Benguela, July 2014.

Men replace streetlamps in an up-market suburb of Lobito in 2014, and a school in a much poorer area is under construction whilst already in use.

A brand-new house in Compão, Lobito, makes a statement against a colonial-era block of flats in 2014.

~ Curiosity ~

CONCLUSION

Attending the Beautiful in the Light of What We Know

[On how to draw maps:] It all depends on what you want the map to show and what use you have for it. People talk about things being lost in translation, but things can, of course, be gained in translation too. A cartographer might add things, such as borders, which may or may not have some physical manifestation on the earth. But even if there is a fence to mark the border in the world, that fence is not the same as the political border represented on the map: A break in the fence doesn't vitiate the political border. After all, the red line on the map doesn't represent the fence and, in fact, the fence itself only represents the border.

But the point of all this is that all these representations or translations begin from needs. Consequently, the loss of information and understanding that every act of representation involved is the effect of an act of destruction that serves a need. We might appear to have taken a step forward, but in fact we took one step back and two steps forward. Every time we want to understand anything, we have to simplify and reduce and, importantly, give up the prospect of understanding at all, in order to clear the way to understanding something at all. This, I think, is true of all human inquiry. (Rahman 2014, 25)

British lawyer and writer Zia Haider Rahman's powerful text *In the Light of What We Know* explores the limits and the possibilities inherent in the act of seeking to understand another person, and another version of the world. For Rahman, the choices made in the acts of cartography, translation, and even writing itself require a willingness to cede any chance of comprehension of the whole, in order to make sense of detail in a meaningful way. His writing rings true for the practice of ethnography, which entails two impossible acts: trying to understand, and then trying to explain.

In this book, I have done my best to share one version of truth about Angola's middle class, and about how the lives of those who belong, however tentatively, to this group are shaped by transnational migration across the southern Atlantic, and also beyond. There is much that I have left out, and potentially much more that I have only partially understood, but it is my hope that colleagues, students, and friends will pick up where this text leaves off, and add to it. There are far more Angolan scholars and writers thinking about these questions than the book does justice to, though interested readers could begin with the work of Ondjaki, Rafael Marques, Angela Mingas, António Tomás, Cláudio Tomás, and Suzana Sousa, amongst others. They know the country and the nuances of its history and contemporary positioning far better than I. Many of them are also members of the emerging Angolan middle class.

Though I have sought to include and draw upon their work, I am very aware of the challenges many Angolan thinkers face. This is due not only to the limits in the infrastructures of knowledge that exist there and the difficulties of publication for a global audience, but also to the realities of living in an environment where one full-time job is not enough to sustain a family, and one's energy is squeezed from every angle. Being middle class in Angola today still means significant struggle to make ends meet, though those ends are centred not on survival but on quality of life. Focusing on a changing quality of life, and understanding its textures, flavors, and links to other places, has been one of my objectives here. This work is therefore offered as a contribution to the conversation, but is certainly neither its beginning nor its end.

It is important here to highlight what is in a sense a political as well as scholarly choice. I have focused on the middle class, and on what is working, in a country where for the majority it is a struggle to simply survive. This is a choice that could contribute to how Angola is known by the outside world, and potentially detract from the very real challenges that many individuals face. I have made that choice carefully, but it is important to be aware of the risk. In *Beautiful Ugly: African and Diaspora Aesthetics*, South African literary scholar Sarah Nuttall observes that so often "beauty is to be found at the limits of the ugly, since it is the ugly which has so often been the sign under which the African has been read" (Nuttall 2006, 17). In this sense, beauty has become dependent on ugliness. What if it were the reverse, and Africa was assumed to be beautiful, not in the fetishistic sense of Western imaginations of sunrises, savannah, and acacia trees (Elliot Ross 2014) but for the everyday works of everyday people, for their world-making, their relationships, their care? This is what this book has tried to highlight, and to open as an imaginative space for readers, building on the work of many, including Michael Taussig, who writes:

> A history of beauty? What would that be? Is it restricted to a human being or should it—must it—include the world around— the streets, the buildings, the cultivated land, and the rivers? and if it—this idea of a history of beauty—spreads like this, from the body to the body of the world, if it is capacious, with these elements and still others feeding into one another, then what of ugliness, and what of the moral quality of ugliness? When I look at the fetid rivers and the crippled land, for instance, how can I split the moral from the aesthetic? (2012, 86)

In the novel *We Need New Names*, Zimbabwean author NoViolet Bulawayo (2013) reflects on the names given to children in early twenty-first-century Zimbabwe, which echo the sociopolitical challenges that country has faced in recent years. The previous chapter in particular, on sight, explored how renaming and rebranding serve to shift both national and international imaginations of a country at peace, and to some extent a book such as this one is an act of naming. Acts of naming can be profoundly uncomfortable, however: remember that Nelson Mandela only became "Nelson" because his primary school teachers could not pronounce his actual name, which was Rolihlala (Mandela 1994). Additionally, as Rahman observes in the quote above, one step forward may actually be two steps forward but one big step back.

In this book, I have engaged the five "kindergarten" senses of Western approaches to knowing the world, as well as proprioception (loosely, movement), to try to deepen readers' ability to place themselves in the position of the people these pages describe. This brings me to the final "sense," which I want to attend to here regardless of whether it appears in primary school textbooks in Euro-America. That is the sense of curiosity—of the ability to be interested in people, processes, systems, and things one does not know. If one can do that, it seems much less likely that one will condone choices that affect others in negative ways, be they political, climatological, economic, or otherwise.

I have tried to understand and to share how people thrive despite circumstances that to outsiders may appear profoundly challenging. I do not wish to suggest that these circumstances are *not* challenging, because they are, and the vast majority of Angolans are well aware that they have been served a historically dense raw deal. Nonetheless, happiness, aspiration, accomplishment, love, and an ethical life well lived (however that is understood [Kleinman 2006]) are just as possible and just as challenging to achieve in Angola as anywhere else in the world, and there, as in other places, energy and resources are expended to achieve them.

I have argued for an understanding of the Angolan economy based in emergent, contested *capitalismo selvagem* that can be entered through movement, hearing, tasting, smelling, feeling, and seeing. It is an economy in which the lines between legal and illegal, formal and informal, free trade and protectionism are largely blurred. In order to succeed, individuals must master the art of reading a given social interaction and utilizing it for the benefit of themselves and their loved ones—the need to negotiate power structures and use one's influence is universal, but the form it takes in Angola is particular to that country. Angolans must know when to place their MPLA membership card on the top of a pile of documents to ensure that it gets processed quickly, and they must know with whom they can voice the inevitable frustrations of everyday life. They must be critical enough of the government that if they spot a gap in service delivery, they can step in with private enterprise to meet it, but they must ensure that criticality is never read as criticism, for that could result in serious sanctions. They must know when to shop in kwanzas and when to use dollars (US), rands (South Africa), or renminbi (China). They must cultivate relationships at clinics, supermarkets, government bureaus, and schools to ensure their children are taken care of, and they must offer favors to others to be able to call them in for themselves when needed.

In a recent series of popular cartoons, the artist "Emma" (2018) has drawn (literally) attention to what is understood in feminist discourse to be the "mental load." By that she means the work of planning, preparing, managing, organizing, and actioning everyday life in the household—something that women, according to studies, do much, much more than men (Folbre 2015). It can be argued that everyday life in Angola is much the same as everyday life elsewhere for those who are part of the "global middle class," but that sustaining it entails carrying a much heavier "mental load" in order to achieve the same results as those whose nation-states have, in the words of Angola's former education minister, "had a longer time to practice" (Interview #55). For example, where infrastructure is weak, electricity unreliable, and the schooling system poor, ensuring the kids get a good education means taking care of their transport, paying school fees, and having to choose between paying for a generator to power the washing machine, paying someone else to do the washing, or spending the time it takes to wash clothes by hand, just to ensure that children are properly dressed going out the door. If food for a child's packed lunch has to be procured not at one supermarket but at several (and the outdoor market as well), and ballet shoes have to be imported from Europe, not bought at the store down the street or on Amazon, the simple task of "sending the children to school" takes on many added dimensions. It is not impossible, but it can be very tiring.

In the transition from socialism to capitalism, albeit a wild version of it (and where, honestly, is capitalism in some way not wild, based on the unfolding of particular histories?), there is tremendous opportunity. As the economy (slowly) diversifies and basic infrastructure is—however problematically—put in place by the government, everyday Angolans are in the process of building and rebuilding their worlds. They use cement to build this world, a substance Lesley Green understands to be *"the* artifact of modernity" (2015, 10, emphasis in original; see also P. Harvey 2015), and they also use glass, wood, and paint in bright colors. One of the things that gave me great joy during fieldwork was to ride my motorbike through the outlying suburbs of Lobito and Benguela early in the morning on the weekends, and take time to observe houses under construction, trees being carefully nurtured, children participating in sports, and the everyday practices of chores, nurturing, worship, and work that have transformed the country and continue to transform it still.

Capitalismo selvagem in Uncertain Times

American anthropologist Anna Tsing (2015) concludes an ethnography entitled *The Mushroom at the End of the World: On the Possibility of Life in Capitalist Ruin* with the following paragraph:

> Without stories of progress, the world has become a terrifying place. The ruin glares at us with the horror of its abandonment. It's not easy to know how to make a life, much less avert planetary destruction. Luckily there is still company, human and not human. We can still explore the overgrown verges of our blasted landscapes—the edges of capitalist discipline, scalability, and abandoned resources plantations. We can still catch the scent of the latent commons—and the elusive autumn aroma. (282)

Seasonal references aside, what Tsing offers in this text is a way of making sense of other globalized processes—in this case Matsutake mushrooms from forest to dinner plate—that do not fit neatly into the buckets of late capitalism (late capitalism is generally accepted to be capitalism since roughly 1945). Angola's landscape has been affected by its civil war, but it is not "blasted" in the way that Tsing describes, despite arguably existing precisely at "the edges of capitalist discipline." It is an interesting country in part because it is one of the few places in the world that has arguably never industrialized in the way most Western readers might understand the term.

There are relatively few factories in Angola, and those that exist flourish less on "ownership of the means of production" than on the trafficking of influence: the strength of political connections that grease the machinery in both the literal and metaphorical senses. That said, profound changes of governance, ideology, and world market insertion have shaped Angola's lived history, which I have argued should be understood within the context of the former Portuguese empire—even more so since João Lourenço assumed presidential office in 2017, dramatically changing the political landscape of Angola after the majority of this research was undertaken.

The Atlantic Ocean has been a primary space for Angola's coming-into-being in a particular way, as a conduit for certain kinds of interactions, and as the locale of one part of a partial history and partial truth. But it is important to bear in mind that oceans themselves are not restricted entities. Instead they blend and fuse with other bodies of water in the processes of transformation: the Atlantic becomes the Indian, the Pacific, the Caribbean, the southern, the Arctic. Rather than using the "chronotope of the ship" described by Paul Gilroy (1993, 225), I suggest the undersea Internet cable deserves attention. People still move, but knowledge moves faster, and this has an impact on the development of new (but nonetheless historically constituted) knowledge practices.

Angola's high-speed Internet comes largely from the South Atlantic Cable System, a 6,100-kilometer cable system stretching from Luanda to Fortaleza, Brazil, that is part of an increasingly important world infrastructure. The country has also been an active participant in Free Basics, Facebook's attempt at "connecting" the two-thirds of the global population who are currently largely offline due to the costs of data (Koebler 2016), a program that has been criticized for the potential within it for Internet censorship, amongst other major concerns (Nyabola 2016). Imperfect as it may be, the Internet cable does give a certain intellectual freedom in Angola, and for those able to access it it changes the limitations placed on what it is possible to know. Throughout this book, the ability to get online (or not) has been an important subtext, and there can be no doubt that digital fluency is now one of the major skills expected of those who aspire to membership of the "global middle class"—however openly or narrowly one might choose to define it (Heiman, Freeman, and Liechty 2011; Lópes and Weinstein 2012).

The Internet—through social media, news, and other content—is now fundamental to how we "see" one another. It is also a critical tool through which Angolans (and others) are affirmed through self-recognition and national branding. As Felicité, a medical doctor in her late thirties completing specialization training in Rio de Janeiro, put it, "The psyche is everything in Angola. People need to feel beautiful, and happy. In Angola being beautiful is important, it is about self-esteem"

(Interview #104). Self-esteem comes through sight, absolutely, but the visual is layered onto the olfactory, the gustatory, the auditory, and the tactile, and is located in space. With increasing self-esteem at a very local level, and an increasingly connected and savvy population who are accustomed to systems that often do not work, Angola has become a place of incredible possibility and opportunity. This book has shown some of those opportunities seized and bearing fruit; others remain works in constant process.

In the Introduction to this book, I set out what is at stake in this text. Reading about Angola provides an example of a disciplined form of curiosity, that increases awareness of and knowledge about people who in some way feel far away. That "far-ness" might be geographical (e.g., Hawaii to Mauritius) or it might be experiential (i.e., based on social class, religion, political or professional affiliation). Yet curiosity provides an entry point that is, hopefully, sincere and open to further exploration.

In using different formats and ways of writing, I hope to connect more deeply with a younger readership (and a changing older readership too ☺) who are increasingly engaged with multiple kinds of media at the same time, who might have been exposed to the Internet from birth. This generation, far from being what William Deresiewicz (2015) so patronizingly named "excellent sheep," are in my experience capable of imagination, empathy, and systems thinking. My hope is that this book enables us all to expand those capabilities to include everyday people in Angola, and that Angolans who read it themselves can engage not as subjects but as co-contributors in transnational dialogue. Many are already writing – it's important that they be read.

The Government Has Gone on Holiday, but Maybe João Lourenço Will Bring It Back

Angola has changed very much already since my original fieldwork was undertaken. In May 2018 when I visited the country again, I found that most people were far worse off than they had been before. In Lobito there had been not only a recession but also the floods that Lino speaks about in the narrative on taste in Chapter 3. Prices for basic commodities had soared as a result of the crash in global oil prices in December 2014, which sparked a major cut in the government's spending ability and in the amount of money entering the country more broadly. At the same time, forex (foreign currency) had been limited by the government so, paradoxically, for anyone earning in dollars the country had become much, much cheaper. The kwanza, however, was almost worthless, and I was told frequently of a spate of people "redoing their bathrooms" with their savings because that was the only way they could see to put the money to some use (Fieldnotes 180527).

Those who had been beginning a journey of upward mobility had largely slipped back into precarity, and those who had already been precarious were suffering more deeply. "There are illnesses now that didn't exist before, and the pharmacies do not have medicine," explained Dono Oniko, continuing, "the government has gone on holiday for now, though it's possible that João Lourenço [the new president] will bring it back" (Fieldnotes 180520).

Most Angolans I have met, both during fieldwork and outside it, express tremendous loyalty to their country of birth. In an interview conducted in Curitiba, Brazil, in October 2014, a young man, here called Rafael, explained to me why he wanted to go back to Benguela as soon as he had finished his degree. He then recited a poem, committed to memory, by Angolan founding father Augostinho Neto entitled *Havemos Voltar* (We must return; see Wolfers 1979), following which he explained:

> Even though we have suffered, Angola is a great country. Angola is the country of the future; it is beautiful, it has a *povo unido*, a united people. When you go to Angola, you always have family, you won't spend anything on food because we know how to take care of people, of one another. We live what the Bible says: we care for strangers.
>
> Angola gives a sense of possibility [*sensação de puder*] that is huge, it is powerful, it has potential. Despite the dust, the rain, the floodwater, and the lack of basic sanitation, it has that power. We love Angola with a terrible passion! With the whole heart! Today I woke up with desire to go home, I had such longing [*saudade*].... I see what happens in Angola, because you know it's the leaders who wreck it [*estragar*], but we Angolans are happy despite the problems. We are not a sad people, there in Angola you won't see sadness on people's faces.... We will improve it. All of this is because of God. We trust that Angola will one day change. (Interview #91)

As of 2019, Rafael has not returned despite his stated desire, because the crisis of 2014 made it impossible to do so with any hope of finding work, and he is increasingly settled in Brazil, where he has now lived the better part of a decade. For all its recent troubles, the Brazilian economy is far more resilient and diverse than the Angolan one, and he is responsible for sending money home each month to support his mother and siblings—one of whom may enter university in Brazil as well. He continues to work as an evangelist with the faith-based organization who sponsored his studies in theology, but he also places a great deal of faith in the Angolan constitution, and his love for his home remains undiminished. He called that love a "terrible passion" because he was aware that his patriotism could at times be blinding and would prevent him from being fully content anywhere else in the world. Yet it is a full love, and utterly sincere, and to him that is very important.

Angola has undergone and is continuing to undergo constant change, and millions of people are contributing in profound ways to that process. This book has shared only a few examples of those contributions, but there are many, many more that merit attention. "Happy," mentioned here by both Felicité and Rafael, is far too simple a word to describe the broad emotional state of an entire nation, but it is worth keeping in mind that a psychological bent toward optimism is generally helpful in living a fulfilling life. National or even global politics have less direct impact on individual well-being than how one chooses to react to them, and happy or unhappy, Angolans—like people everywhere—are doing their best, one day at a time, and in the process quietly rebuilding the country.

José Eduardo dos Santos, president of Angola from 1979 to 2017, was famously referred to as the "architect of peace" (Schubert 2015). Whatever one thinks of his master plans, architects are usually judged by what is actually built and how the buildings are ultimately used. Construction, in Angola, is being carried out by millions of everyday people who of course can only do this if they have money to buy bricks and are healthy enough to lift them. Beyond their homes, everyday life is entangled with material things (Hodder 2011)—both local and global—and the sensory experiences of working with, aspiring to, and enjoying the fruits of labor are how the new realities are known.

Practicing Peace ... Again

In another war, one that ran parallel to the conflict in Angola, Vedran Smailović played his cello in destroyed buildings during the siege of Sarajevo, including in the National Library, pictured in Image C.1. His playing captured the global imagination and inspired a best-selling book by Canadian author Stephen Galloway (which was written without consultation or permission and left Smailović so angry that he told newspapers he wanted to sue [Galloway 2009; Sharrock 2008]). In this instance what seems to have captured the public imagination was arguably the humanizing of a conflict through the actions of a person still seemingly committed to beauty despite the destruction around him. Smailović used the tools he had available to him—in this case a cello—to survive the war, and in some way to help others survive it too.

In writing about the beautiful in Angola, one takes a great risk of occluding attention to the suffering that occurs there. No amount of perfume will ever bring fundamental human rights, nor will trees being planted expunge the fear that permeates many people when they hear elites being criticized out loud. The practices of peace are powerful, but they must nonetheless be seen, as in Image C.1, as a beauty that still remains surrounded by certain kinds of social, economic, and political ruin created not only by national events but by international action and inaction.

What I would like to reiterate here is that *capitalismo selvagem* is not unique to Angola. It instead makes visible dynamics that in other places are harder to see. For any war zone to exist, there must be factories producing bombs, and those factories and the political systems that support them are often surrounded by (metaphorical) white picket fences and the illusions of peace. The conflict in Angola was perhaps one of the last "global wars" that actually included soldiers shooting at one another face to face—after 9/11, conflict in the world has radically shifted (Gusterson 2016; Harari 2018). Lobito, however, where most of this book is based, saw almost no active warfare, but all of the picket fences were breached—not literally, but in terms of how the people who lived around them changed their actions and way of life due to wider dynamics at play in the country, and in the world. They "trafficked influence" in order to secure safety and favor, eating

Image C.1. Vedran Smailović playing in the partially destroyed National Library in Sarajevo in 1992. (Wikipedia, image by Mikhail Evstafiev, © CC BY-SA 3.0.)

cake at Aurea's or creating networks through education in Brazil or Cuba that would foster safety and opportunity for their children.

The practice of peace is enormously challenging. In such times, understanding that practice—which is fundamentally one that begins with self-knowledge, and the awareness of prejudices and the limits of empathy—is absolutely essential if we hope to live on a planet where dignity and human rights may be experienced by all people around the world. Now more than ever, the importance of genuine curiosity, based not on stereotype but on a recognition of a certain fundamental commonality of dream, of aspiration, is ever more critical, with a receptivity to the many unfolding layers of a personhood and experience, as this book has offered for and of the emerging Angolan middle class.

We all need water to survive, but it does not seem unreasonable that many people ask to also drink wine. One does not allow a government to act against people whom one knows one could not only grieve (Butler 2016) but also love: people with whom one experiences—however distantly—some sense of communion. My hope is that through this ethnography of that which is working in contemporary Angola (or at least was working, for a while), readers might find in themselves a desire to know more, and to ask people to explain how it is that their lives are lived, heard, witnessed, and experienced—with regard to the good, the bad, the ugly, and also the beautiful.

> **Why does it matter?**   *Compassion in a burning world*
>
> Ultimately, this is a book that aims to increase compassion—feeling *with*, caring about, engaging at a deep level, and most of all, recognizing that although people are very different, they are also very much the same.
>
> In today's geopolitical context, there is a great deal of emphasis on difference at a global level. Right-wing ideology has become all but mainstream, and increasingly both politicians and individuals cater to the needs of the "tribe" rather than those of broader inclusive collectives. Human rights, which emerged as sacrosanct in the aftermath of the Second World War, are now up for question. Respectful, nuanced dialogue that encompasses true diversity in perspective has become increasingly rare.
>
> This is not accidental. The climate crisis is making large regions uninhabitable or frighteningly insecure, and it is only going to get worse. In many parts of the planet, the water wars have already begun—never mind wine. Unless radical change takes place at every level, millions—realistically, billions—will have their right to life retracted.
>
> The history of humanity makes clear that the easiest way to get groups of people to kill others (or as bystanders, just let them die) is to convince them that those others are not fully "human." In this respect, the dehumanizing of Africans that justified the Atlantic slave trade is no different from the dehumanizing of equatorial peoples across the world that is essential to justifying inaction on climate change today.
>
> Angola is already experiencing the impact of the climate crisis. Droughts and floods are the latest manifestation of devastation in a country that, for the past five centuries, has paid the price for the excesses of others—through slavery, through colonization, through civil war, and now in a literally burning world.
>
> Yet systems can be changed. This is the task of our generation.

Notes

Introduction

1 South African racial classification was an enormously complex process, and there is a vast literature on it (e.g., F. Ross 2010; Mandela 1994). The broad categories used were "White," "Indian" (South Asian), "Black," and "Coloured." "Coloured" included mixed-race individuals and descendants of South Africa's first peoples, the Khoi-San, and slaves from Indonesia.
2 Jonas Savimbi was the leader of the political party UNITA, the União Nacional de Independência Total de Angola—the National Union for the Total Independence of Angola.
3 I use the term "global north" to refer to countries where the majority of citizens experience a high material quality of life, and where human rights are broadly protected. Other terms I could have chosen include "OECD countries," which refers specifically to member states of the Organisation for European Economic Co-operation, or "developed countries," which is extremely vague and based on a Darwinian-inspired idea of poor countries as automatically aspiring to evolve toward an ideal that is overwhelmingly white and capitalist. The phrase "global north" is contradictory and still problematic in certain ways, but I appreciate that if one accepts "north" as equating to economic wealth and stability, within "global north" there is space for the tremendous wealth one also finds *within* countries that in statistical terms are very poor. For example, pockets of South Africa look much like Switzerland (but with sunshine!), and in Angola's capital, the wealthiest think nothing of spending US$200 on a single meal.

4 I use the phrase "capitalist ways of knowing" to describe systems of thinking about, analyzing, and working that have emerged through the spread of global capitalism. These systems originated in Western Europe but have now become global, though in some regions they "hop" (Ferguson 2006) more than in others.

5 In the last few decades, however, the limitations of that framework have been much more clearly recognized. Authors such as Kathryn Linn Geurts have done tremendous work to show that sensory frameworks are culturally specific, usually mastered as children, and often encode moral frameworks by which judgment of one another is made. Thus, clothing might be considered an enormously important reference for judgments of morality in the global north (think of the young black men shot in the United States for wearing hoodies), but in Angola, as this book later explores, how one smelled was deemed far more important than what one wore. In Geurts's (2002) former home in southeastern Ghana, how one walked could also be an indication of the kind of person one was, something that is perhaps more commonly recognized by those familiar with the basics of French sociology using Pierre Bourdieu's (1977) language of *habitus* but that Geurts's work shows is infinitely more complicated.

6 For these calculations I used the tool www.geodatasource.com, which tracks direct distance over the surface of the earth, for international travel and Google Maps for national, road-based travel.

7 In 2014, a liter of processed water was 140 Angolan kwanzas and a liter of gasoline was 130. At that time the exchange rate was 100:1 with the US dollar, meaning US$1.40 and US$1.30 respectively. The exchange rate had significantly changed during the time I was writing this book, however (Fieldnotes and Interview #39). It is also important to note that Angola is a significant player in the global petro-economy (Cardoso 2015; Ovádia 2012, 2013; Reed 2009; Wiig and Kolstad 2011); what will happen with the changing dynamics of oil in the twenty-first century remains to be seen, but there is no doubt the country will feel the effects of any changes.

8 When writing this book, I was unaware of the connotations of the term in French. My friend and colleague, economist Myriam Blin, pointed out that in the Francophone canon *capitalism sauvage* has a very different meaning indeed. There, the term is often used to refer to deregulated capitalism found largely in Anglo-Saxon (UK/US) economic structures, where the welfare state is deprioritized in the interests of the market. This is a fascinating and complex discussion, but it is beyond the scope of this particular book.

9 At the end of my fieldwork, in December 2014, the oil price crashed and Angola entered a recession from which it has yet to recover that dramatically altered the lives of many of my interlocutors. This is addressed in the Conclusion of the book.

10 For those interested in more theoretical and explicitly scholarly debates pertaining to the region, these are essential texts and are included in the Indicative Bibliography on Angola included at the end of this book, which I hope many readers will explore.

1. The Smell of Success

1 *Funge* is the staple carbohydrate of Angola. It is prepared from a dense white powder made of ground cassava that can be cooked in a variety of textures depending on what meal one is preparing.
2 *Kony 2012* was the title of a controversial documentary film released by the US NGO Invisible Children Inc. in March 2012 that quickly went viral. Its intent was to curtail the actions of the Lords' Resistance Army in Uganda, lead by Joseph Kony, largely through his capture. The film galvanized groups of young people across the United States toward civic action, but that proved to be short lived. The presence of the T-shirt in Angola in 2014 is testimony to how quickly the craze both rose and fell.
3 Increasingly attention has been given to smell as an important aspect of research in anthropology. Some of the scholarship is listed in the Indicative Bibliography, but authors include Antonius Robben, Paul Stoller, Cheryl Olkes, Michael Herzfeld, Constance Classen, Anna Tsing, and Lalaie Ameeriar, among many others.
4 Independent schools could choose whether they followed the Angolan national curriculum or the curricula of other learning systems, which were more common in that sector. For example, children at the Portuguese school followed a curriculum set in Lisbon, the French school prepared its students for the International Baccalaureate examinations, and at "the American school" children learned in English and studied United States history. The deliberate choice of the Angolan curriculum was a popular reason for many parents to choose the school.
5 I use the term "poor" here as a commonsense contrast with "rich." In the first draft of this book, I used the phrase "economically marginal"—but my students hated it. They asked what I was trying to achieve by hiding the realities of life behind complex academic language when most people know that to be poor is to have very few choices, and to be rich is to have many choices, and the rest is largely contingent on context. I think they were right to call me out in this way, and so I am using their definition here. Rosemary de Moor, Ahmed Konneh, Liz Mwangi, and Yassmine Eladib—your points are well taken.
6 Race is a culturally constructed category anywhere in the world, and in both Angola and Brazil, race has very particular histories defined to a large extent by the particular forms of Portuguese colonialism. The Portuguese were far more open about "racial mixture" than other European powers (almost always meaning European men sleeping with African or

South American women) and in Angola the descendants of those unions came to form an elite class known as the "creoles" who still dominate certain spheres of Angolan society today. In Brazil, by contrast, the vast majority of people identify as in some way mixed-race and there is a popular national dialogue of racial inclusion and democracy. Over the past two decades, however, that dialogue has been largely interrupted. Irrefutable evidence has shown that police discriminate profoundly based on preconceptions of racial identity in which the darker one's pigmentation is, the more likely one is to be shot. Privilege is largely correlated with light skin. Wealth can also be anticipated to some extent by skin color, thereby revealing both structural and personal-level violence. For Flávia, acknowledging her racial identity indicated an awareness of the prejudice that she would face in the working world. She was not alone: many Angolans explained that in order to *not* be read as working-class Brazilians, they needed to dress and comport themselves in a way that showed an exaggerated belonging to upper and middle class society—much as Claude M. Steele has described in his book *Whistling Vivaldi: How Stereotypes Affect Us and What We Can Do* (2011). Literature that elaborates these themes pertaining to race in Brazil and Angola can be found in the Indicative Bibliography. Of particular relevance is the work of Roberto Kant de Lima (police violence in Brazil), Edward E. Telles and Peter Fry (race in Brazil), and Jacopo Corrado and Ricardo Soares de Oliveira (race in Angola).

2. Touch and the Tactile

1 Scouts in Angola, as elsewhere, are divided into numbered "troops," each associated with a particular district and in Angola also a religious institution. For the sake of anonymity, I have chosen a number at random in this case.
2 Throughout the book I use pseudonyms unless I am referring to a public figure. Hipólito was not a public figure before he died, but in his death became one, so I use his real name.

4. Music, *Fofoca*, and the News

1 Here I use the Commonwealth English word for the five lines that form the basis of Western musical notation. In the United States it is referred to as the staff; the Portuguese word is *partiture*.
2 Stanford University is notoriously difficult to get into, and in 2018 accepted less than 5 per cent of undergraduate applications for just over two thousand places. Anecdotal evidence suggested that the figure for UKB was roughly equivalent, but I could not verify the data. To my knowledge no study has been done on the number of students in less

wealthy countries, particularly in sub-Saharan Africa, who apply to undergraduate institutions there and are turned away for lack of capacity.
3 In Angola vocational training such as teaching and nursing happened in the last period of high school, when students could opt to attend specialized colleges. Tertiary education here means specifically university.

5. National Rebranding

1 Some readers will be familiar with Paul Gilroy's (1993) notion of the "black Atlantic," in which he describes the cultural influences of slaves taken from Africa to the United Kingdom and the United States. Gilroy's Atlantic is all above the equator, though, and scholars such as Miguel Vale de Almeida have written a great deal about the rest of the Atlantic Ocean, which flows in the south and connects Africa to the coast of Brazil. De Almeida calls it the "brown" Atlantic to distinguish it from Gilroy's claims, but also because across the southern Atlantic there was much more racial mixing. This has been a subject of many books, so those interested should see the Indicative Bibliography for further material on it.
2 In anthropology and other related disciplines, the term "the other" has typically been used to refer to entire continents of people, with the assumption being that the "self" is white, straight, and Western. Writers such as Edward Said (1978) and Roberto Kant de Lima (2011) have thoroughly critiqued this assumption, and anthropology now—thankfully—largely consists of scholars who do not meet that definition. I do, though, and the section on ethics that follows reflects on that fact.
3 This line is not my own. James Ferguson, my PhD supervisor, came out with it during one of our meetings in 2016. It was an example of his quick, insightful, and sometimes hilarious guidance. It was a privilege to work with him.
4 This is a wordplay on some famous debates of the 1980s called the "writing culture" debates, where anthropologists started really questioning whether they were doing the work alone, or whether credit should be given to their interlocutors (Clifford and Marcus 1986).
5 A lot of important work has been done on the use of photography in this way. See, for example, Strassler 2011, Vokes 2012, and Hjorth and Pink 2014.
6 The blog *Humans of New York* began in September 2010. Brandon Stanton's (2015) book gathers together his writing on the site.
7 "Armchair anthropology" is the term used to describe scholars' interpretations of the world based on reports and travelogues written in the eighteenth and nineteenth centuries.

Indicative Bibliography

What follows is by no means a comprehensive list, but is included here simply as a starting point for those who would like to do some further reading (or who, perhaps, have been assigned writing projects on the book and aren't sure where to begin). Literature on Angola is constantly changing, and by the time this book is published, the lists below will certainly be out of date. I recommend exploring the "recent publications" of H-Luso-Africa at https://networks.h-net.org/h-luso-africa. The works below are some of those *I* have found most helpful (and, importantly, which have been accessible to me, particularly since leaving the United States). I have chosen only twelve works within each theme, which by necessity means leaving out abundant important material, much of which is cited in the References. Several works listed here speak to more than one category or list as well. My hope is readers will take this list simply as a starting point, and will find much more themselves.

"African" Middle Classes

Cheeseman, N. 2015. "'No Bourgeoisie, No Democracy?' The Political Attitudes of the Kenyan Middle Class." *Journal of International Development* 27(5): 647–64. https://doi.org/10.1002/jid.3057.

Clarence-Smith, W.G. 1980. "Class Structure and Class Struggles in Angola in the 1970s." *Journal of Southern African Studies* 7(1): 109–26. https://doi.org/10.1080/03057078008708022.

Daouda, F.B., P.T.M. Ingenbleek, and H.C.M. van Trijp. 2018. "Living the African Dream: How Subsistence Entrepreneurs Move to Middle-Class Consumer Markets in Developing and Emerging Countries." *Journal of

Public Policy and Marketing 38(1): 42–60. https://doi.org/10.1177/0743915618818575.

Enaudeau, J. 2013. "In Search of the 'African Middle Class.'" *Africa Is a Country*. 5 January. https://africasacountry.com/2013/05/in-search-of-the-african-middle-class/.

Freemantle, S. 2014. "Understanding Africa's Middle Class: Insight & Strategy." *Borgen Magazine*. 18 April. https://www.borgenmagazine.com/understanding-africas-growing-middle-class/.

Heiman, R., C. Freeman, and M. Liechty. 2012. *The Global Middle Classes: Theorizing through Ethnography*. Santa Fe: School for Advanced Research Press.

Lópes, A.R., and B. Weinstein, eds. 2012. *The Making of the Middle Class: Towards a Transnational History*. Durham: Duke University Press.

Melber, H. 2016. "Africa's Rising Middle Class: Time to Sort Out Fact from Fiction." *Pambazuka News*. http://www.pambazuka.org/economics/africa's-rising-middle-class-time-sort-out-fact-fiction.

Mercer, C. 2014. "Middle Class Construction: Domestic Architecture, Aesthetics and Anxieties in Tanzania." *Journal of Modern African Studies* 52(2): 227–50. https://doi.org/10.1017/s0022278x14000068.

Posel, D., and I. Van Wyk. 2019. *Conspicious Consumption in Africa*. Johannesburg: Witwaterstrand University Press.

Rodas, P.A.C., V. Molini, and G. Oseni. 2019. "No Condition Is Permanent: Middle Class in Nigeria in the Last Decade." *Journal of Development Studies* 55(2): 294–310. https://doi.org/10.1080/00220388.2017.1366453.

Southall, R. 2016. *The New Black Middle Class in South Africa*. Johannesburg: Jacana.

The History of Angola

Arenas, F. 2011. *Lusophone Africa: Beyond Independence*. Minneapolis: University of Minnesota Press.

Ball, J. 2015. *Angola's Colossal Lie: Forced Labor on a Sugar Plantation, 1913–1977*. Leiden: Brill.

Birmingham, D. 2015. *A Short History of Angola*. Oxford: Oxford University Press.

Candido, M.P. 2015. *An African Slaving Port and the Atlantic World: Benguela and Its Hinterland*. Cambridge: Cambridge University Press.

Cleveland, T. 2015. *Diamonds in the Rough: Corporate Paternalism and African Professionalism on the Mines of Colonial Angola, 1917–1975*. Athens: Ohio University Press.

De Grassi, A. 2015. "Rethinking the 1961 Baixa de Kassanje Revolt: Towards a Relational Geo-history of Angola." *Mulemba: Revista Angolana de Ciências Sociais* 5(10): 53–133. https://doi.org/10.4000/mulemba.1807.

Ferreira, R. 2012. *Cross-Cultural Exchange in the Atlantic World: Angola and Brazil during the Era of the Slave Trade*. Cambridge: Cambridge University Press.

Fromont, C. 2018. "Common Threads: Cloth, Colour, and the Slave Trade in Early Modern Kongo and Angola." *Art History* 41(5): 838–67. https://doi.org/10.1111/1467-8365.12400.

Heywood, L.M. 2017. *Njinga of Angola: Africa's Warrior Queen*. Boston: Boston University Press.

Marcum, J. 1969. *The Angolan Revolution*, Vol. 1: *1950–1962*. Cambridge, MA: MIT Press.

—. 1978. *The Angolan Revolution*, Vol. 2: *1962–1976*. Cambridge, MA: MIT Press.

Miller, J. 1997. *Way of Death: Merchant Capitalism and the Angolan Slave Trade 1730–1830*. Madison: University of Wisconsin Press.

Contemporary Angola

Agualusa, J.E. 2008. *The Book of Chameleons*. London: Simon and Schuster.

Baptista, J.A. 2018. "Eco(il)logical Knowledge: On Different Ways of Relating with the Known." *Environmental Humanities* 10(2): 397–420. https://doi.org/10.1215/22011919-7156805.

Croese, S. 2019. "'He Will Know How to Explain': Everyday Popular Politics in Postwar Urban Angola." *Comparative Studies of South Asia, Africa and the Middle East* 39(1): 37–48. https://doi.org/10.1215/1089201X-7493755.

Duarte, A.M. 2013. "The Ambivalent Character of Reconstruction: Losers and Winners of the Lobito Transport Corridor Development (Angola)." *Social Science Research Network*. 22 March. https://papers.ssrn.com/sol3/papers.cfm?abstract_id=2237071.

Gastrow, C. 2015. *Negotiated Settlements: Housing and the Aesthetics of Citizenship in Luanda, Angola*. PhD dissertation. University of Chicago.

Moorman, M. 2004. *Intonations: A Social History of Music and Nation in Luanda, Angola, from 1945 to Recent Times*. Athens: Ohio University Press.

Reed, K. 2009. *Crude Existence: Environment and the Politics of Oil in Northern Angola*. Berkeley: University of California Press.

Schmitz, C.M. 2014. "Significant Others: Security and Suspicion in Chinese-Angolan Encounters." *Journal of Current Chinese Affairs* 43(1): 41–69. https://doi.org/10.1177/186810261404300103.

Schubert, J. 2017. *Working the System: A Political Ethnography of the New Angola*. Ithaca: Cornell University Press.

Soares de Oliveira, R. 2015. *Magnificent and Beggar Land Angola since the Civil War*. London: Hurst.

Tomás, A. 2015. "Living Dangerously in Petroluanda." In *African Cities Reader III: Land, Property and Value*, edited by N. Edjabe and E. Pieterse.

Cape Town: Chimurenga. https://africancitiesreader.org.za/reader/chapters/013_LIVINGDANGEROUSLYINPETROLUANDA.pdf.

Vidal, N.C. de F. 2019. "The Historical-Sociological Matrix and Ethos at the Heart and Strength of MPLA's Modern Angola." *Tempo* 25(1): 153–73. https://doi.org/10.1590/tem-1980-542x2018v250108.

Beauty and Ugliness

Ameeriar, L. 2017. *Downwardly Global: Women, Work, and Citizenship in the Pakistani Diaspora.* Durham: Duke University Press.

Bourgois, P., and J. Schonberg. 2009. *Righteous Dopefiend.* Berkeley: University of California Press.

Edmonds, A. 2010. *Pretty Modern: Beauty, Sex and Plastic Surgery in Brazil.* Durham: Duke University Press.

Gama, V. 2018. "Vela 6911 – Explosão, fourth movement." 24 September. https://www.youtube.com/watch?v=vZJxn7oPNCY.

Garcia, A. 2010. *The Pastoral Clinic: Addiction and Disposession along the Rio Grande.* Berkeley: University of California Press.

Gilroy, P. 1993. *The Black Atlantic: Modernity and Double Consciousness.* Cambridge, MA: Harvard University Press.

Nuttall, S. 2006. *Beautiful Ugly: African Diaspora Aesthetics.* Durham: Duke University Press.

O'Dougherty, M. 2002. *Consumption Intensified: The Politics of Middle Class Daily Life in Brazil.* Durham: Duke University Press.

Okri, B. 2015. *A Way of Being Free.* London: Zeus.

Sousanis, N. 2015. *Unflattening.* Cambridge, MA: Harvard University Press.

Strassler, K. 2011. *Refracted Visions: Popular Photography and National Modernity in Java.* Durham: Duke University Press.

Taussig, M. 2012. *Beauty and the Beast.* Chicago: University of Chicago Press.

Capitalism

Appel, H. 2017. "Toward an Ethnography of the National Economy." *Cultural Anthropology* 32(2): 294–322. https://doi.org/10.14506/ca32.2.09.

Ferguson, J. 1994. *The Antipolitics Machine: Development, Depolitization, and Bureaucratic Power in Lesotho.* Cambridge: Cambridge University Press.

Graeber, D. 2011. *Debt: The First 5,000 Years.* New York: Melville House.

Harney, S., and F. Moten. 2013. *The Under Commons: Fugitive Planning and Black Study.* New York: Minor Compositions.

Ho, K. 2011. *Liquidated: An Ethnography of Wall Street.* Durham: Duke University Press.

Hodges, T. 2001. *Angola: From Afro-Stalinism to Petro-Diamond Capitalism.* Bloomington: Indiana University Press.

Miller, J. 1997. *Way of Death: Merchant Capitalism and the Angolan Slave Trade 1730–1830*. Madison: University of Wisconsin Press.
Polanyi, K. 2011. *The Great Transformation: The Political and Economic Origins of Our Time*. New York: Beacon.
Ralph, M. 2015. *Forensics of Capital*. Chicago: University of Chicago Press.
Rofel, L., and S. Yanagisako. 2019. *Fabricating Transnational Capitalism*. Durham: Duke University Press.
Roitman, J. 2004. *Fiscal Disobedience: An Anthropology of Economic Regulation in Central Africa*. Princeton: Princeton University Press.
Tsing, A. 2015. *The Mushroom at the End of the World: On the Possibility of Life in Capitalist Ruins*. Princeton: Princeton University Press.

Methods

Causey, A. 2017. *Drawn to See: Drawing as an Ethnographic Method*. Toronto: University of Toronto Press.
Cerwonka, A., and L. Malkki. 2007. *Improvising Theory: Process and Temporality in Ethnographic Fieldwork*. Chicago: University of Chicago Press.
de Jong, S., R. Icaza, and O. Rutazibwa. 2019. *Decolonization and Feminisms in Global Teaching and Learning*. London: Routledge.
Elliott, D., and D. Culhane. 2017. *A Different Kind of Ethnography: Imaginative Practices and Creative Methodologies*. Toronto: University of Toronto Press.
Getz, T., and L. Clarke. 2015. *Abina and the Important Men: A Graphic History*. Oxford: Oxford University Press.
Narayan, K. 2012. *Alive in the Writing: Crafting Ethnography in the Company of Chekhov*. Chicago: University of Chicago Press.
Pandian, A., and S. McLean. 2017. *Crumpled Paper Boat: Experiments in Ethnographic Writing*. Durham: Duke University Press.
Pink, S. 2009. *Doing Sensory Ethnography*. London: Sage.
—. 2015. *Digital Ethnography: Principles and Practice*. London: Sage.
Robben, A.C.G.M., and J.A. Sluka, eds. 2006. *Ethnographic Fieldwork: An Anthropological Reader*. London: Blackwell.
Ross, F. 2010. *Raw Life, New Hope: Decency, Housing and Everyday Life in a Post-Apartheid Community*. Cape Town: University of Cape Town Press.
Sumartojo, S., and S. Pink. 2019. *Atmospheres and the Experiential World: Theory and Methods*. London: Routledge.

Race in the Southern Atlantic

Alencastro, L.F. de. 2000. *O Trato dos Viventes: Formação do Brasil no Atlântico Sul, séculos XVI e XVII*. São Paulo: Campanha das Letras.
Burdick, J. 2013. *The Color of Sound: Race, Religion and Music in Brazil*. New York: NYU Press.

Cahen, M., and E. Mourier-Genoud. 2012. *Imperial Migrations: Colonial Communities and Diaspora in the Portuguese World*. London: Palgrave Macmillan.

Corrado, J. 2008. *The Creole Elite and the Rise of Proto-nationalism (1870–1920)*. Amherst: Cambria.

de Almeida, M.V. 2007. "O Atlântico Pardo: Antropologia, Pós-colonialismo e o Caso 'Lusófono.'" In *Trânsitos coloniais: Diálogos críticos Luso-Brasileiros*, edited by Cristiana Bastos, Miguel Vale de Almeida, and Bela Feldman-Bianco, 23–37. Lisbon: UNICAMP.

Edmonds, A. 2010. *Pretty Modern: Beauty, Sex and Plastic Surgery in Brazil*. Durham: Duke University Press.

Freyre, G. 1933. *Casa Grande e Senzala: Formação da familiabrasileira sob a regime da economia patriarchal*. Belo Horizonte: J. Olympico.

Fry, P. 2000. "Nationality and the Meaning of 'Race' in Brazil." *Daedalus* 129(2). https://www.jstor.org/stable/20027630.

Matory, J.L. 2005. *Black Atlantic Religion: Tradition, Transnationalism and Matriarchy in Afro-Brazilian Candomblé*. Princeton: Princeton University Press.

Santos, B.D.S. 2002. "Between Prospero and Caliban: Colonialism, Postcolonialism and Inter-identity." *Luso-Brazilian Review* 39(2): 197–293. https://doi.org/10.3368/lbr.39.2.9.

Telles, E. 2005. *Race in Another America: The Significance of Skin Color in Brazil*. Princeton: Princeton University Press.

Williams, R. 2013. "Luso-African Intimacies: Conceptions of National and Transnational Community." In *Imperial Migrations: Colonial Communities and Diaspora in the Portuguese World*, edited by E. Mourier-Genoud and M. Cahen, 197–293. London: Palgrave Macmillan.

The Senses in Anthropology

Classen, C. 1992. "The Odor of the Other: Olfactory Symbolism and Cultural Categories." *Ethos* 20(2): 133–66. https://doi.org/10.1525/eth.1992.20.2.02a00010.

—. 1993. *Worlds of Sense: Exploring the Senses in History and across Cultures*. London: Routledge.

Classen, C., and W.F. Bynum. 2000. "Review: *The Color of Angels: Cosmology, Gender and the Aesthetic Imagination*." *American Historical Review* 105(2): 518. https://www.jstor.org/stable/1571476.

Cox, R. 2018. "Sound, Anthropology of." In *International Encyclopedia of Anthropology*. Hoboken: John Wiley & Sons.

Gershon, W.S., ed. 2019. *Sensuous Curriculum: Politics and the Senses in Education*. Charlotte: Information Age.

Geurts, K.L. 2002. *Culture and the Senses: Bodily Ways of Knowing in an African Community*. Berkeley: University of California Press.

Ingold, T. 2013. "Thinking through Making." Institute for Northern Culture. 31 October. https://www.youtube.com/watch?v=Ygne72-4zyo.

Marks, L.U. 2002. *Touch: Sensuous Theory and Multisensory Media.* Minneapolis: University of Minnesota Press.

Serres, M. 2008. *The Five Senses: A Philosophy of Mingled Bodies.* London: Continuum.

Sparkes, A.C. 2006. "Ethnography and the Senses: Challenges and Possibilities." *Qualitative Research in Sport and Exercise* 1(1): 21–35. https://doi.org/10.1080/19398440802567923.

Stoller, P. 1989. *The Taste of Ethnographic Things: The Senses in Anthropology.* Philadelphia: University of Pennsylvania Press.

—. 2002. *Money Has No Smell: The Africanization of New York City.* Chicago: University of Chicago Press.

References

Abrantes, J.M., and N. Martins. 2010. *Cidades e gentes de Angola/Cities and People of Angola*. Translated by N. Breslin and S. Moreira. Luanda: Angola Solutions.
Adichie, C.N. 2016. "The Danger of a Single Story." TED talk. https://www.ted.com/talks/chimamanda_adichie_the_danger_of_a_single_story.
AEA (Associação de Escuteiros de Angola). 2013. *Manuel Do Caminho*. Luanda: LST, Artes Gráficas.
Agualusa, J.E. 1988. *Creole*. Edited and translated by Daniel Hahn. London: Arcadia.
—. 2006. *The Book of Chameleons*. London: Simon and Schuster.
Alencastro, L.F. de. 2000. *O Trato dos Viventes: Formação do Brasil no Atlântico Sul, séculos XVI e XVII*. São Paulo: Campanha das Letras.
Almeida, M.V. de. 2004. *An Earth-Colored Sea: "Race," Culture, and the Politics of Identity in the Postcolonial Portuguese-Speaking World*. London: Berghahn.
Ameeriar, L. 2012. "The Sanitized Sensorium." *American Anthropologist* 114(3): 509–20. https://doi.org/10.1111/j.1548-1433.2012.01449.x.
—. 2017. *Downwardly Global: Women, Work, and Citizenship in the Pakistani Diaspora*. Durham: Duke University Press.
Ames, M. 2013. "Managing Mobile Multitasking: The Culture of iPhones on Stanford Campus." Paper presented at the Proceedings of the 2013 Conference on Computer Supported Cooperative Work, San Antonio, TX, 23–27 February. https://doi.org/10.1145/2441776.2441945.
Anderson, B. 1990. *Imagined Communities: Reflections on the Origin and Spread of Nationalism*. London: Verso.
Angola. 2012. *Plano Nacional de Quadros 2013–2020*. Luanda: Orgãos Essenciais Auxiliares Do Presidente da República, Casa Civil.

Attali, J. 1977. *Noise: The Political Economy of Music*. Minneapolis: University of Minnesota Press.

Auerbach, J. 2010. "Incapsulating Hands: On the (In)Dependence of Young Adults in the UNHCR's Maratane Refugee Camp." *Social Dynamics* 36(2): 197–293. doi: 10.1080/02533952.2010.483827.

—. 2017. "Landscapes from Fieldwork: A Poetic Series." *Anthropology and Humanism* 42(2): 221–24. https://doi.org/10.1111/anhu.12187.

—. 2019. Review of *A Snake Gives Birth to a Snake. American Anthropologist*, 6 November. doi.org/10.1111/aman.13333.

Auerbach, J., and S. Colégio. 2014. "Happy Lobito." YouTube. https://www.youtube.com/watch?v=vjyz6SIiZdY.

BBC. 2016. "The Persistent Myth That Islam Was Banned in Angola." 18 October. https://www.bbc.com/news/world-africa-37316749.

Biehl, J. 2013. *Vita: Life in a Zone of Social Abandonment*. Berkeley: University of California Press.

Boas, F. 1889. "On Alternating Sounds." *American Anthropologist* A2(1): 47–54. https://doi.org/10.1525/aa.1889.2.1.02a00040.

Bolton, R., A. Parasuraman, and A. Hoefnagels. 2013. "Understanding Generation Y and Their Use of Social Media: A Review and Research Agenda." *Journal of Service Management* 24(3): 245–67. https://doi.org/10.1108/09564231311326987.

Bourdieu, P. 1977. *Outline of a Theory of Practice*. Translated by Richard Nice. Cambridge: Cambridge University Press.

—. 1984. *Distinction: A Social Critique of the Judgement of Taste*. Cambridge, MA: Harvard University Press.

Bulawayo, N. 2013. *We Need New Names*. London: Reagan Arthur.

Bunce, M., S. Franks, and C. Paterson. 2017. *Africa's Media Image in the 21st Century: From the "Heart of Darkness" to "Africa Rising."* London: Routledge.

Buolamwini, J., and T. Gebru. 2018. "Gender Shades: Intersectional Accuracy Disparities in Commercial Gender Classification." *Proceedings of the 1st Conference on Fairness, Accountability and Transparency* 81: 1–15. https://www.media.mit.edu/publications/gender-shades-intersectional-accuracy-disparities-in-commercial-gender-classification/.

Burke, T. 1996. *Lifebuoy Men, Lux Women: Commodification, Consumption, and Cleanliness in Modern Zimbabwe*. Durham: Duke University Press.

Butler, J. 2016. *Frames of War: When Is Life Grievable?* London: Verso.

Cadwalladr, C. 2019. "Facebook's Role in Brexit—and the Threat to Democracy." April. https://www.ted.com/talks/carole_cadwalladr_facebook_s_role_in_brexit_and_the_threat_to_democracy?language=en.

Cain, S. 2013. *Quiet: The Power of Introverts in a World That Can't Stop Talking*. New York: Broadway.

Calvino, I. 1972. *Invisible Cities*. San Diego: Harcourt Brace.

Cardoso, R.V. 2015. "The Crude Urban Revolution: Land Markets, Planning Forms and the Making of a New Luanda." University of California, Berkeley.

Carnegie, D. 2004. *How to Win Friends and Influence People*. New York: Vermillion.

Cerqueira, M., and N. Schul. 2008. "Preface." In *Angola: Um país renascer/ Angola: A Country Reborn*, edited by J. Pinto and N. Schul, 197–293. Luanda: Mundis.

Cerwonka, A., and L. Malkki. 2007. *Improvising Theory: Process and Temporality in Ethnographic Fieldwork*. Chicago: University of Chicago Press.

Chakrabarty, D. 2000. *Provincializing Europe: Postcolonial Thought and Historical Difference*. Princeton: Princeton University Press.

Chant, S., and C. Sweetman. 2012. "Fixing Women or Fixing the World? 'Smart Economics,' Efficiency Approaches, and Gender Equality in Development." *Gender and Development* 20(3): 517–29. https://doi.org/10.1080/13552074.2012.731812.

Chipilica, D. 2014. *Geração da Mudança*. Angola: Self-published.

Classen, C. 1992. "The Odor of the Other: Olfactory Symbolism and Cultural Categories." *Ethos* 20(2): 133–66. https://doi.org/10.1525/eth.1992.20.2.02a00010.

—. 1993. *Worlds of Sense: Exploring the Senses in History and across Cultures*. London: Routledge.

Classen, C., D. Howes, and A. Synnott. 1994. *Aroma: The Cultural History of Smell*. London: Routledge.

Clifford, J., and G. Marcus. 1986. *Writing Culture: The Poetics and Politics of Ethnography*. Berkeley: University of California Press.

Collier, D. 2012. "A 'New Man' for Africa? Some Particularities of the Marxist Homem Novo within Angolan Cultural Policy." In *De-Centering Cold War History: Local and Global Change*, edited by J.E.P. Mooney, F. Lanza, and D. Collier, 187–286. London: Routledge.

Conrad, J. 2010. *Heart of Darkness*. London: Tribeca Books.

Coogler, R., dir. 2018. *Black Panther*. Produced by Marvel Studios. Burbank: Walt Disney Studios.

Corrado, J. 2008. *The Creole Elite and the Rise of Proto-nationalism (1870–1920)*. Amherst: Cambria.

Costa, E. 2016. *Social Media in Southeast Turkey*. London: UCL Press.

Cox, R. 2018. "Sound, Anthropology of." In *International Encyclopedia of Anthropology*. Hoboken: John Wiley & Sons.

Croese, S. 2012. "1 Million Houses? Angola's National Reconstruction and Chinese Engagement." In *China and Angola: A Marriage of Convenience?*, edited by M. Power and A.C. Alves, 124–44. Oxford: Pambazuka.

de Andrade, R.L.F.P. 2010. *Escutismo: Um Método Educativo Não-Formal*. Luanda: Mayamba Editora.

Deresiewicz, W. 2015. *Excellent Sheep: The Miseducation of the American Elite and the Way to a Meaningful Life*. New York: Free Press.

Desjarlais, R. 2003. *Sensory Biographies: Lives and Deaths among Nepal's Yolmo Buddhists*. Berkeley: University of California Press.

de Vries, R. 2016. *Eye of the Firestorm: The Namibian–Angolan–South African Border War—Memories of a Military Commander*. London: Helion.

Du Bois, W. 2005 [1903]. *The Souls of Black Folk*. New York: Barnes and Noble.

Dulley, I. 2015a. "A historiografia sobre a 'conversão' nas colónias portuguesas na África e a trajetória de Jesse Chiula Chipenda." *África São Paulo* 35: 57–86. http://dx.doi.org/10.11606/issn.2526-303X.v0i35p57-86.

—. 2015b. "Cristianismo e distinção: Uma análise comparativa da recepção da presença missionária entre os 'Ovimbundu' e os 'Ovakwanyama' de Angola." *Mulemba: Revista Angolana de Ciências Sociais* 5(9): 185–202. https://doi.org/10.4000/mulemba.404.

Durham, D. 2011. "Youth and the Social Imagination in Africa: Introduction to Parts 1 and 2." *Anthropological Quarterly* 73(3): 197–293.

Edwards, P.N., et al. 2013. *Knowledge Infrastructures: Intellectual Frameworks and Research Challenges*. Report. Ann Arbor: Deep Blue. http://hdl.handle.net/2027.42/97552.

Eisenlohr, P. 2018. *Sounding Islam: Voice, Media, and Sonic Atmospheres in an Indian Ocean World*. Berkeley: University of California Press.

Eltis, D., and A. Tullos. 2013. The Trans-Atlantic Slave Trade Database. www.slavevoyages.org (accessed 30 November 2018).

Emma. 2018. *The Mental Load: A Feminist Comic*. London: Seven Stories Press.

Farquhar, J. 2002. *Appetites: Food and Sex in Post-socialist China*. Durham: Duke University Press.

Farwell, J.P. 2014. "The Media Strategy of ISIS." *Survival: Global Politics and Strategy* 56(6): 49–55. https://doi.org/10.1080/00396338.2014.985436.

Ferguson, J. 2006. *Global Shadows: Africa in the Neoliberal World Order*. Durham: Duke University Press.

—. 2015. *Give a Man a Fish: Reflections on the New Politics of Distribution*. Durham: Duke University Press.

Ferreira Rosa, M. 1936. *O apetrechamento educacional da colónia de angola: Brancos e assimilados*. Luanda: n.p.

Fischer, D. 2016. *The Voice and Its Doubles: Media and Music in Northern Australia*. Durham: Duke University Press.

Folbre, N. 2015. "Valuing Non-market Work." New York: UNDP Human Development Report Office. http://hdr.undp.org/sites/default/files/folbre_hdr_2015_final_0.pdf.

Fox, L., dir. 2007. *The Story of Stuff*. Written by A. Leonard, L. Fox, and J. Sachs. Free Range Studios. https://storyofstuff.org/movies/story-of-stuff/.

Freyre, G. 1933. *Casa Grande e Senzala: Formação da família brasileira sob a regime da economia patriarchal*. Pernambuco, Brazil: J. Olympico.

Friedman, Z. 2019. "30 Fast Facts about the College Admissions Scandal." *Forbes*, 18 March. https://www.forbes.com/sites/zackfriedman/2019/03/18/30-facts-college-admissions-scandal/.
Galloway, S. 2009. *The Cellist of Sarajevo*. New York: Riverhead.
Gastrow, C. 2015. *Negotiated Settlements: Housing and the Aesthetics of Citizenship in Luanda, Angola*. PhD dissertation. University of Chicago.
Geertz, C. 1973. *The Interpretation of Cultures*. New York: Basic.
Gell, A. 1977. "Magic, Perfume, Dream." In *Symbols and Sentiment: Cross-Cultural Studies in Symbolism*, edited by I. Lewis, 15–38. London: Academic Press.
George, E. 2005. *The Cuban Intervention in Angola, 1965–1991*. London: Frank Cass.
Geurts, K.L. 2002. *Culture and the Senses: Bodily Ways of Knowing in an African Community*. Berkeley: University of California Press.
Gilroy, P. 1993. *The Black Atlantic: Modernity and Double Consciousness*. Cambridge, MA: Harvard University Press.
Glick-Schiller, N., and G. Fouron. 2001. *Georges Woke Up Laughing*. Durham: Duke University Press.
Gordon, R. 1987. "Anthropology and Apartheid: The Rise of Military Ethnology in South Africa." *Cultural Survival* 11(4). https://www.culturalsurvival.org/publications/cultural-survival-quarterly/anthropology-and-apartheid-rise-military-ethnology-south.
Green, L. 2015. "Fracking, Oikos and Omics in the Karoo: Reimagining South Africa's Reparative Energy Politics." In *Os Mil Nomes de Gaia* (conference proceedings), 1–15. Rio de Janeiro: academia.edu. https://osmilnomesdegaia.files.wordpress.com/2014/11/lesley-green.pdf.
Gusterson, H. 2016. *Drone: Remote Control Warfare*. Cambridge, MA: MIT Press.
Guyer, J. 2004. *Marginal Gains: Monetary Transactions in Atlantic Africa*. Chicago: University of Chicago Press.
Hammersley, M. 1999. *Taking Sides in Social Research: Essays on Partisanship and Bias*. New York: Routledge.
Harari, Y.N. 2018. *21 Lessons for the 21st Century*. London: Spiegel & Grau.
Harvey, K., ed. 2009. *History and Material Culture: A Student's Guide to Approaching Alternative Sources*. London: Routledge.
Harvey, P. 2015. "Materials." *Cultural Anthropology*. https://culanth.org/fieldsights/materials.
Hatzky, C. 2012. *Cubans in Angola: South-South Cooperation and Transfer of Knowledge, 1976–1991*. Madison: University of Wisconsin Press.
Heiman, R., C. Freeman, and M. Liechty. 2012. *The Global Middle Classes: Theorizing through Ethnography*. Santa Fe: School for Advanced Research Press.
Henshaw, V. 2014. *Urban Smellscapes: Understanding and Designing City Smell Environments*. New York: Routledge.

Hjorth, L., and S. Pink. 2014. "New Visualities and the Digital Wayfarer: Reconceptualizing Camera Phone Photography and Locative Media." *Mobile Media and Communication* 2(1): 40–57. https://doi.org/10.1177/2050157913505257.

Hodder, I. 2011. "Wheels of Time: Some Aspects of Entanglement Theory and the Secondary Products Revolution." *Journal of World Prehistory* 24 (2–3): 175–87. https://doi.org/10.1007/s10963-011-9050-x.

Hoffman, D. 2007. "The Disappeared: Images of the Environment at Freetown's Urban Margins." *Visual Studies* 22(2): 104–19. https://doi.org/10.1080/14725860701507016.

Holmes, S. 2013. *Fresh Fruit, Broken Bodies: Migrant Farmworkers in the United States*. Berkeley: University of California Press.

Hopkins, P., and H. Dugmore. 2000. *The Boy: Baden-Powell and the Siege of Mafeking*. Johannesburg: Zebra Press.

Horst, H.A., and D. Miller. 2012. *Digital Anthropology*. London: Bloomsbury.

INEE (Instituto Nacional para a Educação Especial). 2006. "Plano Estratégico de Desenvolvimento da Educação Especial em Angola 2007–2015." https://planipolis.iiep.unesco.org/sites/planipolis/files/ressources/angola_estrategiaparaeducacaoespecial.pdf.

Ingold, T. 2007a. "Against Soundscape." In *Autumn Leaves: Sound and the Environment in Artistic Practice*, edited by A. Carlyle, 10–13. Paris: Double Entendre.

—. 2007b. *Lines: A Brief History*. Oxford: Routledge.

Jacob, H.E. 1997. *Six Thousand Years of Bread: Its Holy and Unholy History*. London: Lyons Press.

Jain, S. Lochlann. 2013. *Malignant: How Cancer Becomes Us*. Berkeley: University of California Press.

Jansen, J. 2009. *Knowledge in the Blood: Confronting Race in the Apartheid Past*. Palo Alto: Stanford University Press.

Kant de Lima, R. 2011. *A antropologia da academia: Quando os indios somos nos*. Belo Horizonte: Editora UFF. http://www.eduff.uff.br/index.php/livros/144-a-antropologia-da-academia-quando-os-indios-somos-nos.

Klausen, J. 2015. "Tweeting the *Jihad*: Social Media Networks of Western Foreign Fighters in Syria and Iraq." *Studies in Conflict and Terrorism* 38(1): 1–22. https://doi.org/10.1080/1057610x.2014.974948.

Kleinman, A. 2006. *What Really Matters: Living a Moral Life amidst Uncertainty and Danger*. Oxford: Oxford University Press.

Koebler, J. 2016. "Angola's Wikipedia Pirates Are Exposing the Problems with Digital Colonialism." *Vice*, 23 March. http://motherboard.vice.com/read/wikipedia-zero-facebook-free-basics-angola-pirates-zero-rating.

Krog, A. 2000. *Country of My Skull: Guilt, Sorrow, and the Limits of Forgiveness in the New South Africa*. New York: Broadway.

Lane, C., and A. Carlyle. 2015. *On Listening*. London: Uniform.

Lee, K. 2015. "Singapore's Founding Father Thought Air-Conditioning Was the Secret to His Country's Success." *Vox*, 23 March. https://www.vox.com/2015/3/23/8278085/singapore-lee-kuan-yew-air-conditioning.

Lessac, M., dir. 2014. *A Snake Gives Birth to a Snake*. New York: Global Arts Corps.

Lópes, A.R., and B. Weinstein, eds. 2012. *The Making of the Middle Class: Towards a Transnational History*. Durham: Duke University Press.

MacKinnon, I. 2008. Miss Landmine: Exploitation or Bold Publicity for the Victims? *The Guardian*, 22 April. http://www.theguardian.com/world/2008/apr/22/cambodia.internationalaidanddevelopment.

Malan, R. 2000. *My Traitor's Heart: A South African Exile Returns to Face His Country, His Tribe, and His Conscience*. London: Grove.

Malkki, L. 1996. "Speechless Emissaries: Refugees, Humanitarianism, and Dehistoricization." *Cultural Anthropology* 11(3): 377–404. https://doi.org/10.1525/can.1996.11.3.02a00050.

Mandela, N. 1994. *Long Walk to Freedom*. London: Little, Brown.

Marcum, J. 1969. *The Angolan Revolution*, Vol 1: *1950–1962*. Cambridge, MA: MIT Press.

—. 1978. *The Angolan Revolution*, Vol. 2: *1962–1976*. Cambridge, MA: MIT Press.

Maren, M. 1997. *The Road to Hell: The Ravaging Effects of Foreign Aid and International Charity*. London: Free Press.

Marks, L.U. 2002. *Touch: Sensuous Theory and Multisensory Media*. Minneapolis: University of Minnesota Press.

—. 2008. "Thinking Multisensory Culture." *Paragraph* 31(2): 123–37. https://doi.org/10.3366/E0264833408000151.

Marques, N. 2015. "Angola 15++." *GNN*, 19 November 2015.

Marx, K. 1999. *Capital*, Vol. 3: *A Critique of Political Economy*. London: Penguin.

Matory, J.L. 2005. *Black Atlantic Religion: Tradition, Transnationalism and Matriarchy in Afro-Brazilian Candomblé*. Princeton: Princeton University Press.

Max, D. 2008. *Anthropology at the Dawn of the Cold War: The Influence of Foundations, McCarthyism and the CIA*. London: Pluto.

Mazuri Designs. 2016. "A History of African Wax Prints." 4 February. http://mazuridesigns.com/blog/2016/2/4/a-history-of-african-wax-prints.

Mbembe, A. 2001. *On the Postcolony*. Berkeley: University of California Press.

McClintock, A. 1995. *Imperial Leather: Race, Gender and Sexuality in the Colonial Contest*. New York: Routledge.

Mendes, M. da C.B. 2013. *Avaliação da Qualidade e Educação Superior em Angola*. Benguela: KAT Editora.

Menzel, P., and F. D'Aluisio. 2007. *Hungry Planet: What the World Eats*. London: Material Worlds.

Miller, D., ed. 2005. *Materiality*. Durham: Duke University Press.

—. 2016. *Social Media in an English Village: Or How to Keep People at Just the Right Distance*. London: UCL.
Milman, O. 2018. "Americans Waste 150,000 Tons of Food Each Day—Equal to a Pound a Person." *The Guardian*, 18 April. https://www.theguardian.com/environment/2018/apr/18/americans-waste-food-fruit-vegetables-study.
Mintz, S. 1986. *Sweetness and Power*. London: Penguin.
Moorman, M. 2004. *Intonations: A Social History of Music and Nation in Luanda, Angola, from 1945 to Recent Times*. Athens: Ohio University Press.
—. 2015. "What You Need to Know about #free15Angolans." 13 July. https://africasacountry.com/2015/07/free15angolans-what-you-need-to-know.
—. 2019. *Powerful Frequencies: Radio, State Power, and the Cold War in Angola, 1931–2002*. Athens: Ohio University Press.
Morris, P. 2014. *Back to Angola: A Journey from War to Peace*. Johannesburg: Zebra.
Morrison, T. 2007. *The Bluest Eye*. New York: Vintage.
Mourier-Genoud, E., ed. 2012. *Sure Road? Nationalisms in Angola, Guinea-Bissau and Mozambique*. Leiden: Brill.
Mudimbe, V.Y. 2008. *The Invention of Africa: Gnosis, Philosophy, and the Order of Knowledge*. Bloomington: Indiana University Press.
Myers, R. 2011. "The Familiar Strange and the Strange Familiar in Anthropology and Beyond." *Bulleting of the General Anthropology Division* 18(2): 1–9. https://doi.org/10.1111/j.1939-3466.2011.00007.x.
Narayan, K. 2012. *Alive in the Writing: Crafting Ethnography in the Company of Chekhov*. Chicago: University of Chicago Press.
Nielson, R. 1973. "The History and Development of Wax Print Textiles Intended for West Africa and Zaire." In *The Fabrics of Culture: The Anthropology of Clothing and Adornment*, edited by J.M. Cordwell and R.A. Schwarz, 467–596. The Hague: Mouton.
Nuttall, S. 2006. *Beautiful Ugly: African Diaspora Aesthetics*. Durham: Duke University Press.
Nyabola, N. 2016. "Facebook's Free Basics Is an African Dictator's Dream." *Foreign Policy*, 27 October. https://foreignpolicy.com/2016/10/27/facebooks-plan-to-wire-africa-is-a-dictators-dream-come-true-free-basics-internet/.
Ogunnaike, O. 2017. "African Philosophy Reconsidered: Africa, Religion, Race and Philosophy." *Journal of Africana Religions* 5(2): 181–216. https://www.jstor.org/stable/10.5325/jafrireli.5.2.0181.
Ondjaki. 2014. *Os vivos, o morto e o peixe-frito*. Rio de Janeiro: Pallas.
Ortner, S.B. 1973. "On Key Symbols." *American Anthropologist* 75(5): 1338–46. https://doi.org/10.1093/cercor/bhq078.
Orwell, G. 1949. *1984*. London: Secker and Warburg.

Ovadia, J.S. 2012. "The Dual Nature of Local Content in Angola's Oil and Gas Industry: Development vs. Elite Accumulation." *Journal of Contemporary African Studies* 30(3): 395–417. https://doi.org/10.1080/02589001.2012.701846.

—. 2013. "The Reinvention of Elite Accumulation in the Angolan Oil Sector: Emergent Capitalism in a Rentier Economy." *Cadernosde Estudos Africanos* 25: 33–63. https://doi.org/10.4000/cea.839.

Pallasmaa, J. 2005. *The Eyes of the Skin: Architecture and the Senses*. Chichester: John Wiley & Sons.

Parsons, T. 2004. *Race, Resistance, and the Boy Scout Movement in British Colonial Africa*. Athens: Ohio University Press.

Patel, K. 2013. "No, Angola Has Not 'Banned Islam.' It's a Little More Complicated than That." *Daily Maverick*, 26 November. https://www.dailymaverick.co.za/article/2013-11-26-no-angola-has-not-banned-islam-its-a-little-more-complicated-than-that/.

Patel, S. 2010. *Migritude*. New York: Kaya.

Peacock, J.L., and D.C. Holland. 1993. "The Narrated Self: Life Stories in Process." *Ethos* 21(4): 367–83. https://doi.org/10.1525/eth.1993.21.4.02a00010.

Pearce, J. 2005. *An Outbreak of Peace: Angola's Situation of Confusion*. Cape Town: David Philip.

Pearce, J., D. Péclard, and R. Soares De Oliveira. 2018. "Angola's Elections and the Politics of Presidential Succession." *African Affairs* 117(466): 146–60. doi: 10.1093/afraf/adx045.

Péclard, D. 1998. "Religion and Politics in Angola: The Church, the Colonial State and the Emergence of Angolan Nationalism 1940–1961." *Journal of Religion in Africa* 28(2): 160–86. https://doi.org/10.2307/1581711.

Pendergrast, M. 2010. *Uncommon Grounds: The History of Coffee and How It Transformed the World*. New York: Basic Books.

Piot, C. 1999. *Remotely Global: Village Modernity in West Africa*. Chicago: University of Chicago Press.

Pitcher, M.A., and K.M. Askew. 2006. "African Socialisms and Postsocialisms." *Africa* 76(1): 1–14. https://doi.org/10.3366/afr.2006.0001.

Portelli, A. 2003. *The Order Has Been Carried Out: History, Memory, and Meaning of a Nazi Massacre in Rome*. London: Palgrave Macmillan.

Posel, D., and F. Ross. 2015. *Ethical Quandaries in Social Research*. Cape Town: HSRC.

Prensky, M. 2001. "Digital Natives, Digital Immigrants Part 1." *On the Horizon* 9(5): 1–6. https://doi.org/10.1108/10748120110424816.

Price, D. 2016. *Cold War Anthropology: The CIA, the Pentagon, and the Growth of Dual Use Anthropology*. Durham: Duke University Press.

Quercia, D., R. Schifanella, L.M. Aiello, and K. McLean. 2015. "Smelly Maps: The Digital Life of Urban Smellscapes." *CoRR*. http://arxiv.org/abs/1505.06851.

Rahaim, M. 2012. *Musicking Bodies: Gesture and Voice in Hindustani Music*. Middletown: Wesleyan University Press.

—. 2019. "Object, Person, Machine, or What: Practical Ontologies of Voice." In *The Oxford Handbook of Voice Studies*, edited by N. Eidsheim and K. Meizel. New York: Oxford University Press.

Rahman, Z.H. 2014. *In the Light of What We Know*. New York: Farrar, Straus & Giroux.

Reed, K. 2009. *Crude Existence: Environment and the Politics of Oil in Northern Angola*. Berkeley: University of California Press.

Ross, Edward. 1980. *Diary of the Siege of Mafeking*. Cape Town: Van Riebeeck Society.

Ross, Elliot. 2014. "The Dangers of a Single Book Cover: The Acacia Tree Meme and 'African Literature.'" *Africa Is a Country*, 5 July. https://africasacountry.com/2014/05/the-dangers-of-a-single-book-cover-the-acacia-tree-meme-and-african-literature/.

Ross, F. 2001. "Speech and Silence: Women's Testimony in the First Five Weeks of Public Hearings of the South African Truth and Reconciliation Commission." In *Remaking a World: Violence, Social Suffering, and Recovery*, edited by Veena Das, Arthur Kleinman, Margaret M. Lock, Mamphela Ramphele, and Pamela Reynolds, 250–80. Berkeley: University of California Press.

—. 2010. *Raw Life, New Hope: Decency, Housing and Everyday Life in a Post-Apartheid Community*. Cape Town: University of Cape Town Press.

Roxburgh, C., et al. 2010. *Lions on the Move: The Progress and Potential of African Economies*. McKinsey Global Institute. https://www.mckinsey.com/featured-insights/middle-east-and-africa/lions-on-the-move.

Rudder, C. 2014. *Dataclysm: Who We Are When We Think No One's Looking*. New York: Crown.

Said, E.W. 1978. *Orientalism*. London: Vintage.

Schafer, R.M. 1977. *The Tuning of the World*. London: Random House.

Schielke, S. 2011. "Living in the Future Tense: Aspiring for World and Class in Provincial Egypt." In *The Global Middle Classes: Theorizing through Ethnography*, edited by R. Heiman, C. Freeman, and M. Liechty, 197–293. Santa Fe: School for Advanced Research Press.

Scholtz, L. 2016. *The Battle of Cuito Cuanavale: Cold War Angolan Finale, 1987–1988*. London: Helion.

Schubert, J. 2015. "2002, Year Zero: History as Anti-Politics in the 'New Angola.'" *Journal of Southern African Studies* 41(4): 835–52. https://doi.org/10.1080/03057070.2015.1055548.

—. 2017. *Working the System: A Political Ethnography of the New Angola*. Ithaca: Cornell University Press.

Serres, M. 2008. *The Five Senses: A Philosophy of Mingled Bodies*. London: Continuum.

Sharrock, D. 2008. "Out of the War, into a Book and in a Rage." *The Australian*, 17 June. https://www.theaustralian.com.au/arts/out-of-the-war-into-a-book-and-in-a-rage/news-story/dcd310e8a08f2af80c8449892cf23433.

Skuse, A., and T. Cousins. 2008. "Getting Connected: The Social Dynamics of Urban Telecommunications Access and Use in Khayelitsha, Cape Town." *New Media & Society* 10(1): 9–26. https://doi.org/10.1177/1461444807085319.

Smith, M.M. 2006. *How Race Is Made: Slavery, Segregation and the Senses*. Chapel HIll: University of North Carolina Press.

Soares de Oliveira, R. 2015. *Magnificent and Beggar Land: Angola since the Civil War*. London: Hurst.

—. 2016. "The Struggle for the State and the Politics of Belonging in Contemporary Angola, 1975–2015." *Social Dynamics* 42(1): 69–84. https://doi.org/10.1080/02533952.2016.1151108.

Sousanis, N. 2015. *Unflattening*. Cambridge, MA: Harvard University Press.

Stanton, B. 2015. *Humans of New York*. London: St. Martin's Press.

Stoler, P. 1989. *The Taste of Ethnographic Things: The Senses in Anthropology*. Philadelphia: University of Pennsylvania Press.

Strassler, K. 2011. *Refracted Visions: Popular Photography and National Modernity in Java*. Durham: Duke University Press.

Stuart, K. 2016. "Call of Duty Publisher Sued by Family of Angolan Rebel." *The Guardian*, 16 January. https://www.theguardian.com/technology/2016/jan/14/call-of-duty-publisher-sued-by-family-of-angolan-rebel.

Sylvanus, N. 2007. "The Fabric of Africanity: Tracing the Global Threads of Authenticity." *Anthropological Theory* 7(2): 201–16. https://doi.org/10.1177/1463499607077298.

—. 2016. *Patterns in Circulation: Cloth, Gender, and Materiality in West Africa*. Chicago: University of Chicago Press.

Taussig, M. 2012. *Beauty and the Beast*. Chicago: University of Chicago Press.

Thompson, J.B. 2005. "The New Visibility." *Theory, Culture & Society* 22(6): 31–51. https://doi.org/10.1177/0263276405059413.

Thornton, J. 2012. *A Cultural History of the Atlantic World, 1250–1820*. New York: Cambridge University Press.

Tomás, A. 2014. "Mutuality from Above: Urban Crisis, the State and the Work of Comissões de Moradores in Luanda." *Anthropology Southern Africa* 37(3–4): 175–86. https://doi.org/10.1080/23323256.2014.993804.

Tsing, A. 2015. *The Mushroom at the End of the World: On the Possibility of Life in Capitalist Ruins*. Princeton: Princeton University Press.

Udris, D., M. Udris, and J. Der Derian, dirs. 2010. *Human Terrain: War Becomes Academic*. Distributed by Bullfrog Films. Oley, PA: Global Media.

UNDP (United Nations Development Programme). 2014. *Human Development Report 2014*. https://www.undp.org/content/undp/en/home/librarypage/hdr/2014-human-development-report.html.

—. 2018. "Angola: Human Development Indicators." http://www.hdr.undp.org/en/countries/profiles/AGO.

Väliaho, P. 2014. *Biopolitical Screens: Images, Power and the Neoliberal Brain*. Cambridge, MA: MIT Press.

Vansina, J. 1966. *Kingdoms of the Savanna*. Madison: University of Wisconsin Press.
—. 1985. *Oral Tradition as History*. Madison: University of Wisconsin Press.
Veblen, T. 2009 [1899]. *The Theory of the Leisure Class*. Oxford: Oxford University Press.
Vertovec, S. 2009. *Transnationalism*. London: Routledge.
Vokes, R., ed. 2012. *Photography in Africa: Ethnographic Perspectives*. Woodbridge: James Currey.
Walton, M., and Hassreiter, S. 2015. "Real Friends and Fake Friends: Research Relationships in an Era of Global Social Media." In *Ethical Quandaries in Social Research*, edited by D. Posel and F. Ross, 228–49. Cape Town: HSRC.
Weston, K. 1997. *Families We Choose: Lesbians, Gays, Kinship*. New York: Columbia University Press.
Wheeler, R. 2017. "Ruth Benedict and the Purpose of Anthropology." *The Peabody*, 14 January. https://peabody.andover.edu/2017/01/14/ruth-benedict-and-the-purpose-of-anthropology/.
Wiig, A., and I. Kolstad. 2011. "Assigned Corporate Social Responsibility in a Rentier State: The Case of Angola." In *High-Value Natural Resources and Peacebuilding*, edited by P. Lujala and S. Rustad, 197–293. Oxford: Routledge.
WikiHow. 2019. "How to Listen." Co-authored by Moshe Ratson. 11 July. https://www.wikihow.com/Listen.
Williams, P. 2013. "Happy." Miami: Circle House Studios. https://www.youtube.com/watch?v=y6Sxv-sUYtM.
Williams, R. 1977. *Marxism and Literature*. Oxford: Oxford University Press.
Wolfers, M., sel. and trans. 1979. *Poems from Angola*. London: Heinemann.

Index

Abrão, 169–70
Abu Ghraib detention facility, 160
Adichie, Chimamanda Ngozie, 4
AEA (Associação de Escuteiros de Angola, Angolan Scouts Association), 59. *See also* scouting/Scouts in Angola
Africa
  "Africa rising," 174
  beauty of, 183
  middle class emergence, 10–11
  representation and stereotypes, 4–6, 8, 174, 183
  socialism, 127–28
  terminology, 5–6
Africa Scout Day celebrations, 61–62
afterimages of author, 166, 168–74
agriculture and agricultural land, 107
Agualusa, José Eduardo, 48–49, 157
Aimé, 13, 33, 36
air and atmosphere, 34, 37
air-conditioning, 37–38
alternative futures, 157–58
Ameeriar, Lalaie, 48
Anglo-Boer war, 59

Angola
  assets, 16–17
  criticism, 162–63, 184
  generational difference, 76, 136, 163
  history, 9–10, 20, 23–29, 155
  jobs and money, 16
  loyalty to, 189–90
  middle class (*see* middle class in Angola)
  national rebranding, 153, 155–58, 183
  postwar changes and peace, 5, 7–8, 10, 14, 188–89, 190, 191–92
  postwar damage and situation, 3–4
  public *vs.* private views of people, 74
  representation, 4–5, 182–83
  UNDP statistics, 15–16
  who you know, 20
  See also Lobito (Angola); specific topics
Angola, um Pais a Renascer—Angola, a Country Reborn (Cerqueira and Schul), 156
Angola Faz (Angola does), 134, 156

"*Angolanidade*," 90
Anibal (graduate), 43–45
anthropology
    biopolitical life of screens, 153–54, 158–61
    "do no harm," 167–68, 174
    and ethics, 167–68, 174
    individuals *vs.* generalizations, 174
    participant observation, 34–35
    and representation, 181–82
    and smell, 35, 47–48
    social media use, 152, 153, 165–66
    theory and work produced, 14–15
    See also fieldwork of author; methodology and research
apartheid, 1–2, 167
architecture, in photo essay, 178–79
art, in photo essay, 176–77
Askew, Kelly, 127–28
assimilado and *assimilados*, 25, 89
Atlantic Ocean, 11, 12, 187
Aurea's restaurant, 32, 87–89, 107

Baden-Powell, Robert, 59
beating incident, 170–71
beauty, 183, 191
Bela Vista neighborhood, photos, 106, 147
Benguela photo, 176
"birds on campus" (poem), 138
Boas, Franz, 114
bodily senses. *See* senses
body language (gesturing), 117–18
bolo de arroz (rice cake) recipe, 86
Book of Chameleons, The (Agualusa), 157
"border wars" of South Africa, 1, 3
Bourdieu, Pierre, 17
Brazil
    Angolans in social life, 40–41
    economy, 190
    education of Angolans, 130, 131–32
    as fieldwork site, 11, 158–59
    in history of Angola, 24
    and mobility, 103
    and perfume of Angolans, 38–41, 42–43
    race, 197–98n6
"brown Atlantic," 151, 199n1
Bruno (scout leader), 74–75
Bulawayo, NoViolet, 183
business registration, 102–03
"Buying Cloth" (poem), 80

Cain, Susan, 116
Call of Duty: Black Ops III, 162
calulu (grilled fish) recipe, 86
Cameron, Edwin, 172
Caminheiros of Troop No. 21, 59, 72–73
caminheiros Scouts
    author in, 59–60
    and "new man," 70
    role, 71–72
    symbols, 67, 68
    uniform, 65
candonguieros (minibuses), 31–32
capitalism
    transition to from socialism, 10, 19, 118, 120, 127–28, 136, 185
    in universities, 118–19
capitalismo selvagem
    in change and transformation of Angola, 186–87, 188–89, 191
    concept and description, 8, 19–21, 196n8
    critical thinking, 132
    economy and who you know, 19–20, 184
    in everyday life and acts, 184–85
    and listening, 116
    and senses, 184–85
    translation in English, 8, 19
    and universities, 119, 122

carbon from travel, 7, 172
care and love, xxiii, 15, 193
Carnegie, Dale, 116
cars, 13, 18
cassava, 86, 91
Catarina, 35–36
catinga (bad bodily odor), 43–45, 47, 50–51
Catumbela market place, 108
Catumbela river, 107
Celestino, 39–42
Cerwonka, Allaine, 15
child mortality, 19
childhood, in photo essay, 146–47
Chivukuvuku, Abel, 124
Choy, Timothy, 37
Christianity
  in Angola, 7–8, 67
  and "new man," 68–71
Christiano (student/teacher), 121–22
church. *See* religion and church
"Cinema Church" (poem), 143
Cinema Flamingo, 94, 95, 178
Cinema Kalunga, 148, 149, 155
Cities and People of Angola (Abrantes and Martins), 156
civil war in Angola
  children's experience, 73–74, 99
  description and history, 10, 25–28
  Dono Oniko's story, 95
  and education, 128–29
  materiality and symbols, 63
  and "new man," 69, 71
  peace "breakout," 3
  smell, 41
clã (clan) naming by Scouts, 72–74
class, and sound, 135. *See also* middle class
class membership, criteria, 16–19
class mobility. *See* mobility
classical music, 115
"code-switching," 126
Cold War

civil war as proxy (*see* civil war in Angola)
  and universities, 120
College of Stars, 35–37, 121, 122, 146
Collier, Delinda, 69
colonization, 24–25
compassion, 193
concrete elephant, 32, 147
Créole (Agualusa), 48–49
critical thinking, and education, 130–32
Cuba and Cubans
  and education of Angolans, 128–29, 130–31
  as fieldwork site, 11
  university teachers, 119, 123, 125, 128
  in war in Angola, 10, 11, 26, 128
"Cuban Help, The" (poem), 82
Cuito Cuanavale battle, 1
cultural capital, 17
curiosity
  about Angola, 184, 188
  as sense, 184
  for understanding others, 9, 181–82, 184, 192–93

daily life. *See* everyday life and acts
D'Aluisio, Faith, 92
"danger of a single story," 4–5
Daniella (Dr.), 34, 45–46, 176
Das Mingas, Rui Alberto Viera, 69
dead little girl incident, 169–70
de Almeida, Miguel Vale, 151
de Andrade, Luís Falção Pinto, 66–67
decoloniality, 49
"deep hanging out," 87
Diego, Mr. and Dr., 35–36
differences, importance and role, xxiii, 9
digital natives, 163
dinner violence incident, 169
"do no harm" in anthropology, 167–68, 174

dollars (US) *vs.* kwanzas, 16, 19–20, 189
"Dona Inês" (poem), 142
"Dona Maria Serving Soup" (poem), 141
Driver, Elinor, 20, 23–29
"Driver, The" (poem), 83
Dulley, Iracema, 117

economy
  in Brazil, 190
  and *capitalismo selvagem,* 19–20, 184
  jobs and money, 16
  problems in Angola, 188–89
education
  in Angola, 18–19, 35–36
  Angolans in Brazil, 130, 131–32
  and critical thinking, 130–32
  Cuba's role, 128–29, 130–31
  curriculum, 197n4
  degrees and work, 122
  duty and service to government, 129–30
  everyday life challenges, 185
  middle class in Angola, 18
  Scouts, 66–67, 68, 71, 75–76
  and smell, 36–37
  See also universities in Angola
Eisenlohr, P., 113
Emeralda, 171–72
"Emma," 185
Espelanga, Lino (tailor), 93, 98–103
estar and *ser*, 38, 67
"Estrelinha *(Little Star)*" (poem), 137
ethics, and anthropology, 167–68, 174
ethnography. *See* anthropology
everyday life and acts
  vs. big picture, 4
  and *capitalismo selvagem,* 184–85
  challenges and optimism, 185, 188–90, 191
  mental load, 185
  and senses, 9
  and social media, 153
  and transition of Angola, 185–86

Facebook
  Free Basics program, 187
  influence, 164
  joke about leaders, 162, 163
  use of, 152–53, 159–60
Farquhar, Judith, 90–91
"Fatherhood" (poem), 77
"Fátima's Mother, on Christmas Day 2013" (poem), 81
fazer, 134
Félicité (doctor), 187
FESA (Fundação José Eduardo dos Santos), 39, 131
fieldnotes and notebooks of author, 12–14, 50–51, 54
fieldwork of author
  afterimages and ethics, 168–74
  in Angola, 3–4, 10–11, 13–14, 47–48
  and biopolitical screens, 158–61
  in Brazil, 11, 158–59
  in Cuba, 11
  recording, 12–14, 50–56
  sites, 11, 12
  travel done, 7, 172
  See also methodology and research
fire and bonfire, for Scouts, 68
fishing boat, 107
five senses. *See* senses
fixe as word, 117
Flávia
  and perfume, 38–40, 41
  racial identity, 197–98n6
  social background, 41–42
flying by author, 7, 172
fofoca (gossip), 136
food
  distribution and waste, 92
  oral history, 94–98

Index   225

restaurants and owners in Lobito, 87–91
role as marker, 91–92
typical meal ingredients, 106
food writing, 90–91
Free Basics, 187
freedom of speech/expression in Angola, 124, 133, 134–35
funge as food, 91, 197n1
funge recipe, 86

Gabriella (scout), 63–64
Galloway, Stephen, 191
Geertz, Clifford, 47
Gell, Alfred, 44
Geração da Mudança: O despertar de uma geração anestesiada: 32 é muito (Generation of change ...) (Chipilica), 158, 159
gesturing (body language), 117–18
global north, 195n3
Guyer, Jane, 17
gym in Lobito, 53, 54–56

haptic, 58
Harari, Yuval Noah, xxiv
helping incidents, 170–72
higher education. *See* universities in Angola
Hipólito (scout), 57, 69
Hoffman, Danny, 161
Hong Kong, air and air spaces, 37
households, money and labor division, 16
houses in Angola, 17, 18
"Humans of New York" Facebook page and blog, 93, 163

ideological contestation, 136
industrialization, 186
Ingold, Tim, 113
"Insta lies," 164–65
Instituto Superior Jean Piaget de Benguela, 119, 124–25, 133

Internet, 125, 164, 187–88, 193. *See also* social media
interviews by author, xvii–xx, 11–12, 50–51
iPads, 154
Isla de la Juventud (Island of Youth) schools, 128–29
Islam and mosques, 67–68

Jain, S., 76
Jean Piaget. *See* Instituto Superior Jean Piaget de Benguela
JMPLA, 60, 72
João (king), 24
"João, collapsing" (poem), 139–40
Joaquim, Dono, 87, 91–92
Joker restaurant, 95, 97
jornadas científicas ("scientific journeys"), 120, 133–34
journeys, 104
Joyce (mother), and perfume, 42–43, 63

knowledge
  and Internet, 187, 193
  structures in universities, 133, 134–35
  systems, 49
kwanzas *vs.* US dollars, 16, 19–20, 189

language
  Portuguese, 2, 11
  and sound, 114
  and translation, 117
leadership and power, 193
Lee Kuan Yew, 37
leisure, in photo essay, 148–49
life histories. *See* oral histories
listening and how to listen, 116
Lobito (Angola)
  ambient noise, 112
  College of Stars and education, 35–36

226 Index

as fieldwork site, 11
gym, 53, 54–56
on map, 2
old cinema, 96–97
olfactory experience, 31–34
oral histories, 94–103
  in photo essays, 106, 107, 108, 146–47, 149, 177–79
recent problems and changes, 188–89, 191–92
restaurants and their owners, 87–91
Lourenço, João, 10, 29
loyalty to Angola, 189–90
lusophone world, and knowledge system, 49

Magdalena (scout), 72
malaria, 172
Malkki, Liisa, 15, 76
Mandela, Nelson, 2, 183
maps, and representation, 181
Marcos, Dr., 128–29
Maria, Dona, and her restaurant, 89–90, 91–92
Marx, Karl, 17
materiality, 62–63, 76
membership of class, criteria, 16–19
Mendes, Maria C.B., 120
mental load, 185
Menzel, Peter, 92
mercury incident, 169
methodology and research
  fieldnotes and notebooks, 12–14, 50–51, 54
  interviews, xvii–xx, 11–12, 50–51
  objects kept, 51–54
  participant observation, 11–12, 34–35
  participants, 13
  recordings on phone, 50–51
  and relationships with people, 47–48
  structured observations of space, 54–56

and technology, 152
through College of Stars, 36
See also fieldwork of author
middle class
  definition and description, 15–16
  emergence in Africa, 10–11
middle class in Angola
  challenges, 182, 185, 189
  concept and criteria, 15–19
  and education, 18
  emergence, 5
  income and assets, 16–17
  social media and Internet, 187
  as study area, 182–83
Miller, Daniel, 153
"Miss Landmine Angola," 155–56
mobility (class mobility)
  challenges, 189
  concept and considerations, 103–04
  and cultural capital, 17
  and perfume, 41, 43, 46
  and work, 96–98, 100–03, 104
Morrison, Toni, 157
motorbike of author, 13, 53, 170–71
motorbikes in Angola, 13, 17–18
MPLA
  criticisms of, 73–75, 124
  and Scouts, 60–61, 72–75
  and universities, 124, 125
MPLA/UNITA conflict, 25–28. *See also* civil war in Angola
music
  at College of Stars, 35, 36, 121, 122
  instruments in Angola, 111–12
  and noise, 114–15

naming and renaming, 183
Nascimento, Adão, 117–18, 120, 132–35
national anthem of Angola, 68–69, 112
National Library of Sarajevo, 191, 192

national rebranding, 153, 155–58, 183
Neto, Antonio Agostinho, 25
"new man," 68–71
Nina perfume, 36–37
Njinga (queen), 24
noise, and music, 114–15
Nuttall, Sarah, 183

oil and oil crisis, 28–29
Ondjaki, xxi, xxii
Oniko, Dono (chef), 93, 94–98, 189
oral histories (life histories)
    on aesthetic taste, 94, 98–103
    on gustatory taste, 94–98
    use and role, 93–94
Ortner, Sherry, 68

Pallasmaa, Juhani, 58
pano Africano, 101, 102
pano nacional (semakaka), 62
pano trousers for Scouts, 62–63
Parsons, Timothy, 60
participant observation
    in Angola by author, 11–12
    in anthropology, 34–35
    in digital world, 154, 162–64
pasteis de nata (cream pastries), 87, 88, 92
Patal, Shailja, 17
peace
    breakout, 3
    and flavors, 106–09
    learning and practices, 76
    and postwar changes, 5, 7–8, 10, 14, 188–89, 190, 191–92
    as practice, 191–92, 193
    and Scouts, 60, 61, 71, 75
Pedro (scout leader), 59, 62–63
perfume
    Angolans in Brazil, 38–41, 42–43
    as asset, 17
    as focus of research, 47
    lack of, 43–44
    learning through duty-free, 42–43
    as marker, 36–37
    and mobility, 41, 43, 46
    as objects kept, 52, 53, 54
    photo of collection, 176
photo essays, 106–09, 146–49, 176–79
photos
    about Angola, 155–56
    of dead little girl, 169–70
    and digital technologies, 154–55, 160–61
Pitcher, Anne, 127–28
Pizza Shack, 90
Plano Nacional de Formação dos Quadros (National Plan for the Training of Cadres), 122
poems of author, 14, 77–83, 137–45
port of Lobito, 108
Portugal, 24–26, 131
Portuguese language, 2, 11
practice of peace, 191–92, 193
Prensky, Marc, 163
prices in Angola, 8, 16, 196n7
private universities, 121, 122–23
proprioception, 7, 183–84
proxy conflict for Cold War. *See* civil war in Angola
public transportation, 17–18
publicas ("public" universities), 121, 122

race and racial identity, 197–98n6
race in South Africa, 2–3
"Radio Building" (poem), 78
Rafael, 189–90
Rahaim, Matt, 115
Rahman, Zia Haider, 181–82, 183
rationalist views, 6
rebranding of Angola, 153, 155–58, 183
recipes, 86
recording of fieldwork, 12–14, 50–56
religion and church

in Angola, 67–68, 126
and Scouts, 59, 67, 68, 70–71
and universities, 125–26
renaming and naming, 183
Restinga, 88, 96
Ruben (scout leader)
  leader of funeral, 57
  naming of *clã* (clan) and Savimbi, 72–74
  pano pants, 62

Santos, José Eduardo dos (Zedú), 10, 25, 28, 123–24, 158, 190
Sarajevo, 191, 192
Savimbi, Jonas, 3, 28, 72, 73–74, 119, 162
Schafer, R. Murray, 113, 114
"scientific journeys" (*jornadas científicas*), 120, 133–34
scouting/Scouts in Angola
  activities and events, 61–62
  author in, 59–60
  batch of, 52, 53
  description and role, 58–61
  drowning incident and funeral, 57
  education and moral citizenship, 66–67, 68, 71, 75–76
  as inspiration and aspiration, 63–65, 66
  joke on Facebook, 162
  membership and history, 59
  naming of *clã* (clan), 72–73
  and "new man," 68–71
  pano trousers, 62–63
  and peace, 60, 61, 71, 75
  politics and MPLA, 60–61, 72–75
  religion and church, 59, 67, 68, 70–71
  as space for dialogue, 73, 74–75
  and symbols, 62–63, 68
  and touch, 62, 71
  uniform, 58, 63, 65, 67, 75–76
  See also *caminheiros* Scouts

Sebastião, 151
self-esteem and self-recognition, 187–88
semakaka (pano nacional), 62
"sense," as word, 6
senses
  and *capitalismo selvagem*, 184–85
  in chapters of book, 9, 20–21
  in everyday life and acts, 9
  importance and use, 6, 7
  role in book, xxii–xxiii, 7, 183–84
  and ways of knowing, 6–7
  See also specific senses
ser and *estar*, 38, 67
Serres, Michel, 58
"Seven Women" (poem), 79
Sharp, Gene, 163
Sharpeville Massacre, 1
shopping, in photo essays, 108, 109
side gigs, 16
sight
  afterimages, 166
  colors in Angola, 151
  description, 6
  and history of Angola, 155
  new past and alternative futures, 156–58, 162
  and representation, 160–62, 174
  and social media, 151–53
  and truth, 164–65
silence, 118
slave trade, 24, 33, 108
Smailović, Vedran, 191, 192
smell
  in air, 34
  and air-conditioning, 37–38
  in anthropology and research, 35, 47–48
  bad smell, 43–45, 47, 50–51
  and civil war, 41
  College of Stars and education, 35–37
  hygiene and self-care, 44
  importance in Angola, 46–47

as marker and in cultural norms, 36–37, 41–44, 46, 48–49
memories and emotions, 45–46
olfactory experience in Lobito, 31–34
structured observations of space, 54–56
See also perfume
Smith, Mark M., 35
Snake Gives Birth to a Snake, A (Lessac), 166–67
social media
and anthropology, 152, 153, 165–66
biopolitical screens, 158–61
and elections, 164
facts and fiction, 154
and human interactions, 161
joke about leaders, 162, 163
in local and global, 163–64
and sight, 151–53
stories sharing, 93
use of, 151–54, 187
and witnessing, 154
socialism
in Angola, 128–29
demise in Africa, 127–28
transition to capitalism, 10, 19, 118, 120, 127–28, 136, 185
in universities, 118–19
sound
ambient noise, 112
and class, 135
description, 113
keywords and vocabulary, 113–18
in language and translation, 114, 117
music and instruments in Angola, 111–12
spectrographs, 111, 112
and structures of thinking, 135–36
at university, 118
sound blindness, 114, 117
soundscape, 113

Sousanis, Nick, 14
South Africa
Anglo-Boer war, 59
apartheid and ambitions, 1–2, 167
in conflicts in Angola, 1, 3, 10, 26
translators of TRC, 166–67
weapons identification in schools, 2–3
South African Defence Force (SADF), 3
South Atlantic Cable System, 187
spectrographs, 111, 112
Stanton, Brandon, 93, 163
supermarket, 109
sushi, 90, 91–92
Sylvanus, Nina, 63

tailoring, 100–01
taste (aesthetic)
oral history, 94, 98–103
photo essay, 106, 109
taste (gustatory)
Aurea's restaurant, 32, 87–89
oral history, 94–98
and peace, 106–09
photo essay, 106, 107, 109
Taussig, Michael, 183
Tchimboto, Dr., 118, 120, 124–26, 130
Thompson, John B., 160–61
title of book and chapters, 7–8
touch (as emotion), 58
touch (physical), 7, 58, 62, 71
"traffic of influence" or "trafficking influence," 20, 119
translation and translators
and representation, 181
and sound, 117
of TRC in South Africa, 166–67
travel by author, 7, 172
Truth and Reconciliation Commission (TRC) of South Africa, 166
Tsing, Anna, 186
"Two Photographers" (poem), 144

UNDP statistics, 15–16
Unflattening (Sousanis), 14
Union of Soviet Socialist Republics, in Angola war, 1, 26
UNITA/MPLA conflict, 25–28. *See also* civil war in Angola
United States, in Angola war, 1, 26
Universidade Agostinho Neto, 120
Universidade Katyavala Bwila (UKB), 119, 121, 122, 123–24
universities in Angola
  admission and fees, 121, 122
  capitalism and *capitalismo selvagem*, 118–19, 122
  description as sector, 120–23
  emergence and development, 118, 120–21, 133, 134
  ideologies of faculty and teachers, 119–20, 124, 125, 129–31, 133
  knowledge structures, 133, 134–35
  and MPLA, 124, 125
  overseas institutions, 123
  portraits of two institutions, 123–25
  religion and church, 125–26
  science and identity, 132, 133–34
  sound, 118
  teachers from and in Cuba, 119, 123, 125, 128

Väliaho, Pasi, 161
Veblen, Thorstein, 17
Victoria (friend of author)
  "code-switching," 127
  and Dono Oniko's life history, 94
  family and father, 126–27
  as friend, 48
  on people with bad smell, 44
  perfume at College of Stars, 36
video games, 162
voice, 115, 126

war, and technology, 161
war in Angola. *See* civil war in Angola
"Western" ways, senses in, 6–7
White, Bella, 176
whiteness/white people, and smell, 35, 47
William, Raymond, 119

Xavier (chef), 90, 91–92
Xavier (student in Brazil), 159

"Yoga Teacher" (poem), 145
young people, 188
youth movements, 60–61
YouTube, 163

Zedú. *See* Santos, José Eduardo dos
Zulu restaurant, 88

Teaching Culture
UTP Ethnographies for the Classroom

Editor: John Barker, University of British Columbia

This series is an essential resource for instructors searching for ethnographic case studies that are contemporary, engaging, provocative, and created specifically with undergraduate students in mind. Written with clarity and personal warmth, books in the series introduce students to the core methods and orienting frameworks of ethnographic research and provide a compelling entry point to some of the most urgent issues faced by people around the globe today.

Recent Books in the Series

From Water to Wine: Becoming Middle Class in Angola by Jess Auerbach (2020)

Deeply Rooted in the Present: Heritage, Memory, and Identity in Brazilian Quilombos by Mary Lorena Kenny (2018)

Long Night at the Vepsian Museum: The Forest Folk of Northern Russia and the Struggle for Cultural Survival by Veronica Davidov (2017)

Truth and Indignation: Canada's Truth and Reconciliation Commission on Indian Residential Schools, second edition, by Ronald Niezen (2017)

Merchants in the City of Art: Work, Identity, and Change in a Florentine Neighborhood by Anne Schiller (2016)

Ancestral Lines: The Maisin of Papua New Guinea and the Fate of the Rainforest, second edition, by John Barker (2016)

Love Stories: Language, Private Love, and Public Romance in Georgia by Paul Manning (2015)

Culturing Bioscience: A Case Study in the Anthropology of Science by Udo Krautwurst (2014)

Fields of Play: An Ethnography of Children's Sports by Noel Dyck (2012)

Made in Madagascar: Sapphires, Ecotourism, and the Global Bazaar by Andrew Walsh (2012)

Red Flags and Lace Coiffes: Identity and Survival in a Breton Village by Charles R. Menzies (2011)

Rites of the Republic: Citizens' Theatre and the Politics of Culture in Southern France by Mark Ingram (2011)

Maya or Mestizo?: Nationalism, Modernity, and Its Discontents by Ronald Loewe (2010)